Contemporary Issues in Law and Economics

Law and economics is the field of study devoted to understanding laws and legal institutions using the tools of economic theory. This growing subject has become a mainstream area of study in both law schools and economics departments and this book explores the "law and economics" approach to some of the most interesting questions, issues, and topics in law, order, and justice.

Contemporary Issues in Law and Economics considers what economists call the "positive" analysis of the law – that is, using economic theory to explain the nature of the law as it actually exists. As part of this approach the author examines questions such as, what is the economic basis for the predominance of negligence rules in tort law? And, what is the explanation for the illegality of blackmail? Furthermore, another set of questions arises where the law seems to depart from the prescriptions of economic theory, and these issues are also examined in this volume. For example, the deeply rooted norm of proportionality between punishments and crimes, and the use of escalating penalties for repeat offenders, are both explored.

With self-contained chapters written in a non-technical style, this book offers a rigorous discussion of the above themes while remaining accessible to those without formal legal or economic training. It offers the ideal introduction to the field of law and economics while also providing a basis for students in more advanced courses.

Thomas J. Miceli has been a professor at the University of Connecticut since 1987. His research is largely in the area of law and economics, with particular emphasis on land use and property law. He also currently serves as an associate editor for the *International Review of Law and Economics*.

Contemporary Issues in Law and Economics

Thomas J. Miceli

LONDON AND NEW YORK

First published 2018
by Routledge
2 Park Square, Milton Park, Abingdon, Oxon OX14 4RN

and by Routledge
711 Third Avenue, New York, NY 10017

Routledge is an imprint of the Taylor & Francis Group, an informa business

© 2018 Thomas J. Miceli

The right of Thomas J. Miceli to be identified as author of this work has been asserted by him in accordance with sections 77 and 78 of the Copyright, Designs and Patents Act 1988.

All rights reserved. No part of this book may be reprinted or reproduced or utilised in any form or by any electronic, mechanical, or other means, now known or hereafter invented, including photocopying and recording, or in any information storage or retrieval system, without permission in writing from the publishers.

Trademark notice: Product or corporate names may be trademarks or registered trademarks, and are used only for identification and explanation without intent to infringe.

British Library Cataloguing-in-Publication Data
A catalogue record for this book is available from the British Library

Library of Congress Cataloging-in-Publication Data
Names: Miceli, Thomas J., author.
Title: Contemporary issues in law and economics / Thomas J. Miceli.
Description: Abingdon, Oxon [UK] ; New York : Routledge, 2018. |
   Includes bibliographical references and index.
Identifiers: LCCN 2017048910 (print) | LCCN 2017049229 (ebook) |
   ISBN 9781315103976 (Ebook) | ISBN 9781138099753
   (hardback : alk. paper) | ISBN 9781138099760 (pbk. : alk. paper)
Subjects: LCSH: Law and economics. | Law—Economic aspects.
Classification: LCC K487.E3 (ebook) | LCC K487.E3 M525 2018 (print) |
   DDC 340/.1—dc23
LC record available at https://lccn.loc.gov/2017048910

ISBN: 978-1-138-09975-3 (hbk)
ISBN: 978-1-138-09976-0 (pbk)
ISBN: 978-1-315-10397-6 (ebk)

Typeset in Sabon
by Apex CoVantage, LLC

Contents

Preface   vii

1 On the usefulness of economics for understanding law   1

2 Property rights and the Coase Theorem   6

3 The choice between property rules and liability rules   13

4 Does the law evolve toward efficiency?   21

5 Threshold rules in law   28

6 Simultaneous versus sequential care accidents and strategic negligence   36

7 The tort–crime boundary   45

8 Some difficulties with the economic theory of crime   54

9 Escalating penalties for repeat offenders   63

10 The problem with plea bargaining   69

11 The (real) puzzle of blackmail   75

12 Group punishment   81

13 When is a contract enforceable?   89

14 Efficient breach theory	101
15 A question of title: rules for protecting the ownership of land	110
16 Holdups and holdouts	119
17 Eminent domain and the paradox of public use	127
18 Regulatory takings and the compensation question	137
19 Fair use: fair or foul?	148
20 Lawsuits for sale?	154
Bibliographic essay	161
References	166
Index	173

Preface

Law and economics is the field of study devoted to understanding the nature of legal rules and institutions using the tools of economic theory. The field is large and growing, and has become a mainstream course of study in both law schools and economics departments. This book is not intended to be a comprehensive survey of the field, but instead is based on a discussion of issues in law and economics that are centered around two themes. The first involves the usefulness of economic theory for identifying problems that the law is aimed at resolving, and for understanding the solutions that it has arrived at. For example, what is the economic basis for the predominance of negligence rules in tort law? And, what is the explanation for the illegality of blackmail? Providing answers to these types of questions represents what economists call "positive" analysis of the law—that is, using economic theory to explain the nature of the law as it actually exists. I hope to show that an important attribute of this type of analysis is that it reveals the power of economic reasoning to provide a unifying theory of law that transcends traditional legal boundaries.

The second theme concerns problems with the economic approach itself when applied to law, by which I mean instances where the law seems to depart from the prescriptions of economic theory. Examples are the deeply rooted norm of proportionality between punishments and crimes, and the pervasive use of escalating penalties for repeat offenders, both of which are rather difficult to square with the standard economic theory of crime as it has been developed over the past half century. In these cases—where the economic approach apparently fails as a complete description of the law— I will argue that it can nevertheless yield insights into the values or goals, besides economic efficiency, that the law embraces.

Given the preceding objectives, the book is somewhat idiosyncratic, reflecting my perspective, as someone trained in economics but not law, on the usefulness of economics for addressing interesting legal issues. The chapters are written as stand-alone essays that can be read independently and in any order, but there is a rough organization as reflected by the following grouping by legal field (with some overlap): general topics (Chapters 1–5), torts (Chapters 5–7), crime (Chapters 7–12), contracts (Chapters 13 and 14), property (Chapters 15–19), and legal process (Chapter 20). The book can therefore serve as the basis for a topics-oriented introductory course in law and economics, or as a companion book for a more comprehensive survey of the field. It may also be of interest to readers seeking a non-technical introduction to the way that economists think about the law, as motivated by specific examples. A bibliographic essay at the end of the book will direct interested readers to the more technical literature.

I confess up front that there is not much that is new in this book—most of the arguments have previously appeared in some form in scholarly journal articles or book chapters written by me and others. However, all the material is rewritten and reinterpreted in light of the above objectives, which hopefully gives it new life and a coherent theme. The views and arguments expressed herein reflect my many years of reading and writing about law and economics, but I have also benefitted from the insights of many others. My greatest debt is to Richie Adelstein, who first introduced me to the field of law and economics in an undergraduate course, and with whom I have had numerous fruitful conversations on the subject over the years. I have also learned a lot from teaching law and economics for almost three decades at both the undergraduate and graduate levels, which required me to absorb a sufficient amount of law to make the courses credible. I gained most of that knowledge from the various editions of the Cooter and Ulen (1988) and Posner (2014) textbooks, and from an intensive two week course on law offered some years ago by the George Mason University Law School. Finally, I have benefitted greatly from collaborations with my colleagues Kathy Segerson, C.F. Sirmans, and Metin Cosgel, whose insights pervade this book. None of the above, however, should be implicated as endorsing any view, or as being responsible for any errors, that might appear in these pages. Of course, I would be remiss in not thanking my family for indulging the oddities and whims that characterize the working habits of most scholars. I appreciate their support more than I can say.

T.J.M.
Summer 2017

1 On the usefulness of economics for understanding law

The application of economic analysis to law is part of the general expansion of economic reasoning to areas of behavior outside of the traditional market setting. This trend reflects the idea that economics as a discipline is defined by its methodology—the application of rational decision making to human behavior—rather than by its subject matter. Law is an ideal subject for economic analysis because, like economics, it is largely concerned with how incentives affect behavior. The application of economic analysis to law presumes that people view the threat of legal sanctions—monetary payments or imprisonment—as implicit prices aimed at guiding behavior in certain socially desirable ways. From this perspective, laws are devoid of moral content and are instead interpreted solely in terms of how they shape people's decisions.

The assumption of rationality—that people act to maximize their well-being subject to whatever constraints they face—is a foundational component of economic analysis, in whatever context it is applied. It is what allows economists to understand and predict human behavior (albeit imperfectly). Some critics of the economic approach to law may doubt that rationality applies to legal settings, but in its absence the law is only understandable in a strictly backward looking sense, serving to do justice in individual cases after the fact. And while this is surely one of its functions, it also takes on an important instrumental role if, by remedying past wrongs, it serves to inspire or encourage people to behave better in the future. That is the perspective the economic approach to law takes.

It is instructive to compare this view of law to that espoused over a century ago by the great American judge, Oliver Wendell Holmes, Jr., who in his classic essay, "The Path of the Law," articulated a theory of law that in many ways presaged the economic approach (Holmes, 1897). The key figure in Holmes's theory is the so-called "bad man," who is an amoral decision maker whose only interest is in learning what the law is and what the consequences will be from breaking it. As Holmes argues, "If you want to know the law and nothing else, you must look at it as a bad man, who cares only for the material consequences which such knowledge enables him to predict" (Holmes, 1897, p. 459). This "prediction theory" of the law is law seen through the eyes of an economist. This is not to say that all people do or should act in this way—indeed, most people obey the law based on a sense of moral obligation or a devotion to righteousness—but to paraphrase James Madison, laws are not designed to restrain angels, only those who choose to act like angels for fear of punishment. It is these people—the "bad men"—on whom the economic analysis of law focuses, for it is them to whom the law acts as a binding constraint.

Other critics of the economic approach to law argue that efficiency is an inappropriate, or at least an insufficient, norm for evaluating legal rules. The principal goal, they contend, should be justice or fairness. Defenders of the economic approach counter that justice, or distributional equity as it is often defined in practice, is a value that economists also embrace, and while economic theory offers no special insight into what constitutes a just or fair society—that is ultimately a political question—it surely has much to contribute to prescribing how such an outcome can be achieved with the least sacrifice of resources. Further, economists note that justice or fairness, to the extent that people care about those values and however they are measured, can be incorporated, along with efficiency, into the social welfare function that society seeks to maximize. In that sense, values besides efficiency are perfectly compatible with economic analysis. Finally, staunch defenders of the economic approach to law might argue, as Richard Posner has, that one definition of justice *is* efficiency because "in a world of scarce resources waste should be regarded as immoral" (Posner, 2003, p. 27).

It is nonetheless true that economic analysis of the law, as it has most commonly been practiced, focuses on the specific objective of wealth maximization. (This is also sometimes called Kaldor-Hicks efficiency, which is a relaxed version of Pareto efficiency, the standard efficiency concept in economics.) Although changes in legal rules, and indeed in any economic policies, however narrowly focused, will generally affect the distribution of wealth in society, in most cases it will be quite difficult to ascertain the specific winners and losers from the proposed change. Even when the effects can be traced, tinkering with legal rules will not generally be the best way to achieve a desired redistribution. A better approach, it seems, would be to focus on making individual laws operate as efficiently as possible in the hope that, across the set of all laws, people who lose from the effects of one law will benefit from the effects of others, and that all people will benefit on average as the law is made to operate more efficiently. To the extent that some residual unfairness exists, it can be corrected by policies whose primary purpose is redistribution, such as progressive income taxes. This perspective reflects the idea that people, choosing from behind a "veil of ignorance," would consent to such an approach to legal rulemaking.[1]

In terms of fully understanding the insights that economics can bring to the study of law, it will be useful to distinguish between what I will call the "economic analysis of law," and "law and economics." Although these labels may appear to be synonymous, I will argue that they represent distinct perspectives on the relationship between the two disciplines.

By "economic analysis of law" I mean the use of the tools of economics to evaluate legal rules. In this perspective, law becomes the subject matter for economic analysis. This is the program first undertaken in a systematic way by Richard Posner in his seminal treatise, now in its ninth edition (Posner, 2014). This type of analysis comes in two varieties: positive analysis and normative analysis. Positive analysis studies the law as it is, focusing on how it affects behavior. The interpretation of the rules of tort law, or of criminal penalties, as inducing people to internalize the harms they create when engaged in potentially harmful activities are classic examples. (The fact that torts are usually accidental harms and crimes are usually intentional harms, while an important common-sense distinction, apparently plays no role in the economic view of the respective sanctions—see Chapter 7.) A stronger version of positive analysis of the law goes further to assert that the common law as a whole broadly reflects an economic logic—in other words, that efficiency has somehow become embedded in the law. This is not a claim that judges or other participants in the legal arena consciously pursue the goal of efficiency, but rather that the common law process embodies market-like tendencies that propel it in that direction. (The logic of this argument is the presented and evaluated in Chapter 4.)

Normative analysis, in contrast, asks how the law can be made more efficient. All policy-making, whether in law or other areas, represents a kind of normative analysis. The application of normative economic analysis to law specifically relies on the assumption that efficiency is a norm that the law *should* pursue, possibly in conjunction with other norms (as noted previously), and that the tools of economic analysis (mathematical models and optimization) provide the means by which this is accomplished. As an illustration, consider the proposed enactment (or repeal) of "three-strikes" laws for repeat criminal offenders. Positive analysis answers the question of how these laws would (or do) affect the crime rate, while normative analysis goes further to say that these laws should be enacted (or repealed) because such a decision would lower the overall cost of crime.

The other use of economics for understanding law, what I am calling "law and economics," does not treat law as a subject for economic study, but instead asks how legal institutions and markets interact as co-equal social mechanisms for coordinating human behavior. Thus, while "economic analysis of law" seems to place law in a subservient position relative to economics, "law and economics" actually reverses the hierarchy by recognizing that markets cannot function without the prior existence of a stable background of laws to protect property rights and enforce contracts. Most economists, when teaching principles, take this background of legal rules as given (if they mention it at all), in the same way that they take tastes and technology as given. However, law and economics scholars have shown that much insight into the operation of both the legal system and markets can be learned by fully appreciating, and thus seeking to understand, the interrelationship between these two institutions. The starting point for this inquiry is the classic essay on social cost by Coase (1960), coupled with the also-classic paper by Calabresi and Melamed (1972) on the choice between property rules and liability rules for protecting legal entitlements. The next two chapters examine the insights contained in these papers, and describe how they combine to create a coherent theory of law and markets that has become known as the General Transaction Structure.

I conclude this introductory chapter with a word on the use of economic models. Economics, as a social science, relies on mathematical models to simplify the world, and although I will avoid formal mathematics in this book, most of the conclusions presented here were first derived in that way. The use of such models, like controlled experiments in laboratories (which generally are not available to social scientists), allows researchers to disentangle the myriad of factors that influence the operation of complex social institutions like the market or the legal system. The manner in which models simplify the world is by means of their assumptions, which are meant to exclude extraneous factors while isolating the issues of interest. One measure of the quality of an economic model is the reasonableness of its assumptions—do they highlight only the essential questions? Another measure is the extent to which the model succeeds in explaining the world and predicting behavior.

Economic models can apply to a wide range of questions—this is a consequence of the above-mentioned expansion of economic analysis beyond the traditional market setting—but they all share certain features. First, as noted earlier, they posit rationality on the part of decision makers, at least part of the time. This implies that individuals engage in optimizing behavior, which in practice is manifested by their use of *marginal analysis* to maximize their well-being, however that is described, subject to the constraints that they face. Second, economic models rely on *equilibrium analysis*, which means that decision makers whose interests strategically interact, whether in the marketplace or the legal arena, make choices that are simultaneously in their individual self-interests and are mutually compatible. Thus, once an equilibrium is reached, no one wants to change their behavior, and the system is said to be "at rest." The point here is that observed social institutions are presumed to reflect outcomes from which people have no reason to deviate, given their knowledge and beliefs. In other words, the world as we see it is taken to be an "equilibrium outcome." Law is particularly concerned with social interactions, in many cases involuntary ones, and an important function of legal rules in the economic perspective is to establish sustainable (equilibrium) outcomes. An example is the interaction of injurers and victims in potential accident settings, as governed by the applicable rule for assigning liability. Third, economic models distinguish between positive and normative analysis, as described previously. Both varieties of analysis appear throughout this book.

The specific application of economic analysis to law has a long history, but the application of formal mathematical models is fairly new, dating to the 1960s. Since then, the field has expanded to the point where law and economics is a major field in both economics and law. The following chapters hopefully illustrate the reasons for the success of this enterprise.

Note

1 This reflects the approach to social justice taken by Rawls in his classic treatise (Rawls, 1971).

2 Property rights and the Coase Theorem

Property law is that body of court-enforced rules governing the establishment, use, and transfer of rights to land and other assets. From an economic perspective, the goal of property law is to maximize the value of these assets by providing incentives for people to make efficient investments in them (especially in the case of land) and to transfer them to higher valuing users. Secure property rights represent an important pre-requisite for the efficient operation of markets, and are therefore fundamental to all economic activity. In this sense, law is a *complement* to markets.

Markets do not always function smoothly, however, even when property rights are clearly defined and enforced. An important source of what economists call "market failure" is the problem of incompatible property rights, which represent situations in which one person's unrestricted use of his or her property imposes costs on others, or conflicts with the unrestricted use of their property. For example, some uses of property necessarily cause pollution in the form of smoke, noise, or discharge of waste, while other uses endanger the habitat of wildlife or deprive society of land that is potentially valuable for public use. These "externalities," as economists call them, potentially lead to inefficient land uses, thus providing a possible justification for government-imposed restrictions on land, such as zoning, environmental regulations, or takings. Much of property law, whether in the form of common law rules or government regulation, is aimed at limiting the detrimental effects of externalities. In this way the law (ideally) corrects for market failure by coercively allocating resources in a more efficient manner. In serving this purpose, the law *substitutes* for the market as the principal mechanism for allocating property rights efficiently.

This distinction—between law as supporting markets and law as regulating markets—reflects the philosophical perspective advanced in the previous chapter under the heading of "law and economics"; namely, that law and economics are co-equal institutions aimed at solving the fundamental economic problem faced by society regarding the efficient allocation of scarce resources. This view will culminate, in the next chapter, in the derivation of the "General Transaction Structure," which represents an heuristic framework for understanding the manner in which legal rights are defined and exchanged. As a first step in that effort, we need to be more specific about the nature and economic function of property rights.

Property rights are a creation of society in the sense that they define those things that people can and cannot do with the economic resources under their control. Normally, however, economists and lawyers interpret "ownership" of property not as a single right but as a bundle of rights consisting of (1) the right to *use* the asset in question, (2) the right to *exclude* others from using it, and (3) the right to sell or *transfer* ownership of it. In the case of agricultural land, for example, an owner can grow and sell crops, exclude trespassers, and sell or lease the land to a willing buyer/renter. The law enforces these rights, but not absolutely: as noted, when an owner's use of his or her rights conflicts with another owner's use, the law will impose limits on one or both parties' rights. These limits can take the form of regulations or the threat of financial liability for imposing harm.

In some situations, owners may *choose* to limit their rights by voluntarily transferring one or more "sticks" from their bundle of rights to another person or persons in a consensual (market) exchange. For example, a lease involves the temporary transfer of *use* rights from the owner of a piece of property (the landlord) to the user (the tenant). The law enforces such transactions as long as they are voluntarily made based on the premise that division of property rights enhances the value of the underlying asset.

At the opposite extreme from private property is what is called an *open access resource*, which describes a situation in which there is a complete absence of property rights. In this case, which is often associated with the "state of nature" (the period before property law institutions arose), the equilibrium outcome generally involves overuse of the asset, possibly resulting in complete "dissipation" of its value. For example, a mineral deposit is prematurely depleted, or a fishing ground is exhausted as users compete for the scarce resource. This outcome is referred to as the "tragedy of the commons." Property rights institutions solve the tragedy of the commons by creating incentives for owners to use a resource efficiently, either individually or collectively (as in the case of group ownership).

Following this line of reasoning, it is useful to think about the problem of externalities as arising when property rights are absent or not well-defined. In the canonical example of a polluting factory, the undefined property right is over the good health of nearby residents who are forced to ingest the polluted air or water. The right of victims to sue for damages in tort law, or the imposition of government regulation of harmful emissions by the EPA, represent alternative ways that the law (both private and public) tries to internalize the externality by implicitly or explicitly assigning the property right to victims of the harm.

The seminal economic analysis of the origin of property rights in the state of nature, by Harold Demsetz, is specifically based on their role in internalizing externalities. Demsetz argued that property rights will emerge "when the gains from internalization become larger than the costs of internalization"

(Demsetz, 1967, p. 350). The gains consist of the prevention of harm from the externality (e.g., pollution), and the costs are the victim's costs of avoiding the harm (e.g., moving away from the polluting factory), the injurer's cost of abating it, or both.

Prior to 1960, economists typically viewed government intervention as a necessary response to externalities. This approach, commonly associated with the economist Arthur Pigou, recognized that an externality results in too much of the harm-creating activity (pollution), and therefore needs to be controlled by a coercive government action. Economists usually prescribe a so-called "Pigovian tax," which forces the party causing the externality to internalize the resulting harm. (The use of tort liability accomplishes the same purpose.)

To illustrate the impact of an externality and the manner in which a Pigovian tax corrects the resulting inefficiency, consider the classic example of a railroad whose tracks border a farmer's land, resulting in fire damage caused by sparks emitted from passing trains. According to the traditional perspective, the externality results in too many trains being run from a social point of view because the railroad does not account for the cost borne by the farmer. This point is illustrated in Figure 2.1, where the downward sloping curve labeled MB is the railroad's private marginal benefit from running trains (and is also the social marginal benefit, assuming that the

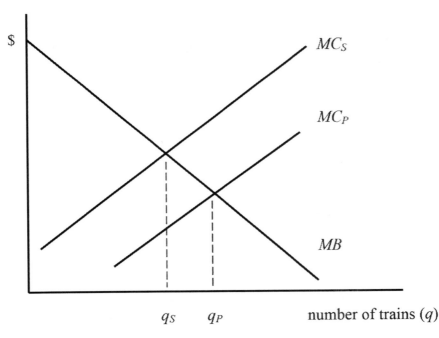

Figure 2.1 Pigovian tax approach to externalities

railroad internalizes all of the benefits to its customers of running trains). The upward sloping curve labeled MC_p is the railroad's private marginal cost, reflecting the cost of its inputs (coal, employees, maintenance of the train and tracks, etc.). The privately optimal number of trains—the level that maximizes the railroad's profit—therefore occurs at the intersection of these curves (where the railroad's marginal benefit equals its marginal cost), and is denoted q_p.

The curve labeled MC_s is the marginal social cost of running trains, reflecting the railroad's private costs *plus the damage suffered by the farmer in the form of crop damage*. In other words, MC_s equals MC_p plus the external damage (added vertically in the graph). The socially optimal number of trains occurs where the marginal social cost curve intersects the MB curve, at the point labeled q_s. The social optimum therefore involves fewer trains compared to the railroad's profit maximizing choice.

The Pigovian solution to this inefficiency is to impose a tax (or liability) on the railroad to force it to internalize the external harm. If the tax is on a per-train basis, then the amount of the tax should equal the amount of the harm caused per train—that is, it should equal the vertical distance between the MC_s and MC_p curves in Figure 2.1. (The calculation of the tax is more complicated if the externality is not a fixed amount per train.) Faced with the tax, the railroad will run the socially optimal number of trains because the profit-maximizing outcome now coincides with the social optimum (i.e., the railroad's private marginal cost, including the tax, now equals the social marginal cost).

In the case where the farmer is purely passive, it does not matter whether the revenue from the tax is given to the farmer as compensation for his damage or if it is used for some other purpose; its only function in the current setting is to provide incentives for the railroad to behave efficiently. Note that a tax differs from liability in this respect because under tort law, the damages paid by the railroad would have to be given to the farmer. In the current example, however, this issue is irrelevant in terms of the impact of the tax/liability on the railroad's behavior. (In Chapter 5 we examine situations in which both the injurer [railroad] and victim [farmer] can take steps to avoid the external harm—so-called "bilateral care" problems. In that case, what is done with the revenue *will* affect efficiency.)

In his famous paper on social cost, published in 1960, the economist Ronald Coase re-examined the Pigovian approach to externalities as just described by challenging two of its underlying assumptions (Coase, 1960). These are, first, that there is a single "cause" of the harm, and second, that some form of government intervention (coercion) is needed to internalize that harm. We consider these two challenges in turn.

Regarding the issue of causation, note that the Pigovian perspective implicitly assumes that the railroad is *the* cause of the harm and therefore must be held financially responsible for the damages. In other words, the causal direction is "one way." According to our earlier definition of an externality as an undefined property right, this perspective amounts to awarding the right to be free from harm to the farmer. The Pigovian tax, or strict tort liability, enforces that right by putting a price on it, which the railroad (injurer) then "purchases" up to the point where the benefit of spewing additional sparks just equals its social cost (as reflected by the tax or liability payment). The efficient outcome is achieved in this way by bringing the railroad's private costs in line with social costs. In this case, where the railroad is identified as the cause of the harm, the Coasian analysis just re-affirms the efficiency of the traditional Pigovian view.

But suppose that the disputed property right is assigned to the railroad rather than to the farmer. That is, suppose the railroad is allowed to spew sparks without incurring any tax or liability. According to the Pigovian view, this would involve *no* solution to the externality, and hence, it is assumed that the railroad, which is free to ignore the external harm, would simply expand the number of trains to its profit-maximizing level, q_p in Figure 2.1, resulting in an inefficient outcome. Coase argued, however, that this may not be the final outcome, because there is room for a bargain between the railroad and the farmer.

To see why, note that, starting from the railroad's privately optimal outcome (q_p in the graph), the last train yields zero marginal profit to the railroad because $MB=MC_p$, but it imposes positive marginal damages on the farmer in an amount equal to the vertical distance between the MC_S and MC_P curves at that point (the amount of the externality). Thus, the farmer would be willing to pay up to this amount to "bribe" the railroad to cut back on the number of trains, and the railroad would accept any amount greater than zero (the private value of the marginal train) to do so. In other words, the farmers would be willing to "buy" the right to prevent the marginal train from running. Such bargaining would in theory continue as long as the value of the marginal train to the farmer in the form of reduced crop damage (the vertical distance between MC_S and MC_P at any given point between q_P and q_S) exceeds the value of the marginal train to the railroad (the vertical distance between MB and MC_P at that point). Bargaining will therefore take place up to the point where $MC_S-MC_P=MB-MC_P$, or where $MB=MC_S$, which is exactly the efficient point.

Note that in this scenario, although the disputed property right was initially awarded to the railroad, the farmer was able to purchase it up to the point where it was equally valuable at the margin to the two parties. This is the opposite of what happened under the Pigovian approach, where the railroad had to purchase the right. Importantly, however, the outcome in both cases was the same—namely, the efficient number of trains operated. This conclusion—that the outcome will be efficient regardless of the initial assignment of rights provided that the parties can bargain—is an example of the *Coase Theorem.*

Now recall the first assumption implicit in the Pigovian approach to externalities: that there is a unique cause of the harm. The preceding analysis shows that this is not true. In fact, both parties, the railroad and the farmer, are simultaneously causes in the sense that if either party were absent, the harm would go away. In this sense, as Coase observes, the causal relation is "reciprocal" rather than being one-way. It follows that it is not necessarily optimal to assign the legal right in a dispute to one or the other of the parties. If the parties are able to bargain, *it does not matter for efficiency how the right is assigned*, the efficient number of trains, q_s, will operate either way.

While the assignment of rights does not matter with respect to the number of trains that will run, it *does* affect the distribution of wealth between the railroad and the farmer. In particular, when the right is assigned to the farmer (as under the Pigovian view), the railroad must pay in order to run trains up to the efficient number, whereas when the right is assigned to the railroad, the farmer must pay to reduce the number of trains down to the efficient number. Thus, each party would prefer to possess the property right in question, which is not surprising because it is, after all, a valuable right. What this conclusion implies is that in assigning the right, courts need not worry about efficiency (provided that the conditions of the Coase Theorem are met), but can focus instead on which party is the more deserving in a distributional sense. In other words, there is no conflict between efficiency and fairness regarding the assignment of the right.

The ability of the parties to bargain to an efficient outcome is, of course, by no means guaranteed, an observation that limits the usefulness of the Coase Theorem for practical purposes. For example, if land along the tracks is owned by several farmers, then awarding them the right to be free from crop damage collectively may prevent any trains from running because it would first be necessary for the railroad to obtain the permission from *all farmers* along the route, and such transactions would be costly. Conversely, if the right were assigned to the railroad, the farmers would have to organize to act collectively to buy the rights to inefficient trains, which would also be costly. In these cases, the initial assignment of rights becomes critical for achieving the efficient outcome in an externality setting because Coasian bargaining is unlikely.

This conclusion is perhaps the most important implication of the Coase Theorem with regard to actual legal rulemaking; namely, that when transaction costs are high, the initial assignment of rights will probably decide final ownership. In this circumstance, the law matters for efficiency. This observation brings us to the second of the implicit Pigovian assumptions: that government intervention is necessary to internalize an externality. This assumption turns out to be true in a world of high transaction costs precisely because Coasian bargaining is not possible in that case. Thus, the assignment of rights that the government, or the court, imposes will most likely be the final one, and it must therefore be chosen explicitly with efficiency in mind (assuming that is the desired goal). In that case, we would say that a corollary to the Coase Theorem is that *when transaction costs are high, property rights should be assigned to the party that values them most*.

In the railroad-farmer example, this would actually argue for "dividing" property rights to trains so that the railroad has the unencumbered right to run q_S trains, but the right to run further trains implicitly lies with the farmers. The question is how the farmers would enforce their right if the railroad tried to run more than q_S trains. Given the assumption of high transaction costs, they would not be able to act collectively to bribe the railroad to cut the number of trains back to q_S. And if these costs also prevented the farmers from collectively filing a damage suit, the government would have to act on their behalf to enforce the right, either through a direct regulation on the railroad limiting the number of trains to q_S, or by the imposition of a properly calibrated Pigovian tax on the railroad.

The comparison of the low- and high-transaction cost scenarios in the railroad-farmer example illustrates a larger point regarding the role of bargaining (consensual trade) versus the law (coercion) in achieving an efficient allocation of resources. This is a fundamental insight because it defines the scope for legal intervention in markets; in other words, it determines when the law matters. The next chapter picks up on this theme and carries it to its logical conclusion by examining in more detail rules for protecting the assigned property rights.

3 The choice between property rules and liability rules

An important extension of the Coasian perspective on externalities from the previous chapter concerns the choice of legal rules for protecting the assignment of property rights. This choice was first examined in the classic article by Calabresi and Melamed (1972) in which they distinguished between *property rules* and *liability rules*. These two enforcement rules differ in terms of how they protect a legally defined "entitlement," meaning control over some asset or portion of an asset. For example, in the railroad-farmer dispute, the setting of the entitlement determines how many trains the railroad can legally run without facing some form of sanction. Once that entitlement is established, however, it is equally important to specify how it will be protected and, what amounts to the same thing, how it can be legally transferred. Let us say that the farmer wins the entitlement to be free from any crop damage (i.e., the initial entitlement point is zero trains). If that entitlement is protected by a property rule, then the only way that the railroad can legally impose crop damage is by negotiating with the farmers to purchase the right to run its trains. In the absence of such an agreement, the farmers can (collectively) seek an injunction ordering the railroad to cease running trains under penalty of law. Alternatively, if the farmers' entitlement is protected by a liability rule, the railroad can run its trains without first obtaining the farmers' permission as long as it is willing to pay compensation to the farmers for the resulting crop damage. In other words, the railroad can "take" the farmer's entitlement in a forcible transfer by paying a "price" set by the court.

As these examples illustrate, the key difference between a property rule and a liability rule concerns the manner in which entitlements can be legally exchanged. Under a property rule, exchange can only occur by means of a consensual (market) transaction, whereas under a liability rule it can occur by means of a forced (but legal) exchange. Property rules therefore require *consent* whereas liability rules do not. Much of the analysis in Calabresi and Melamed's article concerns the choice between these two enforcement rules. The decision turns on the dual-edged nature of consent: on one hand, consent ensures mutual gains in a transaction, but on the other it can result

14 Property rules and liability rules

in high transaction costs. The choice between property rules and liability rules reflects this trade off.

To illustrate, return to the railroad-farmer dispute. If there is a single farmer along the tracks, it is conceivable that the railroad and farmer would be able to engage in bargaining with each other over the assignment of the entitlement in such a way as to maximize the joint value of their activities. In this case, use of a property rule would be preferred because it sets the stage for such bargaining, and, according to the Coase Theorem, this will necessarily lead to the efficient outcome. In contrast, if there are multiple farmers along the tracks, bargaining becomes much more costly, and so there is no assurance that an efficient outcome will be achieved by consensual means. In this case, use of a liability rule to protect the farmers' rights would be preferred because it removes the need for the railroad to negotiate with each farmer before running its trains. Instead, the court sets the price of the entitlement, thus saving the costs of bargaining. (It would still be necessary for the farmers to file suit for damages, perhaps in the form of a class action suit.) It is important to note, however, that attainment of an efficient outcome under a liability rule hinges on the ability of the court to set the price correctly, which means that it has to accurately measure the farmers' damages.

As an illustration of the preceding argument, consider a numerical example of the railroad-farmer dispute, the details of which are summarized in Table 3.1. The first column shows the number of trains run by the railroad; the second column shows the railroad's profit; the third column shows the resulting crop damage to farmers along the route; and the fourth column shows the net gain (profit minus damages). Obviously, the railroad maximizes its profit by running two trains, but the socially optimal outcome, that which maximizes the railroad's profit less the crop damage is for only one train to run.

Suppose initially that there is a single farmer who sustains all of the damage, and that bargaining between the railroad and the farmer is therefore possible. Further, suppose that the court assigns the entitlement to the farmer and protects it with a property rule. Thus, the farmer can obtain an injunction to prevent the railroad from running any trains. The railroad, however, would be willing to offer the farmer up to $50 to be allowed to run the first train, and the farmer would accept any amount above $40.

Table 3.1 Illustration of the choice between property rules and liability rules

Number of trains	Railroad profit ($)	Crop damage ($)	Net gain ($) (=profit–damage)
0	0	0	0
1	50	40	10
2	100	95	5

Thus, there is room for a bargain, and the first train would run. The parties would not, however, be able to reach a bargain that would allow the *second* train to run. Although the railroad would again offer up to $50, its incremental profit from running the second train (=$100–$50), the farmer would demand at least $55, his incremental crop damage (=$95–$40). Thus, no transaction would be possible. The final outcome is that only one train would run, which is the efficient result. This is confirmed by the fourth column, which shows that the net social gain is maximized when only one train runs. (Note that the second train is inefficient even though it yields a positive net benefit.)

Now suppose that bargaining between the parties is not possible because there are several farmers along the tracks whose aggregate damages are the amounts shown in the table. In this case, protecting the farmers' collective right to be free from damage with a property rule will not lead to an efficient outcome because, by hypothesis, the railroad will not be able to negotiate individually with the farmers to lift the injunction. As a result, no trains would run. Suppose, therefore, that the court protected the farmers' entitlement with a liability rule and set the price equal to the farmers' aggregate damages. The railroad could therefore acquire the entitlement to run its trains without having to negotiate with the farmers, provided it was willing to pay the damages set by the court (and, as noted, assuming the farmers filed suit). In this case, the railroad would again run only one train because its net profit, including the court-imposed damages, coincides with the net social gain. The railroad therefore internalizes the externality and the outcome is efficient.

The preceding example shows the advantage of liability rules over property rules when transaction costs are high. Specifically, they allow the court to mediate the transfer of entitlements by setting the price that the railroad must pay, given that negotiations between the parties are not possible. The importance of the court's setting the correct price, however, should be clear. Suppose, for example, that the court over-estimated the damage from the first train to be $60. In that case, the railroad would not have been willing to run that train. Conversely, if it correctly estimated the damage from the first train at $40 but under-estimated the damage from the second train to be $45, the railroad would have run both trains. Either way, the outcome is inefficient. The point is that the possibility of legal error limits the usefulness of liability rules for achieving an efficient allocation of rights. We therefore conclude that courts should only use liability rules in those situations where transaction costs between the parties to an externality are high.

A classic illustration of the logic underlying the choice between property rules and liability rules is offered by the well-known case of *Boomer v. Atlantic Cement Co.*[1] The case involved a factory whose operation caused noise and smoke that harmed a group of nearby residents. The victims collectively filed suit seeking an injunction to have the factory shut down, but the court opted instead to allow the factory to continue to operate provided it paid damages to the residents. In other words, the court found for the plaintiffs by awarding them an entitlement to be free of the harm, but instead of granting the injunction—which would have amounted to protecting the entitlement with a property rule—it awarded damages; that is, it protected the entitlement with a liability rule. In defending its ruling the court argued that issuing an injunction likely would have caused the plant to shut down, resulting in the loss of the value of the plant (estimated at $45 million) as well as hundreds of jobs, as compared to the $185,000 in damages suffered by the plaintiffs. In contrast, use of a damage remedy allowed the plant to continue operating provided it was willing to pay the damages (which in this case it certainly would have).

The court's choice of a liability rule (damages) over a property rule (an injunction) in this case reflects the belief that costly bargaining between the plant owner and the residents would have been necessary to lift an injunction and allow the plant to continue operating. The situation is similar to the multiple-farmer example given previously. The use of a liability rule removed that obstacle and allowed the efficient outcome to be achieved.

A final point is that, although large numbers are usually an indication of high transaction costs, small numbers do not always assure *low* transaction costs. In the *Boomer* case, even if there had been a small number of plaintiffs, transaction costs between the plant and the plaintiffs might have been high because the range of bargaining was so large. In theory, the plant would have been willing to pay up to $45 million to stay open, while the plaintiffs as a group would have accepted anything above $185,000 to drop an injunction. Economists refer to situations like this as a *bilateral monopoly* because each side has no choice but to bargain with the other side. When the bargaining range is large, negotiations can be very costly. Thus, in externality settings, we usually suppose that large numbers are a sufficient but not a necessary condition for bargaining costs to be high.

The Coasian perspective on controlling externalities as described so far has emphasized the choice between property rules and liability rules as alternative ways of governing the transfer of entitlements. However, Calabresi and Melamed also discuss a third rule for protecting entitlements, referred to as an *inalienability rule*. When an entitlement is protected by an inalienability rule, the holder cannot legally transfer or surrender it *under any circumstances*. For example, the Declaration of Independence states that citizens of the United States have an "unalienable" right to life, liberty, and the pursuit of happiness, and the U.S. Constitution protects basic freedoms, such as speech, religion, and the right to vote from any infringements. Thus, no person can part with those rights, even in a consensual transaction. In addition, the law forbids certain other transactions, such as the sale of one's labor for a wage below the statutory minimum, the sale of body parts, or the sale of one's body for sex.

Inalienability rules pose a challenge to the preceding perspective because they represent an absolute ban on consensual exchange, even when transaction costs are low. In some cases, one can appeal to externalities as the rationale for prohibiting such transactions. For example, the sale of drugs may be consensual at the time of purchase, but the use of drugs can create an addiction that robs the user of free will in the future (an intertemporal externality), and drug use may lead to crimes as addicts seek to support their habit. In other cases, however, arguments based purely on efficiency simply cannot explain the restrictions. For example, minimum wage laws are surely aimed at altering the distribution of wealth rather than improving the efficiency of the labor market, and absolute protections of certain fundamental civil and human rights are based on moral or ethical, rather than economic, considerations. These factors represent the limits of economic analysis of law, at least based on the norm of efficiency.

Let us return to the consideration of alienable entitlements and conclude the current discussion by summarizing the arguments in this and the preceding chapters by means of the "General Transaction Structure," which represents a unified framework for understanding the relationship between markets and law. Table 3.2 provides a schematic depiction of this structure within the context of the railroad-farmer dispute. The table depicts four possible outcomes of the dispute, depending on which party is *assigned* the entitlement (in this case, the right to control the number of trains that will run), and how that entitlement is *enforced*, whether by a property rule or a liability rule. If the court assigns the entitlement to the farmer (left-hand column), it can either protect it with a property rule (upper left cell), in which case the farmer can seek an injunction stopping any trains; or with a liability rule (lower left cell), in which case the farmer can only seek damages for the lost crops. Conversely, if the court assigns the entitlement to the railroad (right-hand column), it can protect it with a property rule (upper right cell), in which case the railroad is free to run as many trains as it wants; or with a liability rule (lower right cell), in which case the farmer can compel the rancher to run fewer trains, but it must pay the railroad's forgone profit.

As emphasized previously, the choice among these various options depends, in part, on the ability of the two parties to bargain with one another. Suppose first that they can bargain costlessly. In that case, we have argued that a property rule is preferred to a liability rule because a property

Table 3.2 The General Transaction Structure

		Assignment	
		Farmer	*Railroad*
Enforcement	*Property rule*	Farmer can enjoin trains	Railroad can run trains
	Liability rule	Farmer can seek damages for lost crops	Railroad can seek compensation for lost profit

rule promotes a consensual resolution of the dispute rather than leaving it in the hands of the court. As for the initial assignment of the right, that choice determines the direction of any payments and therefore is primarily a distributional issue. If, for example, the farmer wins the case, he can enjoin the running of trains, and the railroad must pay the farmer to lift the injunction. Conversely, if the railroad wins, it can run any number of trains and the farmer must pay it to reduce that number. Either way, though, the efficient outcome is achieved through Coasian bargaining, with the role of the court being limited to enforcing any transactions.

If on the other hand transaction costs are thought to be high, a liability rule is preferred, with the court taking on the role of both assigning the entitlement (i.e., deciding the winner), and setting the price at which it can be transferred. In this case, if the farmer wins, he cannot force the railroad to cut back on the number of trains but can only seek damages for lost crops. As long as the court sets the amount of the damages equal to the value of the crops, the railroad will run the efficient number. Conversely, if the railroad wins, the farmer can compel it to cut back on the number of trains, but he must pay for the lost profits. Again, if the court sets the damages equal to forgone profits, the efficient number of trains will run.

Note that the preceding argument outlines a division of responsibilities between the market and courts. Specifically, it prescribes that when market (consensual) transactions are feasible, they are the preferred method for allocating resources, and the court should therefore remain in the background. In this case, the law acts as a complement to market exchange by enforcing property rules. However, when transaction costs are likely to prevent bargaining, the court takes on a greater role in allocating resources by setting the price of exchange, and then allowing non-consensual transactions by means of liability rules. In this case, the law substitutes for markets.

With this framework in mind, let us return to the traditional economic treatment of externalities from the previous chapter, which we referred to as the Pigovian approach. Notice that this represents only one of the four possible outcomes in Table 3.2—specifically, it corresponds to the lower left cell, where the railroad, in the role of the "injurer," is compelled to pay damages equal to the harm suffered by the farmer, playing the role of the "victim." (In this case, it doesn't matter for efficiency if the damages are in the form of tort liability or a Pigovian tax, for, as argued in the previous chapter, they have the same effect on the incentives of the injurer.) The *Boomer* case similarly corresponds to the outcome in the lower left cell, given that the factory in that case was cast as the injurer and was therefore ordered to pay damages to the victims as a condition for remaining in operation.

The upper left cell reflects the assignment of the entitlement to the farmer, protected by a property rule (injunction). This would be efficient in cases where it is expected that the two parties can negotiate fairly easily, as when the numbers are small. In actual case law, this outcome represents application of the law of trespass, where victims (farmers) can enjoin unwanted physical intrusions onto their property (by railroad sparks). Here, the small numbers involved suggest that a consensual resolution of the dispute under such a rule would be feasible.

The right-hand side of Table 3.2, which represents cases where the railroad wins, effectively reverses the roles of injurer and victim by requiring the farmer to pay for any "damages" that the railroad incurs by having to cut back on the number of trains. (Recall that in the Coasian perspective, the roles of injurer and victim were relative.) In the upper right cell, this assignment is protected by a property rule, meaning that the farmer has to "bribe" the railroad to reduce the number of trains. In other words, the railroad is not liable for any crop damage—in fact, the payment will go in the other direction if the farmer chooses to pay the railroad to cut back on the number of trains. In the law, this outcome coincides with the common law doctrine of "coming to the nuisance," which grants pre-existing land users priority over newcomers when their uses are incompatible. The lower right cell represents the same assignment of the entitlement, but protected with a liability rule.

A famous illustration of this last outcome is the case of *Spur Industries, Inc. v. Del E. Webb Development Co.*,[2] which involved a land developer who encroached upon a pre-existing cattle feedlot and sued to have it shut down as a nuisance. The court granted the developer's request, but ordered him to pay the feedlot's relocation costs. Note that under this ruling, the feedlot actually "won" the case because its entitlement to remain in operation was legally recognized, though it was only protected by a liability rule. The developer could therefore shut the feedlot down by paying its lost profits (damages). The *Spur* case thus turns the Pigovian view of externalities on its head by reversing the roles of injurer and victim, thereby exemplifying the reciprocal nature of causation first pointed out by Coase. (The court's use of a liability rule in *Spur* might, perhaps, be questioned on the grounds that only two parties were involved, and hence transaction costs should have been low.)

I conclude this discussion of the General Transaction Structure, and the choice between property rules and liability rules, by suggesting how criminal law might fit into the overall framework (a connection first suggested by Calabresi and Melamed). Consider a thief who steals someone else's property. When the thief is apprehended, what should the punishment be? Suppose that he is assessed a fine equal to the cost of the stolen property. By the logic of the above argument, only thieves who value the property more than the owner would therefore ever commit the theft, and the result would be an efficient exchange (albeit non-consensual) in the sense that the property ends up in the hands of the higher-valuing owner. In other words, the theft is efficient. An interesting question is how this example of an "efficient theft" differs (if at all) from the outcome of the *Spur* case. After all, both represent non-consensual transfers of an entitlement, with the deprived owner being fully compensated for the loss. Intuition suggests that they are different, but the question is, how?

The resolution of this paradox is that the theft allowed the thief to transform the property rule into a liability rule—that is, to violate the Transaction Structure, whereas the ruling in *Spur* was compatible with it. The thief's behavior is not desirable because under that structure, the entitlement in question was specifically protected by a property rule for the reasons cited previously; namely, because when transaction costs are low, society has deemed market (consensual) exchange to be the preferred means of exchanging entitlements. However, a theft converts that property rule into a liability rule by making the exchange non-consensual. The labelling of such unwanted conversions as "crimes" identifies them as illegitimate transfers and attaches a punishment above and beyond the value of the stolen item (a "kicker") in an effort to deter them. In contrast, transfers governed by liability rules, while also non-consensual, are deemed legitimate by the Transaction Structure.

If this argument makes sense for entitlements to ordinary property, it would seem to be all the more compelling for acts that involve bodily injury or the deprivation of civil rights—cases where the violator attempts to transform an inalienability rule into a liability rule. These acts also need to be labelled as crimes and the perpetrators to face criminal sanctions. I will pursue this argument further in Chapter 7 as one way of identifying the boundary between torts and crimes.

Notes

1   26 N.Y.2d 219, 309 N.Y.S.2d 312, 257 N.E.2d 870 (Court of Appeals of New York, 1970).
2   494 P.2d 701 (Ariz. 1972).

4 Does the law evolve toward efficiency?

Chapter 2 referred to the positive economic analysis of law, which in its strong form asserts that the common law, meaning the body of laws or precedents emanating from judicial rulings, reflects an economic logic. Much of the literature comprising the "economic analysis of law" (including several chapters in this book) is devoted to marshalling evidence in support of this conjecture. Because the common law has arisen gradually and without any obvious direction, however, it is natural to ask how that state of affairs, if true, could have arisen. This chapter offers some possible answers to that question.

While it would be implausible to argue that any of the major players in the legal process—particularly, litigants and judges—consciously pursue the goal of efficiency, it would be equally implausible to propose a theory that ignored the role of those agents, each acting in pursuit of their own self-interests, in shaping the direction of legal change. A proper theory must therefore account for the influence of all parties involved in the litigation process. Initially, we will focus solely on the behavior of litigants—plaintiffs and defendants—deferring until later a consideration of the impact of judicial decision making on the evolution of the law.

The first step in examining how the law evolves is to recognize that the vast majority of civil cases—indeed more than 95 percent—end up settling before they ever reach trial. And since the output of the legal process (precedents) comes entirely from appellate court decisions of cases that initially went to trial, the evolution of the common law depends solely on those few cases that reach trial and beyond. Thus, examining the manner in which these cases are "selected" for trial is a first step in understanding how the law evolves. This selection effect depends crucially on the bargaining between plaintiffs and defendants, in consultation with their lawyers, during the pre-trial period. We therefore begin our analysis by reviewing the economic theory of the settlement-trial decision.

Cases settle when the parties are able to agree on a monetary payment from the defendant to the plaintiff that allows them to avoid the costs of a trial. This will usually happen when the parties substantially agree on the likely outcome of a trial, such as when there is little disagreement about the facts of the case and the prevailing legal standard. The process of discovery—the procedural rules governing the exchange of information prior to trial—facilitates this outcome by compelling the parties to produce witnesses and respond to questions, thereby resolving many of the disagreements, especially over facts. The set of cases reaching trial are therefore primarily those for which the outcome remains uncertain, which raises the question of where this residual uncertainty comes from. The two principal economic models of litigation and settlement attribute it to *mutual optimism* and *asymmetric information*.

According to the mutual optimism model, trials result when the plaintiff and defendant each assess a high probability of victory at trial. Priest and Klein (1984) have argued that this situation is most likely to be true when the merits of the case put it close to the applicable legal standard, implying that, based on legal merit, each side believes it has an approximately equal chance of winning. This theory has given rise to the so-called "50 percent rule"—the prediction that cases reaching trial should result in a roughly 50 percent win rate for plaintiffs (and obviously, therefore, a 50 percent win rate for defendants).

The asymmetric information model instead attributes trials to the existence of some residual private information held by the plaintiff or the defendant, which results in the two parties' holding divergent beliefs about the outcome of a trial. According to this theory, the set of cases reaching trial depends on which side holds the private information. If it is the plaintiff, the theory predicts that cases reaching trial will be those for which there is a high probability of plaintiff victory because plaintiffs with weak cases would have already settled. If, however, the asymmetry is reversed and it is defendants who have private information about the strength of their cases, the theory makes the opposite prediction—namely, that only defendants with strong cases will go to trial, implying that cases reaching trial should have a low probability of plaintiff victory. Because either scenario is possible, the theory makes no specific prediction about the cases that will reach trial—it depends on the particular information structure. Putting this together with the prediction of the optimism model we are forced to conclude that, from a theoretical perspective, *any* probability of plaintiff victory at trial is possible (Shavell, 1996).

Although economic theory offers no clear prediction regarding the plaintiff win rate for cases that reach trial, we can draw some conclusions. Most importantly for present purposes, both the mutual optimism and asymmetric information models predict that cases with higher stakes (i.e., larger plaintiff damages) are more likely to be tried rather than settled. This is true because the stakes of the case magnify any disagreement over the outcome, which therefore makes it harder for the parties to find common ground. To illustrate, suppose that both the plaintiff and defendant assess that their probability of winning is .7 (meaning that the defendant assesses his probability of *losing* to be .3). Thus, both are optimistic. Also suppose that a trial costs $1,000 for each party, and the stakes of the case—the amount that the plaintiff is suing for—is $3,000. The expected value of trial for the plaintiff is therefore (.7)($3,000)−$1,000=$1,100, which represents the minimum amount she would accept in a settlement. The corresponding expected cost of trial for the defendant is (.3)($3,000)+$1,000=$1,900, which is the maximum amount he would offer in a settlement. The parties would therefore both benefit from any settlement amount between $1,900 and $1,100. If they split the gains evenly, they would settle for $1,500.

Now suppose that the stakes were raised to $10,000 but everything else remains the same. In this case the plaintiff's expected value of trial is (.7)($10,000)−$1,000=$6,000, while the defendant's expected cost of trial is (.3)($10,000)+$1,000=$4,000. Thus, a settlement is no longer feasible because there is no amount that the defendant would be willing to offer that the plaintiff would accept in lieu of trial. The greater likelihood of trial as the stakes increase turns out to be a crucial element for assessing the direction of legal change according to one influential theory.

That theory, first proposed in a pair of papers by Paul Rubin (1977) and George Priest (1977), relies on an Invisible Hand-type explanation along the lines of Adam Smith's proposition that markets achieve efficiency despite the self-interested behavior of individual participants. I illustrate the logic of this argument with a simple example. Suppose that legal rules can be categorized as being either *efficient* or *inefficient*. As an example, consider an accident setting in which either the injurer or the victim can prevent the accident by investing in some precaution (referred to as "alternative care" accidents). It is therefore efficient for the party with lower costs of care—the so-called "least cost avoider"—to make the investment. (It would be wasteful for both to invest in care since, by assumption, either can avoid the accident acting alone.) In this setting, strict liability is the efficient rule if injurers have lower costs, and no liability is the efficient rule if victims have lower costs.

Now suppose that the rule currently in place (it does not matter which) is inefficient. In order for the more efficient rule to be put in place, some lawsuits must be filed, and at least some of those cases must proceed to trial—and ultimately to appeal—so that judges can have the opportunity to evaluate the existing rule and possibly replace it with the other (more efficient) rule. Accident victims decide whether to file suit based purely on their self-interest. Still, their decision to file initiates the process that may ultimately lead to a change in the law.[1]

Once a case is filed, the next step is the pre-trial period during which the plaintiff and defendant negotiate over a possible settlement, as described above. Now recall that a common prediction of the two prevailing economic models of settlement was that cases involving higher stakes are more likely to result in a trial. Based on this conclusion, Priest (1977, p. 67) has reasoned as follows:

> For the set of all legal disputes, the stakes will be greater for disputes arising under inefficient rules than under efficient rules. Inefficient assignments of liability by definition impose greater costs on the parties

subject to them than efficient assignments. . . . It follows, therefore, that other factors held equal, litigation will be more likely for disputes arising under inefficient rules than for those arising under efficient rules.

If we combine this *selective litigation* argument with an assumption that judges are not biased *against* efficiency (it does not matter what they are *for*), we can show that the common law will evolve in the direction of efficiency. I illustrate the logic of this claim with a numerical example.

Suppose that at some point in time, the common law consists of ten rules, five of which are efficient in the above sense, and five of which are inefficient. (This could reflect ten jurisdictions, or ten areas of law within a given jurisdiction.) Then, over a fixed time period, litigation takes place which, given the selective litigation result, involves four of the inefficient rules and two of the efficient rules being evaluated at trial. In each case, a judge examines the applicable rule and decides whether to *uphold* it, or *overturn* it, where overturning an existing rule means replacing an efficient rule with an inefficient one, and vice versa. To minimize the role of judges (for now), I assume that they decide cases without regard for efficiency. Thus, both efficient and inefficient rules are upheld (or overturned) with probability one-half (though any fixed probability will do).

Given this simple setting, we can calculate that, after the litigation process has concluded, the number of efficient rules will have increased from five to six, where the latter consist of the three original rules that were not litigated (and hence remained in place); one that was litigated and upheld (the other having been overturned); and two inefficient rules that were litigated and overturned. The number of inefficient rules will have correspondingly decreased from five to four. This same result will occur in each subsequent period. We can therefore conclude that the process of selective litigation—which differentially subjects inefficient rules to litigation—combined with judicial indifference to efficiency, will cause the law to evolve in the direction of efficiency.

Intuitively, laws filter through the judicial process and are randomly replaced. Thus, the greater the chance that a particular law is subject to this filtering, the greater is its chance of being replaced. And because the economic theory of settlement implied that inefficient laws will be disproportionately litigated according to Priest's argument, they will be replaced with efficient laws at a higher rate than the opposite change, even though there is no conscious preference on the part of judges in favor of efficient rules. The result is a kind of "natural selection" of efficient rules.[2]

The preceding analysis is, of course, over-simplified and therefore needs to be qualified in several ways. First, notice that it is not a claim that the law *is* efficient at any point in time—only that it will evolve in that *direction*. Second, if the costs associated with inefficient laws are highly dispersed so that most victims are deterred from bringing suit by the high cost of doing so, then inefficient laws may not be litigated at a higher rate than efficient laws. Likewise, if the costs of efficient laws are concentrated, then victims may make a concerted effort to overturn them. Finally, judicial adherence to precedent will tend to inhibit any sort of legal change because it reflects a bias in favor of existing law, whether or not it is efficient. Thus, precedent will act to slow legal change, though without imparting any particular bias to it.

While decision by precedent may slow the march of the law toward efficiency, the practice offers some advantages as a decision-making strategy. These include saving on the costs of duplicate evidence gathering, adjudication, and legal error. These benefits must be weighed against its tendency to enshrine bad laws. An economic approach to decision by precedent reflects an optimal balancing of these factors.

To be specific, note that in the absence of precedent, judges have complete discretion to decide each case based on its merits. In an ideal world with fully informed and rational judges, this would be the optimal decision-making structure because it would allow judges to tailor decisions to individual circumstances. In this setting, the law would evolve optimally. However, in a world of imperfect information and error-prone or self-interested judges, a limitation on judicial discretion may be socially desirable. In general, constraining judges to follow precedent rather than exercising discretion will be beneficial in three circumstances: first, when judges cannot reliably respond to a changing environment, either because they lack the ability or knowledge to distinguish new situations, or because they seek to impose their own biases on the law; second, when the cost of wrongfully selecting a new rule is high; and third, when the environment is relatively stable, as in areas of the law that are not changing.

Another claimed benefit of decision by precedent, apart from its role in limiting legal error, is that it promotes predictability of the law. As Posner (2003, p. 553) characterizes it, precedents serve as "a stock of knowledge that yields services over many years to potential disputants in the form of information about legal obligations." Although the value of this knowledge depreciates over time as the environment changes, stability of the law per se is an important feature of an efficient legal system because, apart from its content, it provides a predictable background against which Coasian bargaining can take place. And, as discussed in Chapter 2, when such bargaining is feasible, resources will be allocated efficiently regardless of the content of the law.

In most areas of the law, however, the content matters because transaction costs preclude such bargaining. Fortunately, the above analysis of legal change implies that as precedents decay over time, meaning laws become less efficient, the litigation rate will likely increase because legal disputes will involve increasingly larger stakes. As a result, judges will have more opportunities to review existing legal rules, which will eventually result in their being replaced by more efficient rules according to the above evolutionary theory (again, assuming unbiased judges). In this way, the law operates as a self-correcting system.

The remaining wild card, of course, is the role of judicial preferences. Unfortunately, this remains a somewhat under-developed area in the literature, largely because of our incomplete understanding of what motivates judges. In seeking to develop a theory of judicial behavior, the first impulse of economists is to suppose that judges behave like any other economic agents by pursuing their self-interests (i.e., maximizing their utility). This approach is complicated, however, by the fact that judges for the most part have security of tenure, and their income is not directly tied to their performance. Even if it were, judicial performance is difficult to evaluate since many legal rulings have implications that will only be felt over a long time frame, making the effects of those decisions difficult to disentangle from other factors. Such considerations have led Richard Posner, the originator of the claim that the common law embodies an economic logic, and himself a federal judge, to lament that "it is the unique insulation of federal appellate judges from accountability that makes their behavior such a challenge to the economic analysis of law" (1995, p. 112). Nevertheless, there is a nascent and growing economic literature on judicial decision making that has begun to shed some light on their role in shaping the law.

One approach supposes that judges are concerned with enhancing their reputations. Specifically, judges are assumed to derive utility from deciding cases in accordance with their own personal preferences (so-called judicial "activism"), and from having future judges cite their opinions. At the same time, they suffer disutility from being overturned by a higher court. Thus, judges will tend to be more activist as their disutility from following precedents with which they disagree increases, and as their aversion to reversal decreases. But even judges who are strongly inclined to activism will want to maintain a healthy respect for precedent because "by refusing to follow their predecessors' decisions and thus weakening the practice of decision according to precedent, they reduce the likelihood that their successors will follow their decisions" (Posner, 1995, p. 121). Even activist judges will therefore likely pick and choose when to depart from precedent.

Judges are also subject to scrutiny by the legislative branch. If, for example, judges are perceived as having overstepped their bounds in terms of "legislating from the bench," Congress may seek to counteract their decisions by enacting legislation. (The response to the *Kelo* takings case, as will be discussed in Chapter 17, is an example.) The possibility of legislative oversight of the judiciary raises the question of judicial independence. The more independent the judiciary is from other branches of government, the more its decisions are insulated from political influence and rent-seeking, which should promote better judicial decisions, or at least remove one source of bad decisions. But offsetting this is the fact that greater independence gives judges more scope for imposing their own preferences on the law. It follows that there is an optimal degree of judicial independence. However, there would seem to be no mechanism to ensure that the degree to which judges actually exercise their discretion, and in what circumstances, will correspond to this ideal.

Finally, we might ask if any direct link can be drawn between judicial self-interest and the efficiency of the law. This is an important question because judicial bias, if unrestrained, can affect the direction of legal change. One hopeful suggestion is that judges actively promote efficiency as at least one of their many objectives. As Posner (1995, p. 132) notes,

> Efficiency—not necessarily by that name—is an important social value and hence one internalized by most judges, and it may be the only social value that judges can promote effectively, given their limited remedial powers and the value pluralism of our society. So it should be influential in judicial decision-making when judges are called upon to exercise the legislative function.

When judges' preferences do not align with efficiency, we can nevertheless seek comfort in the fact that, as long as these preferences are not *contrary* to efficiency, at least they will not divert the law away from its trend toward becoming more efficient. That was the message of the Invisible Hand arguments, which showed that selective litigation will drive the law toward efficiency as long as judges are neutral regarding efficiency and precedent is not an absolute constraint. At the moment, that may be the best we can say.

Notes

1 If the rule in place is strict liability, victims file in hopes of affirming the rule (i.e., of receiving compensation), whereas if the rule is no liability, they file in hopes of overturning it.
2 The analogy is to Darwinian evolution in biology, which results in organisms becoming better suited to their local environments over time (i.e., becoming more "efficiently" designed).

5 Threshold rules in law

This chapter examines the pervasiveness in law of what I call "threshold rules," or rules that condition the imposition of a legal sanction on whether or not a person has met (or surpassed) a threshold, or standard of behavior. The prototypical example of this is the negligence rule in tort law, which subjects an injurer to liability for the resulting damages if he or she failed to exercise reasonable, or "due," care to avoid the accident. This is in contrast to strict liability, which imposes damages on an injurer regardless of how careful he or she was (assuming it has been established that the injurer in fact caused the accident). In this chapter I will argue that there is a good economic reason for the prevalence of threshold rules. I will argue, in particular, that when properly structured, they provide an ingenious solution to the sort of bilateral incentive problems that commonly arise in the context of legal disputes. These represent situations in which the two parties to a potential dispute (an accident, say) both have the ability to take steps to reduce the likelihood of its occurrence, for example by investing in care. An important function of the governing legal rule in such settings is to provide incentives for the parties to undertake those steps in an efficient (cost-minimizing) manner, and I will show that threshold rules can achieve precisely that result. I will specifically demonstrate this conclusion in the context of tort law, and then provide examples from other areas of the law, some of which will show up later in the book, to illustrate the generality of the result.

The economic theory of tort law is based on the idea that imposing liability on injurers serves as a means of deterring unreasonably risky behavior. In this sense, tort liability performs the same function as a Pigovian tax—a similarity that we noted in Chapter 2—given that accidental harm is a type of externality. (The deterrence function of tort liability also has much in common with the economic theory of criminal law, as will be explored in Chapter 7.) An important difference is that tort law, because it is a private legal action initiated by the victim, is also concerned with compensating the victim, so any liability assessed against an injurer must be awarded to the victim as compensation. In contrast, the revenue from a Pigovian tax is not necessarily passed on to those bearing the external harm—a point that I will return to later. Indeed, the compatibility of these two functions of tort law—deterrence and compensation—will figure prominently in this chapter, especially as it relates to the negligence rule.

Negligence is the predominant basis for tort liability in the U.S. today, but that has not always been the case. Negligence only emerged as a separate cause of action during the early to mid-nineteenth century. Prior to that time, claims for negligence were limited to certain "public" callings—such as common carriers, innkeepers, blacksmiths, or surgeons—who were contractually obligated to provide proper service, and were subject to liability for failing to do so. It also applied to sheriffs, who were held negligent when they allowed debtors to escape custody. In none of these areas, however, did negligence carry the modern meaning of a failure to take "reasonable care." Rather, it connoted "nonfeasance," or failure to perform a pre-existing, usually contractual, duty. The broader realm of accident law involving accidents between parties not in a pre-existing contractual relationship (so-called accidents between "strangers") was a relatively unimportant field of law prior to the industrial revolution, with few cases coming before the courts. In those that did, there was "considerable uncertainty" over whether they were governed by strict liability or some form of negligence (Landes and Posner, 1987, pp. 2–3). The rise of the modern concept of negligence, meaning the failure to take reasonable care (which means the same thing as being "at fault"), coincided with the onset of industrialization and the resulting explosion of accidents caused by mechanization.

Richard Posner (1972) was the first to propose an explicitly economic theory of negligence law based on the due care standard famously advanced by Judge Learned Hand in the case of *U.S. v. Carroll Towing Co.*[1] According to the eponymous "Hand test," the determination of negligence is to be based on three factors: the probability that an accident will occur (P), the damages, or loss, in the event of an accident (L), and the burden of precautions necessary to prevent the accident (B). As asserted by Judge Hand, a defendant who failed to take precaution was negligent if the burden of that precaution was less than the expected damages, or if $B<PL$. As Posner demonstrated, this test creates exactly the right incentives for injurers to invest in the efficient level precaution—that is, the level that minimizes the sum of the cost of precaution plus expected harm—if it is applied in its correct *marginal* form. Specifically, B must be interpreted as the marginal cost of the precaution in question, and PL must be interpreted as the expected marginal reduction in accident costs.

Table 5.1 Data for accident example

Care level	Cost of care ($)	Expected damages ($)	Care plus damages ($)
Low	10	100	110
Moderate	20	85	105
High	30	80	110

To illustrate this point, consider the following numerical example in which a potential injurer can invest in care to reduce the risk of an injury. The relevant data for the example are shown in Table 5.1. The injurer can choose among three possible levels of care: "low," "moderate," and "high," which cost, respectively, $10, $20, and $30, as shown in column two of the table. Greater care reduces expected damages, but at a decreasing rate, as shown in column three. The socially optimal level of care is that which minimizes the sum of care plus damages. This occurs at the moderate level of care, as shown in column four, indicating that this level of care is the efficient choice.

Now let's consider the injurer's incentives to invest in care, first under a rule of strict liability, and then under a rule of negligence. As noted, strict liability, like a Pigovian tax, imposes the full damages on the injurer, and thereby creates exactly the right incentives for him to choose the efficient care level. The reason is that the injurer's costs coincide with the social costs in column four, which are minimized at the moderate care level. At the same time, the damages paid by the injurer are awarded to the victim, who is thereby fully compensated for her losses. The two objectives of tort law, deterrence and compensation, are therefore perfectly compatible under strict liability.

Now consider negligence as applied according to the Hand test. We first need to determine how B, P, and L correlate to the numbers in the table. Suppose initially that we interpret the cost of care in column two to be B, and the expected damages in column three to be PL. In that case, it would appear that the injurer would be found negligent if he chose anything other than "high" care because $B<PL$ for all three options. However, this turns out to be an incorrect application of the rule. The correct *marginal* application applies it instead to successive care choices. To illustrate, consider first the injurer's choice between "low" and "moderate" care. The cost of increasing care from low to moderate is $10 (=$20–$10), while the resulting reduction in expected accident costs is $15 (=$100–$85). Treating the *increase* in costs as B and the *reduction* in damages as PL, we see that $B<PL$, so it is efficient for the injurer to take moderate rather than low care. Now apply the same analysis to the decision of whether the injurer should further increase his care from moderate to high. The increase in costs (B) is again $10 (=$30–$20), but the reduction in damages (PL) is now only $5 (=$85–$80). In this case, $B>PL$ and the extra care is *not* efficient. It follows that the injurer should not take the extra care, meaning that moderate care is the optimal choice.

The proper application of the marginal Hand test in the more general case where care is continuously variable is illustrated in Figure 5.1, where units of care, denoted x, are measured on the horizontal axis. The horizontal line labeled B is the marginal cost of care, again assumed to be constant, and the downward sloping curve labeled PL is the marginal reduction in care, assumed to be decreasing. The intersection determines the optimal (cost-minimizing) level of care, x^*. With the negligence standard set at this level of care, the injurer will be found negligent if $x<x^*$, which coincides with $B<PL$; and he will be found non-negligent if $x>x^*$, which coincides with $B>PL$.

The way that the negligence rule induces injurers to comply with the due care standard of x^* (or moderate care) is by imposing the victim's damages on him *only if he fails to meet or surpass the threshold of due care*. In the above example, the injurer would therefore be found negligent, and hence liable, if he took a low level of care, but he would not be found negligent, and hence would avoid liability, if he took either moderate or high care. Table 5.2 compares the injurer's costs under strict liability (column two) and negligence (column three) for the different care choices. Note that his costs are minimized when care is moderate under both rules, indicating that

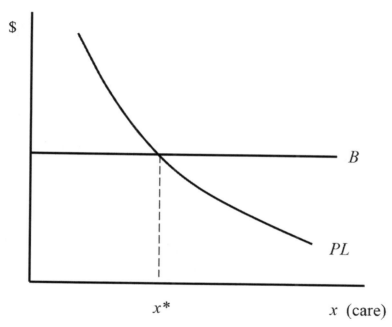

Figure 5.1 The marginal Hand test

Table 5.2 Injurer's costs under strict liability and negligence

Care level	Strict liability ($)	Negligence ($)
Low	110	110
Moderate	105	20
High	110	30

both rules induce optimal care. The difference, however, is that the injurer must pay the victim's full damages regardless of his care choice under strict liability, but he escapes paying damages as long as his care choice meets or exceeds the efficient care level under negligence.

It should be clear from this example that the injurer has a strong incentive to just *meet* the efficient care level under negligence because by doing so he avoids a large jump in his costs, from $20 to $110. However, he has no incentive to *exceed* the efficient level, as this would increase his cost of care from $20 to $30 with no corresponding savings in liability. Thus, the injurer minimizes his costs by choosing moderate care.

The two liability rules differ, however, regarding compensation of victims. Note in particular that when the injurer meets the due standard under negligence, *the victim does not recover her damages*. Thus, deterrence is achieved at the expense of leaving victims uncompensated. This would seem to be a strong argument in favor of strict liability over negligence, and it therefore presents something of a puzzle regarding the predominance of negligence law. I will now argue that the resolution of this puzzle is found by turning to accident settings in which victims can also invest in care against accidents, referred to as "bilateral care" accidents.

It should be obvious that in many accident settings, victim care is at least as important as injurer care in reducing accident risk. For example, pedestrians should stop and look both ways before crossing a busy street, consumers of dangerous products should only use them for their intended purposes, and patients should follow the doctor's instructions prior to surgery. In these bilateral care contexts, imposing strict liability on injurers is not generally efficient because then victims would have little or no incentive to be careful. In the language of economics, strict liability creates a moral hazard problem for victims, precisely because they are fully compensated for their losses. In contrast, we will now show that a properly structured negligence rule creates incentives for both injurers and victims to invest in efficient accident care.

As demonstrated previously, the due care standard creates a strong incentive for injurers to meet, but not to exceed, the due standard in order to minimize their costs. It follows that any residual accident losses will remain on the victim. Since victims rationally anticipate that this will be the case—specifically, that injurers will invest in due care and will therefore not have to pay damages—they (victims) have an incentive to invest in efficient accident precaution themselves so as to minimize their expected losses. The negligence rule thus induces efficient care by both injurers and victims because it combines two mechanisms for creating efficient incentives—on one hand, it sets a threshold level of care so that the injurer can *avoid liability* by meeting that threshold (as shown earlier), while on the other, it *imposes the full damages* on the victim. The result is an efficient equilibrium in which accident costs are minimized.

The preceding argument illustrates the superiority of negligence over strict liability regarding cost-minimization in bilateral care accident settings, but the logic of the argument has implications beyond tort law. As I have suggested, it reveals the general usefulness of threshold rules for creating bilateral incentives. As noted, the problem with a rule of strict liability was that the awarding of compensation to victims eliminated any incentives for them to avoid the accident because they (theoretically) expect to be made whole. This moral hazard problem is a direct consequence of the dual function of liability to both deter dangerous activities by injurers and to compensate the victims of those activities. While we saw that deterrence and compensation are perfectly compatible when only injurers can take precaution, in those situations where victims can also take precaution, the compensatory and incentive functions are necessarily in conflict. Cooter (1985) has referred to this as the "paradox of compensation," in recognition of the adverse impact on victim incentives of imposing strict liability on injurers.

The problem underlying the paradox of compensation is the legal requirement that any money paid by the injurer in the form of liability must be passed on to the victim as compensation. As a result, only one party can face the full damages—either the injurer under strict liability, or, symmetrically, the victim under "no liability." A Pigovian tax can resolve this paradox by imposing the victim's damages on the injurer, but then *not passing the revenue from the tax on to the victim*. In this way, both parties in effect face the full damages and so take efficient care. Tort rules cannot achieve this kind of "bilateral responsibility," however, because of the constraint that what the injurer pays the victims must receive. In recognition of this problem, some economists have advocated "de-coupling" liability from compensation—in effect adopting a Pigovian tax approach to tort liability.[2]

The brilliance of the negligence rule is that it resolves the paradox of compensation by establishing a standard of behavior that the injurer can meet to avoid liability, which then leaves the victim to bear her own damages, thereby simultaneously giving both parties an incentive to invest in efficient care. This requires, of course, that the due standard be properly set, which highlights the importance of the Hand test for the economic theory of negligence. Beginning with Brown (1973), economists have formally shown that the threshold feature of negligence law, coupled with the marginal Hand test to determine that threshold, works perfectly to induce efficient bilateral care in accident settings.

The manner in which the negligence rule coordinates the behavior of injurers and victims was described by Grady (1988, p. 16) as follows: "if each party is placed in a position where its conduct is judged on the assumption that the other side has taken appropriate precautions, then it would act in the socially appropriate manner." What this says is that both injurers and victims, acting in ignorance of each other's behavior (i.e., prior to the accident), nevertheless have an incentive to choose the socially optimal care levels. In other words, it is not necessary that the parties explicitly coordinate with one another, or observe what the other is doing—it is sufficient that each acts under the *presumption* that the other party is behaving optimally.

What's more, the law of negligence compels parties who find themselves in risky situations to hold such presumptions; that is, to assume that any other parties with whom they may come in contact are taking efficient (due) care. As Justice Holmes wrote in the case of *LeRoy Fibre Co. v. Chicago, Milwaukee & St. Paul Ry.*: "as a general proposition people are entitled to assume that their neighbors will conform to the law ... and therefore ... are entitled to assume that their neighbors will not be negligent."[3] In this way the law facilitates the attainment of the efficient equilibrium by compelling people to behave *as if* everyone else is acting efficiently. It turns out that matters get substantially more complicated when one of the parties *can* observe what the other is doing before choosing his or her own action. In this case, strategic behavior becomes possible, as will be discussed in detail in the next Chapter.

I will conclude this chapter by briefly noting some other examples of threshold rules in the law, and suggesting that they are similarly responses to bilateral care problems. The first example, also from tort law, is the doctrine of proximate cause, which limits the liability of injurers to those accidents that were the *reasonably foreseeable* consequences of their actions. In other words, a reasonable person, standing in the position of the injurer prior to the occurrence of the accident, must have been able to foresee the victim's damages as resulting from his action or failure to act. If not, then the victim is barred from recovery, even if the injurer was negligent according to the Hand test. Proximate cause thus establishes a threshold based on reasonable foresight that exists alongside, and theoretically in opposition to, the Hand test for negligence. In fact, the reasonable foresight test can be conceptualized using the same marginal analysis as the Hand test, and therefore can serve the same economic purpose in terms of creating efficient bilateral incentives for injurers and victims. It is an interesting, and open, question as to why tort law includes both seemingly redundant tests.

Robert Cooter (1985) used the economic model of accidents (what he called the "model of precaution") to extend the logic of accident avoidance to other areas of law. The key insight, referred to earlier, is that most legal conflicts, regardless of the subject matter, can be conceptualized as bilateral care problems in the sense that they involve a dispute between two parties (a plaintiff and defendant), where each usually possesses the ability to take some pre-emptive of precautionary action to avoid or mitigate the resulting "damages." Cooter illustrated this approach in the context of both contract and property disputes. I will elaborate on both of these applications in later chapters and so will only sketch the arguments here.

In contract law, Cooter modeled the breach of a contractual promise as an "accident," where the breaching party (the promisor) plays the role of the "injurer", and the party to whom the promise was made (the promisee) plays the role of the "victim". The promisor's "care" in this setting is the decision of whether (or when) to breach the contract,[4] and the promisee's "care" is how much to invest in reliance on performance, which then determines the amount of her loss in the event of a breach. In this context, awarding victims full damages for breach is like strict liability in that it creates efficient incentives for promisors to avoid breach, but it simultaneously creates a moral hazard problem for promisees regarding their choice of mitigation—specifically, because they expect to be fully compensated, they will overrely on performance. Cooter showed, however, that a rule that limits damages to the amount that promisors could have *reasonably foreseen*—which he defined to be damages computed at the efficient level of promisee reliance—will create efficient incentives for both parties. (See the further discussion of this limited liability rule in Chapter 14.) While the rule is not structured exactly like negligence, it is nevertheless a threshold rule that works for the same reason.

Cooter's application of the model of precaution to property law concerns government regulations of private property, which fall under the law of eminent domain. In this context, the "injurer's" care corresponds to the government's regulatory decision, while the "victim's" care represents the landowner's initial investment in improvements to the land, which determines the value of the lost property in the event of a regulation. (This assumes that any improvements will be lost as a result of the regulation.) As will be detailed in Chapter 18, the application of a threshold rule to the question of whether a regulation ever rises to the level of a taking, thus requiring compensation (a "regulatory taking"), induces both efficient regulatory decisions by the government, and efficient land use decisions by the landowner. I will also argue there that the threshold aspect of the rule offers significant insights into the way courts have treated these cases.

Two other examples of threshold rules in subsequent chapters include the prohibition on unreasonable searches and seizures in criminal law (Chapter 7), and the fair use standard for unauthorized copying in the law of intellectual property (Chapter 19), both of which can be conceptualized using a modified Hand test. Both of these examples illustrate the usefulness of economic theory for providing a unifying framework for understanding disparate areas of law. Although the actual rules that have arisen in these different areas address very different sorts of legal problems, and the rules themselves often vary in their outward form, it can be seen that they embody a common structure when viewed through the lens of economic theory. In this sense, the law has converged on similar solutions to a common set of economic problems.

Notes

1 159 F.2d 169 (2d. Cir. 1947).
2 See, for example, Polinsky and Che (1991).
3 232 U.S. 340, 352 (1914).
4 It doesn't matter for current purposes that the breach is an "intentional" act. See the discussion of this point in the context of the tort–crime distinction in Chapter 7.

6 Simultaneous versus sequential care accidents and strategic negligence

The discussion of accident law in the preceding chapter involved situations in which potential injurers and victims made their care choices simultaneously, or more precisely, in ignorance of each other's decisions. The principal finding of that analysis was that, under a properly structured negligence rule, both parties have an incentive to behave efficiently—that is, to choose their cost-minimizing levels of precaution. Because each party had to act without first observing the actions of the other party, they had to form expectations about what the other was doing. For the resulting choices to constitute an equilibrium in game-theoretic terms (a Nash equilibrium), those expectations had to be fulfilled. In other words, each party's expectation about what the other party was doing had to turn out to be correct. The ingenuity of the negligence rule (and threshold rules in general) is that, when properly structured, it yields an equilibrium that is also efficient.

One can, of course, question the realism of this argument, relying as it does on the ability of potential injurers and victims to correctly anticipate what other parties, about whose actions they are ignorant, might be doing. The inability to observe the actions of others leading up to an accident, one supposes, would greatly impede the actual attainment of an efficient outcome. In contrast, if injurers and victims acted in sequence so that the second mover could first observe, and then respond to, the first mover's action, one might expect that an efficient outcome would become more likely. As it turns out, however, sequential care accidents are in fact more susceptible to opportunistic behavior.

An important reason for this paradoxical conclusion is the legal requirement, noted in the previous chapter, that parties must behave *as if* other parties with whom they might come into contact are exercising proper care to avoid accidents. By compelling this presumption, the law actually promotes the attainment of an efficient Nash equilibrium in simultaneous care accidents because it fixes the belief that parties must hold about what others are doing—namely, that they are exercising efficient care. When parties move in sequence, however, the second mover has time to react to the *actual* care that he or she observes, which may deviate, for whatever reason, from the efficient level. As a result, it turns out that inefficient behavior may actually become more pervasive.

In the prototypical sequential accident, one party—it could be either the injurer or the victim—moves first and chooses a care level. The other party, after observing the first party's care, then makes his or her care choice. If the first party took due care, then the incentive for the second party under the standard negligence rule is also to take due care, and the outcome is identical to that for simultaneous care accidents. The difference arises when the first party, whether by inadvertence, error, or intent, chooses an inefficiently low level of care (i.e., is negligent). The question then is whether the second mover still has an incentive to take due care, or better yet, to take extra precaution to avoid an accident. While it is desirable from an economic point of view for the second mover to take such "compensating precaution," the risk is that if the law compels people to respond in this way, first movers may have an incentive to be "strategically negligent" as a way of shifting some avoidance costs onto second movers.

The possibility of this sort of strategic behavior is well-illustrated in F. Scott Fitzgerald's classic novel, *The Great Gatsby*, by an interesting exchange between the narrator, Nick Carraway, and the professional golfer Jordan Baker. Nick was a passenger in Jordan's car when she nearly collided with some workmen on the road, after which the following conversation ensued:

> "You're a rotten driver," [Nick] protested.
> "I am careful."
> "No you're not."
> "Well, other people are," she said lightly.
> "What's that got to do with it?"
> "They'll keep out of my way," she insisted. "It takes two to make an accident."

Jordan evidently has adopted a strategy of being a reckless driver because she expects other drivers to avoid her. In other words, she is being strategically negligent. From an economic perspective, the question is how the law should deal with this sort of behavior.

Normatively speaking, the criteria for efficient behavior in sequential care accident settings can be stated as follows: (1) the party moving first (whether the injurer or the victim) should have an incentive to take efficient care; (2) when the first mover makes the efficient care choice, the second mover's best response should also be to take efficient care; and (3) when the first mover chooses too little care (i.e., is negligent), the second mover should have an incentive to respond by taking compensating precaution. The first two of these criteria are the same as those that we applied to simultaneous move accidents when asking whether two parties acting in ignorance of each other's choices have an incentive to take efficient care. The new criterion, number three, concerns the incentives of a party to respond to prior negligence by taking more than "ordinary" precaution to avoid an accident. (This of course is not possible in simultaneously care accidents.) This is what I mean by "compensating precaution." Economically speaking, this is a desirable thing to do because it mitigates the effect of the first mover's negligence (no matter why that happened), which is a sunk decision. However, it turns out to be quite difficult to satisfy this third criterion while still maintaining the first.

To see why, let us begin by considering the incentives created by a simple negligence rule in a sequential accident setting. In the previous chapter, we saw that this rule creates incentives for both parties to be careful in simultaneous accidents, assuming the due standard is set at the injurer's efficient level of care. The reason, recall, is that injurers have an incentive to meet the due standard to avoid liability, and victims, correctly anticipating that injurers are being careful, also have an incentive to take care to minimize their damages (which they expect to bear in equilibrium). In sequential accidents where injurers move first, they still have an incentive to be careful to avoid liability, and victims, who now *observe* injurers exercising due care, likewise have an incentive to be careful. Thus, the outcome is again efficient. So far so good.

But now suppose the injurer, moving first, does *not* take due care, for whatever reason. (We will return to the first mover's incentives.) In the simultaneous care case, this would not change the behavior of victims because, as noted, they must act based on the *presumption* that injurers will meet the due standard. The fact that some injurers fail to be careful therefore can have no effect on victims' behavior. Even if victims expect some injurers to be negligent, the law compels them to behave as if all injurers were being careful. In the sequential accident case, however, things are different because the victim *observes* the injurer's prior negligence. As a result, under a simple negligence rule she no longer has an incentive to be careful because she knows the injurer will bear the full liability as a consequence of his prior negligence. The simple negligence rule therefore creates no incentives for victims to be careful in the presence of negligent injurers.

The old English case of *Butterfield v. Forrester* addressed a situation like this.[1] The injurer had negligently placed an obstruction in the street, which the victim struck while riding his horse. The victim sued for damages based on the injurer's negligence, and he would have won under an ordinary negligence rule, but the court denied recovery because of the victim's own failure to exercise due care in the face of the obstruction. The court specifically said that "One person being in fault will not dispense with another's use of ordinary care for himself." In other words, victims confronted with prior negligence by injurers cannot automatically recover damages; they must also meet a due care standard of their own. The decision in this case thus established the concept of *contributory negligence* for victims, which subsequently became a standard component of negligence law.

Economists have shown that the pairing of negligence with contributory negligence—that is, the creation of a due standard for both injurers and victims—does not disrupt the efficiency of simple negligence in simultaneous care accidents (criteria one and two given previously), but it has the added benefit of compelling victims to be careful when confronted with negligent injurers in sequential accidents (criteria three). In other words, the contributory negligence standard creates an incentive for victims to take care in the presence of prior negligence. (It is not clear whether contributory negligence requires compensating precaution or just ordinary precaution in this case.) Landes and Posner (1987, p. 76) have argued that this logic provides an important economic justification for adding contributory negligence as a defense to the simple negligence rule.

The preceding argument applies to situations in which injurers move first, but victims can also move first; indeed, this may be the more common scenario. As an illustration, consider another old English case, *Davies v. Mann*,[2] which is similar to *Butterfield v. Forrester* except that the victim moved first. Specifically, the victim owned a donkey that he had tied up on the side of a highway. The injurer subsequently drove his wagon down the highway and hit the donkey, killing it. The court found that both parties were negligent in this case: the victim for having tied his donkey up on the side of the street, and the injurer for traveling at an excessive rate of speed. Under the new contributory negligence standard, the victim would therefore have been barred from recovery, in spite of the injurer's negligence, because of his own prior negligence. (In cases where both parties are negligent, the contributory negligence defense prevails.) As a result, injurers who confront a negligent victim not only have no incentive to take compensating precaution, they have no incentive to take ordinary precaution. In this case, a simple negligence rule would have worked better because it would have compelled the injurer to be careful regardless of the victim's prior negligence.

What these two cases show is that standard negligence rules fall short of satisfying the three criteria listed. It appears that they can satisfy at most two of the three. While both negligence and negligence with contributory negligence satisfy criteria one and two in the sense that they both create incentives for the parties to take ordinary care in the first place, neither provides "general purpose" incentives for a second mover to take compensating precaution (criteria three). Under simple negligence, a victim will have no incentive to be careful when confronting a negligent injurer, and under negligence with contributory negligence, an injurer will have no incentive to be careful when confronting a negligent victim. Since both scenarios are possible, it is hard to argue that either rule is superior to the other in dealing with sequential accidents.

The court in *Davies v. Mann* attempted to address this problem by articulating a kind of "catch-all" rule that became known as "last clear chance." Simply stated, the rule placed the burden on the party moving last to take any reasonable steps to avoid the accident, irrespective of any duties implied by the applicable negligence rule. Thus, in the *Davies* case, the court allowed the owner of the donkey to recover, despite his contributory negligence, because of the injurer's failure to take compensating precaution.

If the doctrine had been applied in the *Butterfield v. Forrester* case, it would have barred the victim's recovery on account of his negligence, despite the injurer's prior negligence. (In this case, last clear chance therefore would have had the same effect as contributory negligence, whereas in the *Davies* case, it would have defeated contributory negligence.) Although last clear chance has faded in importance with the advent of comparative negligence (more about which later), one can still admire the court's attempt to introduce a general duty by the second mover in sequential accident settings to take compensating precaution—that is, to provide a general purpose response to criterion three.

For this reason, the introduction of last clear chance would seem to have been a useful innovation in accident law in sequential care accident cases. But now let's consider the incentives of a "strategic" victim moving first under the last clear chance doctrine, where by strategic we mean a victim who acts rationally to minimize her costs while correctly anticipating the response of injurers given the prevailing legal rules. (The same logic would apply to cases where the injurer moves first.) Suppose first that the applicable rule is simple negligence coupled with last clear chance. If the victim takes ordinary (efficient) care, the injurer will respond by meeting the due standard to avoid liability. The outcome is therefore efficient (that is, criteria one and two are satisfied), and the victim bears her own damages. But can she do better by being strategically negligent? If the victim, moving first, takes less than ordinary care, the injurer will have to respond by taking compensating precaution under the last clear chance doctrine; because he will be held liable if he fails to do so, he as a strong incentive to comply. The victim still bears her damages under this outcome, but because her strategic underinvestment in precaution succeeded in shifting some of the costs of precaution to the injurer, she lowers her overall costs. Strategic negligence is therefore a rational decision by a victim moving first, knowing that the injurer has a duty to take compensating precaution. What this logic shows is that, although last clear chance creates an incentive for compensating precaution, the duty of compensating precaution itself undermines incentives for first movers to be careful. In other words, there is a fundamental conflict between criteria one and three.

Would the addition of a contributory negligence defense resolve this conflict, given that it creates a duty for victim precaution? The answer is no for the simple reason that last clear chance defeats a contributory negligence defense for the injurer. As we saw in the *Davies v. Mann* case, if the injurer confronts a negligent victim, he would have no incentive to take precaution if a contributory negligence defense were available. Thus, last clear chance must defeat contributory negligence if its purpose is to create an incentive for compensating precaution for injurers. But then we are back in the same situation as under simple negligence with last clear chance; that is, first movers in accident cases will have an incentive to be strategically negligent in order to shift some costs onto second movers. It seems that Jordan Baker, a self-proclaimed strategic victim/injurer, had an intuitive understanding of non-cooperative game theory (perhaps owing to her experience as a professional golfer!).

Mark Grady (1988, p. 19) has examined the last clear chance doctrine in light of the trade-off between criteria one and three and has concluded that

> When someone has been negligent in the first place—one hopes, through inadvertence—the best thing left to do is to get the other party to make up for it. But there is a flip side to the coin. If the second party must compensate for errors, the first party may think about the payoff from being deliberately negligent.

He argues that courts were in fact sensitive to this problem and therefore limited the duty of compensating precaution to those cases in which strategic negligence was not a serious problem. According to Grady, strategic negligence requires the following conditions to be satisfied: (1) the victim's negligence must be easily observed by the injurer; (2) the injurer must have ample time to react to it (that is, the "reaction time" must be sufficiently long); and (3) the strategic victim must be able to conceal her intention. The first two conditions are straightforward because they are objective criteria of the accident setting and therefore are easily observed by the court. Condition three, in contrast, is problematic because it requires knowledge of the victim's motivation at the time she made her care choice. Distinguishing between inadvertence and intent will therefore not generally be an easy task for the court.

Given this difficulty, it would seem to be preferable to apply last clear chance selectively, based on a more objective criterion that could possibly serve as an observable proxy for the victim's motivation. It turns out that a candidate for such a criterion emerges from an examination of the types of cases to which last clear chance was typically applied.

Historically, courts allowed negligent victims to recover in two types of cases: those in which the victim was *helpless*, and those in which the victim was merely *inattentive*. It seems fairly obvious that truly strategic victims, those whose actions are dictated by a strategic goal of shifting costs onto would-be injurers, would not want to put themselves into a helpless position from which they could not escape if an injurer did not "cooperate" by taking compensating precaution. Such a strategy would involve a very risky gamble that would put the victims' safety in the hands of a stranger. In contrast, supposedly "inattentive" victims are much more likely to be feigning inattentiveness (as opposed to helplessness), while still leaving themselves an out if the injurer does not take the expected compensating precaution. The greater risk of strategic behavior in this type of case suggests that the costs of invoking last clear chance may outweigh its benefits.

As an example, consider the case of *New York Cent. R. Co. v. Thompson*,[3] which concerned a woman who, while walking home one night, caught her foot in some railroad tracks. An approaching train saw her predicament but did not brake, injuring her. The court held the train liable for her damages under last clear chance, despite her obvious contributory negligence, because it found that the train had sufficient time to react and did not. It seems that the doctrine was efficiently invoked in this case because the gain from creating an incentive for trains to stop in the face of truly helpless victims outweighs the risk of strategic negligence. Who in their right mind, after all, would intentionally get stuck on railroad tracks merely in an effort to shift accident avoidance costs onto the railroad?

In another case, *Anderson v. Payne*,[4] the court denied recovery under last clear chance by an accident victim who had been walking on the wrong side of the street when she was struck by a car. The court reasoned as follows:

> The plaintiff, possessing all of her faculties, was at the time able to prevent the mishap by the exercise of ordinary prudence. Instead of doing so, she deliberately and knowingly elected to walk on the forbidden side of the road and thus actively exposed herself to danger.
>
> (p. 86)

Although courts have allowed recovery in similar cases, in this case it did not. The ruling reflects the much greater likelihood of strategic behavior by supposedly inattentive victims, and therefore offers a reasonable compromise in the application of last clear chance.

As if to further confuse matters, courts have sometimes relied on the "proximate cause" doctrine to assign liability in sequential accident cases. For example, they reason that the failure of the injurer, acting last, to take compensating precaution, is therefore the proximate cause of the victim's injury. Grady (1984) has specifically suggested that the *direct consequences* doctrine can be understood as an effort to compel compensating precaution by second movers:

> The purpose of the direct-consequences doctrine of proximate cause is to increase the pecuniary incentives of persons other than the original wrongdoer, such as the last wrongdoer, to take precautions that compensate for the original wrongdoer's lack of care.
>
> (pp. 416–417)

By finding the last "wrongdoer" to be the proximate cause, this doctrine functions exactly like last clear chance, but of course, it has the same drawback of reducing the incentives for care of the first mover. That is, it involves the trade-off between criteria one and three.

The jumble of liability rules we have discussed up to this point has been, or is in the process of being, replaced by comparative negligence, which apportions liability between injurers and victims based on their relative fault. The rise of comparative negligence seems to have been largely motivated by dissatisfaction on fairness grounds with so-called "all-or-nothing" rules that assign the full damages to one or the other of the two parties, even when both are negligent. This development may or may not disrupt the desirable incentive properties of negligence rules in simultaneous accident cases, depending on whether the applicable version of comparative negligence retains the "threshold" feature. (There are multiple versions, depending on the state.) If it retains this feature—that is, if the injurer can still avoid all liability by taking efficient care—then it can achieve an efficient Nash equilibrium in simultaneous accident cases (though it presumably also loses some of its appeal on fairness grounds as a consequence).

As to the effect of comparative negligence in sequential accident settings, it satisfies criterion three if it incorporates (implicitly or explicitly) a duty for compensating precaution. To the extent that it does, it effectively replicates the function of last clear chance, but in so doing, it creates the same trade-off between criteria one and three. Specifically, if victims moving first expect injurers to take compensating precaution, they will have an incentive to be strategically negligent. But this conclusion just reinforces the fundamental nature of the conflict between these two properties in sequential accident settings.

As a final point, economists have sought to design liability rules that satisfy all three criteria, but the results turn out to be complex mechanisms that would be difficult to implement in practice. An example is the rule proposed by Donald Wittman (1981), which he calls "marginal cost liability." To describe this rule, note first that all of the rules we have discussed so far (indeed all tort liability rules) are based on liability for *actual* costs—that is, the responsible party bears the actual damages, and each party must pay his or her own actual costs of precaution. Under marginal cost liability, in contrast, the responsible party (the first mover) would be held liable for the "cost-effective" (i.e., efficient) precaution the other party *should* have taken, plus any damages that would occur at that efficient care level. The other party (the second mover) is then liable for the excess of his actual care beyond the efficient level, and any residual damages above the first mover's liability. For example, when the victim moves first, she is responsible for her own costs of care, plus the injurer's efficient care cost, and the damages that would arise from this combination of care choices. It is possible to show that under this rule, both parties have an incentive to act efficiently (criteria one and two), and the injurer, acting second, also has an incentive to take compensating precaution in the face of prior negligence by the victim (criterion three). In other words, it satisfies all three of the proposed criteria.

The reason for describing this rule is not to suggest that it is a practical option—it clearly is not. Rather, it is to illustrate the difficulty of the problem, which requires a fairly sophisticated mathematical model to solve.

It should also serve to command admiration for the efforts of courts to fashion workable rules for dealing with the problem of strategic negligence long before economists thought to study it.

Notes

1 11 East 60 (K.B. 1809).
2 10 M. & W. 545 (Ex. 1842).
3 21 N.E.2d 625 (1939).
4 54 S.E.2d 82 (1949).

7 The tort–crime boundary

Crimes and torts are both harmful acts that society views as unlawful, but they are handled in very different ways. While tort law is privately enforced by means of lawsuits filed by victims seeking compensation for their losses, criminal law is publicly enforced by the state, with police and prosecutors acting as agents of the victim. Penalties are also very different in the two areas. Tort liability is exclusively in the form of monetary damages, whereas criminal penalties can take the form of monetary fines or imprisonment (or both). Finally, procedural rules also differ, such as in the standard of proof for conviction ("preponderance of the evidence" for tort liability versus "beyond a reasonable doubt" for criminal sanctions), as well as rules regarding self-incrimination and the admissibility of evidence.

Despite these outward differences, when viewed from an economic perspective the two areas of law appear to be serving essentially the same social purpose—namely, to prevent people from imposing unwanted harm (external costs) on others. Thus, we may ask, why are both categories needed and why are they structured so differently? And correspondingly, how does society choose those acts it labels as "crimes" and those acts as "torts"? In other words, where is the dividing line between tort law and criminal law? This chapter offers some possible answers, and then uses those answers to offer insights into the structural differences between the two areas.

The most obvious answer to the question of what distinguishes crimes and torts is that crimes are *intentional* harms whereas torts are *accidental* harms. Individuals engaged in socially beneficial activities such as driving, performing medical procedures, or manufacturing inherently dangerous products (like chain saws) will sometimes cause harm to others as an unintended by-product of those lawful activities, and tort law is the means by which they are required to compensate their victims. In contrast, criminal acts involve an intent to cause harm, as motivated by a guilty mind (*mens rea*), which thereby justifies the imposition of "punishment" to deter the act, as opposed to mere liability for the harm caused. And because only the state has the power to punish someone, especially when it involves imprisonment, criminal law must be administered publicly.

But what does "intent" really mean in this context? For example, might we not argue that someone who acted negligently by failing to take reasonable precautions in some sense "intentionally" caused the resulting accident? If not, at what point does negligence shade into recklessness, and recklessness into willfulness? What about the case of an injurer—say the manufacturer of a chain saw—who takes all reasonable precautions but still knows with virtual certainty (due to the Law of Large Numbers) that its activity will cause some predictable number of accidents over a given period of time? Such harm, if not intentional, is at least anticipated as a necessary consequence of engaging in an otherwise legal activity. The point is that the potential harm-causing actions of injurers lie along a continuum that is only arbitrarily divisible into "accidental" and "intentional."

In any case, it is not clear that such a categorization even matters when it comes to fashioning an efficient legal remedy, as there seems no reason why the motives of injurers should be relevant for purposes of creating incentives for them to internalize the harms they cause. The efficient solution is the same whether the harm was intentionally or accidentally imposed—namely, impose the victim's harm on the injurer. Whether that happens by means of a liability payment, a criminal fine, or a Pigovian tax, the incentive effects should be exactly the same regarding decisions of whether or not to engage in harmful activities, and how carefully to engage in them. Based on this logic, it would appear criminal and tort law are redundant mechanisms, at least as regards the incentives of injurers.

A different explanation for public enforcement of criminal law therefore focuses on the cost to victims of identifying and bringing suit against the party responsible for their injuries. When that cost is high, or if the harm is dispersed across a large number of victims so that none finds it worthwhile to pursue a claim, some injurers will escape punishment under a purely private system of enforcement. In addition, some injurers may deliberately attempt to cover up their identity, thereby reducing their chances of facing liability for their actions. (Note that this explanation may indirectly reflect "intent" in the sense that individuals who intentionally plan to inflict harm will be more likely to take steps to avoid detection.) Public enforcement overcomes these problems by transferring responsibility for prosecution and punishment to the state.

There are, however, private solutions to the under-detection problem. One is suggested by the economic theory of *punitive damages*, which is also based on the problem of inadequate detection of some injurers. Suppose, for example, that only one in three injurers expects to face liability for the harm they impose. This would appear to result in under-deterrence, but suppose that the court simply inflates by a factor of three the amount of liability imposed on those injurers who are detected. All prospective injurers would therefore face an *expected* liability equal to the harm they impose and would therefore have the correct incentives to be careful. Formally, let the probability of detection be p and the actual harm be h. The liability assessed on those injurers who are caught should therefore be set at h/p, which results in *expected liability* of $p\bullet(h/p)=h$ for all injurers. Thus, deterrence is optimal.[1]

Another solution to the under-detection problem is the class action suit, which bundles several related claims into a single lawsuit, thereby economizing on litigation costs. A related solution is to allow victims to sell their claims to individuals who specialize in the apprehension and prosecution of offenders. (See the further discussion of this idea in Chapter 20.) However, this sort of "bounty system" would likely be inefficient for several reasons. First, there are significant scale economies associated with the detection and apprehension of offenders, which arise from the high fixed costs of establishing a police force and the avoidance of duplicative activities concerning the collection and maintenance of a registry of information about current and past offenders. Thus, as in the case of a natural monopoly, it is efficient for a single agency to emerge to perform these functions, and organizing it as a public agency would prevent monopoly exploitation of victims by a single private firm. Natural monopolies in certain industries characterized by large scale economies, such as utilities, are usually regulated by the government for the same reason.

A second inefficiency arising from specialized private enforcers is that the harm from some acts extends beyond the immediate victims, also imposing "public harm." Public harm will be especially severe for those acts that create sympathy among non-victims for fear that they may suffer the same kind of harm in the future, and general moral outrage. The problem that public harm creates is that victims, or private enforcers working on their behalf, will not account for the full extent of the harm an offender causes and therefore will devote too little effort to apprehending him.

In theory, this problem can be overcome by a quasi-public system in which the government establishes rewards, or bounties, that reflect the true social cost of a given act, and then leaves it to private enforcers to apprehend offenders in return for the right to collect the reward. Under such a system, the government would in effect subsidize the efforts of private enforcers to account for the full social benefit of apprehension. Such a system is often associated with law enforcement in the American West, but it poses exactly the opposite problem—it would likely result in *over*-enforcement.

To see why, consider an arrangement whereby the state sets the fine, and a group of profit-maximizing enforcement firms (or bounty hunters) undertakes the task of enforcement. If the first firm to apprehend an offender collects the fine, then firms will have an incentive to overinvest in enforcement in a "race" to be first. Specifically, the actual probability of apprehension, p, will be determined by the combined efforts of enforcers, and although an appropriate choice of the fine/reward, f, can be set so that offenders face the correct expected liability, pf, in equilibrium, too much effort will be devoted to enforcement from a social point of view. Only if the government takes control of both the reward and apprehension effort (i.e., the choice of p and f)

can the optimal outcome be achieved. But this reflects the situation under a public enforcement system.

A final problem with purely private enforcement of fines is the possibility that an offender, even if apprehended, may lack the resources to pay the required liability. This so-called "judgment-proof problem" is a serious impediment to a system based purely on monetary sanctions for wrong-doing. For example, it is often cited as a source of inefficiency in the tort system. The availability of imprisonment as a supplement to fines is therefore an advantage of public enforcement. Again, however, there are some possible private solutions to the judgment-proof problem. One is indentured servitude or wage garnishment from offenders unable to pay fines, but either of these approaches would likely require some sort of public administration.

Another possibility would be to allow potential victims of harmful activities to sue for *expected damages* before an actual harm occurs (and therefore, before the injurer becomes judgment proof). In other words, a "tort for risk" could be created that would allow people, for example, to sue a polluting firm for exposure to a toxic substance rather than having to wait for an illness to arise, or to sue speeders before they cause an accident. (The potential injurer's liability would then be correspondingly discounted by the likelihood that the harm would materialize.) The obvious drawback of this approach, of course, is that would-be injurers would be subject to a flood of litigation that would overwhelm the court system and may drive them into premature bankruptcy, or deter them from engaging in the activity. It would also present challenging procedural issues regarding the proof of causation and the measurement of damages.

Finally, I offer a different kind of explanation for the co-existence of criminal and tort law based on an argument that was first proposed in Chapter 3. This explanation relates not to differences in the motives of injurers or practical problems in holding them responsible for their harmful acts, but rather to the role of criminal sanctions in enforcing the General Transaction Structure. Recall that this structure represented the institutional arrangement by which legal entitlements (or rights) are both defined and exchanged based on the goal of maximizing their economic value. A key element of that structure concerned the choice between property rules and liability rules. Property rules, remember, only allow consensual (market) transfers, whereas liability rules allow court-ordered (coercive) transfers, with the choice between them depending on the magnitude of transaction costs. Specifically, when transaction costs are low property rules should be used, thereby channeling exchange through the market, whereas when transaction costs are high liability rules are preferred, thereby allowing court-ordered exchange. The role of criminal law within this framework is to provide a mechanism for enforcing this arrangement.

Suppose, for example that an individual owns an entitlement to a piece of property, a watch, for example, and it is protected by a property rule. If someone else values the watch more than the owner, she can only legally acquire it by market exchange—that is, by offering a price that exceeds its value to the owner. If instead she steals the watch and the court orders her to pay a fine equal to the owner's loss as compensation, the thief would have succeeded in transforming the owner's property rule protection into liability rule protection, which is a violation of the transaction structure. A similar violation occurs when someone transforms an inalienability rule into a liability rule (as when a person physically assaults another person), or into a property rule (as when someone tries to buy another person's vote). In all of these cases, the role of the criminal law is seen as deterring the attempted transformation by imposing an additional penalty (a "kicker") on top of compensatory damages. In this way, a criminal sanction is interpreted as a *penalty* for attempting to carry out an *illegitimate* transaction, rather than court-imposed *compensation* for completing a *legitimate* one. The attraction of this distinction between criminal law and tort law is that it incorporates criminal law into a larger economic framework that views the market and the law as institutional structures whose common goal is to define and mediate the efficient exchange of legal rights within society. (It also restores the idea of criminal law as being punitive rather than merely serving as a system of prices.)

As noted earlier, tort law and criminal law differ in the nature of the available penalties, but also in terms of procedure—that is, the manner in which those penalties are imposed. These procedural differences, I will argue, stem largely from two sources, both by-products of considerations discussed previously. The first is the availability of prison as a sanction for criminal violations (which is itself a response to the judgment-proof problem); and the second is the stigma associated with criminal conviction, which is a consequence of society's decision to label certain acts as illegitimate and hence worthy of moral opprobrium. The particular procedural issues that I will consider here are the differing standards of proof for conviction in criminal and tort law, the rule against self-incrimination, and the exclusionary rule (the latter two being unique to criminal procedure).

The standard of proof establishes the minimum degree of certainty that a court must reach before it renders a guilty verdict or a finding of liability. As noted, the standard is different for criminal and civil cases, with a much higher degree of certainty required for criminal conviction. This difference, I will argue, can be largely understood as reflecting the higher perceived cost of wrongful conviction in a criminal case as compared to a civil case.

To understand this aspect of the standard of proof, it is first important to recognize that a trial is nothing more than a procedure for making decisions under uncertainty. In a trial, whether involving a civil or criminal violation, the two sides (the plaintiff and defendant) present their best possible cases, and then the fact-finder—the judge or the jury—decides which will prevail.[2] It does that by first hearing the evidence from both sides and then implicitly assessing a probability—a number between zero and one—that the defendant is guilty. It then compares this assessment with the standard of proof, which represents the minimum level of defendant guilt that will result in a conviction. In civil procedure that standard is *preponderance of the evidence*, which is a threshold of just over 50 percent, whereas in criminal procedure that standard is *beyond a reasonable doubt*, which is a much higher threshold, say 90 percent. (There is no set numerical value.) In order to account for this difference, we need to understand the nature of legal errors that may arise at trial.

As a starting point, it seems logical to suppose that the court's assessment of a defendant's guilt will be larger for defendants who are truly guilty because there will generally be more evidence against them, and vice versa for truly innocent defendants. However, this will not be true in every case. Some truly guilty defendants will have done a good job of covering their tracks or otherwise avoiding detection, while some truly innocent defendants will be framed or implicated by circumstantial evidence. Thus, it is an unavoidable consequence that trials will result in two types of errors: wrongful convictions (type I errors) and wrongful acquittals (type II errors). According to economic theory, the optimal standard of proof should be chosen to minimize the expected costs of these two errors. This calculation involves consideration of both their relative probabilities and impacts.

Note first that it is impossible to simultaneously lower the probability of both types of errors merely by adjusting the standard of proof. Any change in the standard of proof in either direction can only reduce the probability of one type of error at the expense of increasing the probability of the other. For example, a stricter standard of proof will reduce the number of false convictions but will necessarily also increase the number of false acquittals. A more lenient standard of proof will have exactly the opposite effect. It follows that an intermediate standard of proof is necessary to balance the incidence of the two types of errors, but exactly how stringent it should be will depend on their relative costs. In assessing these costs, one might reasonably suppose that the cost of wrongful convictions is increasing in the severity of the sanction for conviction (i.e., it is costlier to wrongfully impose a more severe punishment), while the cost of wrongful acquittals is increasing in the severity of the offense (i.e., it is costlier to wrongfully acquit someone who committed a more harmful offense). Thus, given our hypothesized objective of minimizing error costs, the optimal standard of proof should be strengthened as the threatened sanction becomes more severe and relaxed as the offense becomes more severe, all else equal.

The differing standards of proof for civil and criminal cases can be understood in this light. Specifically, the higher standard in criminal cases suggests a strong aversion to wrongful punishments as compared to wrongful acquittals, holding the severity of the offense constant. This makes sense in view of the possibility of imprisonment for criminal conviction, along with the stigma associated with having a criminal record. Society is therefore willing to tolerate a disproportionate number of wrongful acquittals in order to avoid wrongful convictions. As far back as the 1760s, for example, William Blackstone, in his *Commentaries on the Laws of England*, famously wrote "that it is better that ten guilty persons escape, than one innocent person suffer."[3] In contrast, there is no reason to believe that either of the two types of errors is more costly than the other in a civil (tort) context because changing the standard at the margin will only have a distributional effect—that is, it will shift money from one party to the other. Further, the deterrence effects of shifting civil liability will also be symmetric, assuming injurers and victims have roughly equal abilities to invest in accident avoidance.

Within the category of criminal cases there is no formal way to further refine the standard of proof to reflect differences in the seriousness of crimes or differences in threatened punishments. However, there is anecdotal evidence that judges, juries, and prosecutors use their considerable discretion to effectively adjust the actual interpretation of "beyond a reasonable doubt" to reflect these case-specific considerations. For example, Shepherd (2007, p. 558) observes that "[n]ot wanting to impose a long sentence on a seemingly low-risk defendant, a prosecutor may decide not to prosecute, or a judge or jury may dismiss charges or acquit." The practice of plea bargaining (see Chapter 10) and jury annulment are examples of this type of case-specific tailoring.

Consider next the Fifth Amendment rule against self-incrimination, which gives criminal defendants the right to refuse to testify without having that refusal interpreted by the court as evidence of guilt. (No such right exists in civil procedure.) On its face, the rule presents something of a puzzle because it seems to protect the guilty, given that innocent defendants will presumably always protest their innocence. Thus, for example, without the rule, guilty defendants would either be forced to lie, or to incur the negative inference of guilt. The requirement that juries *not* be allowed to draw such an inference would therefore seem to reduce the ability of the court to distinguish the innocent from the guilty, thereby reducing the ability of a trial to produce a correct verdict.

One explanation for the rule, however, is that it provides yet another safeguard against wrongful criminal convictions. A careful economic analysis reveals that the right to silence can actually benefit the innocent by making their protestations of innocence more believable. To see how, suppose that the protection was not available. Then, as noted, guilty defendants would be forced to take the stand and lie in order to avoid the inference of guilt. The result is a situation in which claims of innocence have no informative power. If, however, defendants were allowed to remain silent without the negative inference, some guilty defendants would choose to remain silent rather than lie, resulting in some beneficial sorting that makes the claims of innocence by the truly innocent, if not determinative, at least more believable.

As an example, suppose that out of 100 defendants, 25 are truly innocent. If all defendants protested their innocence on the stand, then the claim of

52 The tort–crime boundary

any one defendant would be believable only 25 percent of the time. However, if under a rule against self-incrimination, two-thirds, or 50 of the 75, guilty defendants chose *not* to testify (i.e., did not claim innocence), then a claim of innocence by a given defendant would be believable 50 percent of the time (i.e., 50 defendants would choose to testify—all professing innocence—and 25 would be telling the truth).

Finally, consider the Fourth Amendment prohibition of unreasonable searches and seizures, which places restrictions on the ability of the police to gather evidence against criminal defendants. The application of a "reasonableness" standard here suggests (along the lines of the argument in Chapter 5) a balancing of costs and benefits—a kind of Hand test—for determining when searches should be allowed. To be specific, let the cost of a search be C, which is the cost of invasion of a suspect's privacy, including the reputational loss from the inference of guilt people draw from mere suspicion, and let the benefit of a search be the product of the probability that probative evidence of a crime will be found, P, and the benefit from a conviction, B. A search is therefore reasonable if the cost is less than the expected benefit, or if $C<PB$.

The principal means of enforcing this requirement is that, with some exceptions, police must obtain a warrant from a judge before conducting a search. The function of the warrant is that an impartial judge (i.e., someone not directly connected to the investigation) has to make a determination that there is *probable cause* to believe that the target of the search was involved with the crime. This provides an important safeguard against random searches, or "shots in the dark." In terms of the above formula, it requires that P must be sufficiently large so that the product, PB, outweighs the cost of the invasion of privacy.

The remedy for unlawful searches is the "exclusionary rule," which holds that any evidence gathered in an unlawful search (usually meaning a search without a warrant) cannot be used in a trial against the target of the search. The rule is a controversial one because, like the rule against self-incrimination, it seems to help the guilty by sometimes resulting in evidence of the defendant's guilt being disregarded. But again, the rationale can be understood as limiting the ability of the state to use its resources to unduly invade the privacy of innocent people. In fact, the rule probably over-deters the police from conducting searches. Suppose, for example, that the court interprets "probable cause" to mean $P \geq .5$ and therefore refuses to issue a warrant in cases where $P<.5$. This will result in some otherwise efficient searches—those for which $P<.5$ but $C<PB$—being forbidden. (This can obviously happen if the benefit of a conviction, B, is very large.)

Recognizing this problem, some authors have proposed replacing the exclusionary rule with a rule that imposes tort liability on the offending officer but does not exclude use of the illegally obtained evidence. The idea is that the threat of tort liability will deter inefficient searches while not preventing prosecutors from using the evidence to obtain a conviction. Guilty defendants therefore do not gain an advantage, which, it is argued by critics, was never the intention of the Fourth Amendment. There are at least two drawbacks of the tort remedy, however. One is that juries may be reluctant to assess liability against a police officer who turned up important evidence, albeit illegally, against a truly guilty defendant. A second reason is that tort liability will not deter the planting of evidence by police (and may encourage it), given that as a practical matter courts will not be able to distinguish such evidence from legitimate evidence after the fact. In contrast, the exclusionary rule with a warrant requirement requires police to convince an impartial judge that probable cause exists *before the fact*, which makes planting of evidence much more difficult. Thus, when some police officers may be corrupt, the exclusionary rule enhances the ability of courts to distinguish the innocent from the guilty while also protecting the privacy rights of citizens.

This chapter has reviewed economic arguments for the existence of a separate category of law aimed at enforcing the prohibition of certain harmful acts that society has chosen to label as crimes. The arguments presented here have dispelled some traditional explanations as unconvincing while finding others more consistent with observed differences between criminal and tort law. The next chapter continues the analysis of criminal law with the objective of comparing the prescriptions of the economic model to actual practice.

Notes

1 The amount of damages imposed in excess of h, which is equal to $(h/p)-h$, represents the amount of punitive damages. As an example, if one in three injurers, each causing harm of $1,000, is caught, that injurer should face a liability judgment of $3,000. Of that amount, $1,000 is compensatory damages and $2,000 is punitive damages.
2 This reflects the adversarial nature of the Anglo-American procedural system.
3 See Blacksone (1766), Book 4, p. 358.

8 Some difficulties with the economic theory of crime

Although eighteenth-century writers such as Jeremy Bentham and Cesare Beccaria anticipated many of the basic insights of the economic theory of crime and law enforcement, Gary Becker (1968) was the first to give it a firm theoretical foundation. Since then, two generations of scholars have expanded on the theory's basic insights to create a highly polished product, but there remains a question as to how well it describes reality. That question is the subject of this chapter.

The distinguishing feature of the economic theory of crime is the idea that the objective of criminal penalties is to achieve optimal deterrence. This does not mean that all crimes should be deterred; only those that impose more harm than it would cost to deter them. It follows that there is an "optimal level of crime," which is usually not zero—a concept that is sometimes difficult for those untrained in economics to grasp. (The same response would greet an economist's argument that there is an optimal level of pollution or any other external harm.)

A crucial feature of the economic model, one that is also at odds with many people's commonsense notions of crime, is that offenders are rational, at least some of the time. The idea that crime is an irrational act that is only committed by the mentally impaired or those motivated by passion is a commonly held view, but when challenged, most people will concede that some crime must be rational, such as that motivated by financial gain. If further pressed, they will likely admit that the idea of using criminal punishment as a deterrent only makes sense if criminals respond to the costs of their actions; in other words, that the demand curve for crime slopes downward.

This last point, that the crime rate is inversely related to punishments, is substantially supported by the available evidence, thereby providing a solid empirical foundation for the economic theory. And yet, there is a fundamental paradox underlying the reliance of this theory on deterrence as the principal justification for criminal punishment. To understand this "paradox of punishment," let us accept the premise that the objective of punishment is to deter crime. It follows that once a crime has been committed, the purpose of punishing that particular offender is no longer valid! It doesn't matter whether the offender acted irrationally (i.e., was undeterrable), or acted perfectly rationally in the sense that he viewed the private gain from committing the act as exceeding the expected cost (i.e., it was an "efficient crime"). Once the act is done, the threatened punishment has served its purpose of signaling the harmfulness of the act to the offender, and so it makes no sense, going forward, to incur the cost of actually imposing it.[1]

One answer to this paradox is the need for society to establish credibility regarding enforcement of laws. If rational offenders anticipate that punishments will *not* be imposed, they will commit inefficient as well as efficient crimes. Thus, enforcers need to make credible commitments to carry out the threatened punishments after the fact. (Private enforcement [tort law] overcomes this problem by relying exclusively on monetary punishments, and by allowing enforcers [victims] to keep the money they collect.) In this sense, punishment is forward-looking because there are always future potential offenders.

Criminologists refer to this rationale as "general deterrence"—that is, deterring future crime by punishing prior wrongdoers—as opposed to "specific deterrence," which is deterrence of a particular individual by threatening to punish him or her. Some philosophers of crime object to the idea of general deterrence, however, because it violates the Kantian imperative that punishing individuals should only be justified based on acts that they themselves committed, and should not be used to promote other objectives (such as to deter future offenders). In contrast, general deterrence is perfectly compatible with a utilitarian approach to law enforcement, as advocated by Bentham and Becker, which is aimed at maximizing overall well-being.

One theme of this chapter is that the paradox of punishment as just described arises as a consequence of looking at the criminal process at different points in time, which potentially involves the application of different social values. To see this, note that deterrence is by its nature a forward-looking concept that is primarily concerned with how the threat of punishment affects future decisions. From this perspective, optimal punishment reflects expectations about uncertain events. In contrast, the actual imposition of punishment necessarily takes place after a particular defendant has been apprehended, at which time he is a real person rather than a hypothetical villain. Thus, what was threatened beforehand may no longer seem appropriate to the facts as they now appear.

The resulting inconsistency is exemplified by a comparison of the prescriptions of the economic theory of crime, which in its purest form reflects optimal deterrence, with the concept of proportionality of punishments, which seems to be the leading alternative theory. As Oliver Wendell Holmes wrote over a century ago, "The main struggle is between [retribution and deterrence]. On one side is the notion that there is a mystic bond between wrong and punishment; on the other, that the infliction of pain is only a means to an end" (Holmes, 1881 [1963], p. 37).

The idea of proportionality, or retribution, is indeed a deeply held human value. In primitive societies, this impulse manifested itself in the form of retaliation by one kinship group against another according to the principle of *lex talionis*, and the concept became enshrined in the legal and religious traditions of virtually all known cultures including the Hammurabi Code, Roman law, and the Old Testament ("an eye for an eye"). Although Holmes saw retribution merely as "vengeance in disguise" (1881 [1963], p. 39), the concept is so ingrained that it continues to be a guiding principle in modern penal codes, though generally transmuted to reflect an enlightened desire to limit overly severe punishments rather than to inflict equivalent pain.

In practice, the objective of proportionality manifests itself in the discretion of prosecutors not to pursue charges carrying what are perceived to be excessive sentences; of judges to exercise sentencing discretion within allowed legal bounds; and of juries to engage in nullification. For example, Dawson (1969, p. 201) notes that "there is judicial resistance to imposition of mandatory maximum sentences that seem unduly long in relation to the circumstances of the crime." The prominent legal theorist, H. L. A. Hart (1982, p. 164) likewise observes that it is through judicial discretion that "the ideas of fitness and proportionality have had their fullest play." And yet it is not clear exactly what "proportionality" means in this context. There are several possibilities.

The first is that punishment should somehow "equal" harm in a kind of one-to-one correspondence. For example, Adelstein (1981, p. 7) characterizes punishment in the Anglo-American criminal justice system as follows: "Over the years, ours has been a legal order of retributive punishment tempered by the norm of proportionality, one which seeks to exact an eye, but only that, for an eye." Similarly, Hart (1982, p. 161) observes that "In its crudest form [proportionality] is the notion that what the criminal has done should be done to him." In other words, the punishment should cause the criminal to suffer an equal amount of harm as he imposed on the victim. Hart quickly adds, however, that such a prescription, if taken literally, will often lead to impractical, absurd, or even barbarous punishments that would be at odds with most people's sensibilities, not to mention the Constitutional ban on cruel and unusual punishments. In practice, therefore, the idea of equating punishments to harms more commonly serves as the motivation for arguing against punishments that are deemed to be excessive in relation to the crime in question. Such logic, for example is undoubtedly behind recent efforts to roll back "three-strikes" laws that subjected serial offenders to particularly lengthy prison terms for relatively minor third offenses, as well as the trend toward the decriminalization of medicinal or recreational drug use.

A second possible meaning of proportionality is that punishments should increase with harms. According to this interpretation, it is not the specific form or level of punishment that matters, but rather the relationship of punishments to harms across the range of crimes. Again, as Hart (1982, p. 162) describes it,

> What is required is not some ideally appropriate relationship between a single crime and its punishment, but that on a scale or tariff of punishments and offenses, punishments for different crimes should be "proportionate" to the relative wickedness or seriousness of the crime. For though we cannot say *how* wicked any given crime is, perhaps we can say that one is *more* wicked than another and we should express this ordinal relationship in a corresponding scale of penalties.

In other words, the punishment should increase in proportion to the crime. Although this relies on a ranking of the seriousness of crimes, which may itself present difficulties, once that ranking is established, whatever form of punishment is chosen should follow a corresponding scale.

Two other concepts of proportionality mirror the previous ones but recognize the uncertainty of punishment from the perspective of individuals contemplating committing criminal acts. What matters to these would-be offenders is the *expected* punishment, which equals the actual punishment for a particular crime, f, multiplied by the probability of apprehension and conviction, p, or pf. It is this quantity which, according to the economic theory of crime, is relevant for deterrence purposes.

This concept is illustrated in Figure 8.1, which plots p on the horizontal axis and f on the vertical axis. The downward sloping, convex curve shows those combinations of p and f such that their product equals a constant—here set at \$500.[2] Thus, any combination of p and f on the curve will deter crimes worth less than \$500 to the offender. (It is therefore sometimes called an iso-crime line.)

In this context, the above concepts of proportionality can be re-interpreted in terms of the relationship between the *expected punishment* and the harm—what we might call ex ante proportionality, as opposed to ex post proportionality, which is the relationship between the actual punishment, f, and the harm. The crucial distinction, as we shall see, is that under the concept of ex ante proportionality, there is no necessary relationship between actual punishments and harms—it depends on whether or how the probability of punishment varies with harm.

Having described the various concepts of proportionality, let us turn to the question of how well the prescriptions of economic theory reflect them. In answering this question, I will focus on the pure deterrence version of the model as originally described by Becker, which takes as its goal the maximization of a welfare function that depends on the net harm from the crime plus the costs of enforcement. (It is of course possible to extend the model to explicitly incorporate a social preference for fairness or proportionality of punishment, but the objective here is to evaluate the compatibility of the goals of deterrence and proportionality.)

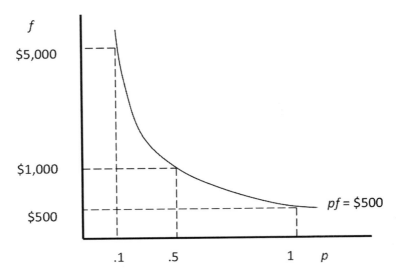

Figure 8.1 Iso-crime line

As a benchmark, we first consider the prescriptions of the economic model when the probability of apprehension, p, is taken as given, and so the only choice of the enforcer is the magnitude of the sanction, f. (This does not mean that $p=1$, only that it is not a choice variable.) In that case, the model prescribes that the actual punishment, whatever form it takes, should be set equal to the harm caused by the act, denoted h, divided by the probability of apprehension, or $f=h/p$. (The theory sidesteps the above question of how to "equate" punishments and crimes by denominating both in dollars.) Thus, for example, if the harm caused by an act is $500, and one half of offenders are expected to be caught and punished (i.e., $p=.5$), then assuming punishment takes the form of a fine, the optimal fine would be $1,000, as shown by the middle point in Figure 8.1, which is $500 divided by .5. The intuition is that would-be offenders then face an *expected fine* of $500=(.5)×($1,000), which is equal to the harm that the act would impose on society. As a result, offenders face the full cost of their actions in expected terms, which gives them exactly the right incentives when deciding whether to commit the act.

In terms of proportionality, however, this result is clearly inconsistent with the first concept—that actual punishments should equal crimes—because of the need for "probability scaling," which "unfairly make[s] specific individuals instruments for the achievement of larger social ends" (i.e., optimal deterrence) (Adelstein, 1981, p. 19). In particular, observe that this scheme in effect punishes those individuals who are caught for the actions of those who are not caught, with the requisite scaling up of ex post punishments being seen, in many people's eyes, as excessive (unless, perhaps, the individual in question is a habitual offender who has himself escaped capture in the past). In the example, one of two offenders is caught and pays a fine of $1,000, which is the harm imposed by both his act and the act of the offender who got away.

Note, however, that the optimal fine in this context *is* consistent with the other concepts of proportionality. Specifically, the actual fine is increasing in the harm (i.e., it rises in proportion to $1/p$), and the expected fine is both equal to, and increasing in, the harm (given that p is held constant). The principal departure of the current version of the economic model of crime and the norm of proportionality therefore concerns ex post proportionality, given the need for probability scaling.

Now let us expand the model to allow the enforcer to optimally choose both the level of the punishment and the probability of detection. The latter choice amounts to choosing the amount to invest in policing and the court system, as well as the formulation of the rules of criminal procedure, such as the standard of proof for conviction and admissibility of evidence. Introducing this additional choice variable turns out to have a rather dramatic effect on the optimal policy that emerges, especially as it relates to proportionality. I will describe the result here for the case of a fine, though the logic extends, in a less intuitive way, to the use of imprisonment.

The principal prescription of the economic model in this case is that the optimal fine—the actual punishment imposed on convicted offenders—should be "maximal." That is, it should be the largest amount that they can feasibly pay (for example, their wealth). Then, given the maximal fine, the probability of apprehension should be set at the point where the last dollar spent on apprehension yields exactly one dollar in deterrence benefits (i.e., reduced harm from crime). In Figure 8.1, this might correspond to the point where $p=.1$ and $f=\$5,000$.

Though it sounds odd at first, on reflection, the thinking behind this result is clear. Because would-be offenders are assumed to respond to the expected sanction, pf, then the crime rate will depend only on that magnitude. Thus, if the probability is lowered and the fine is proportionately raised—that is, pf is held constant—then the crime rate will remain unchanged. Since it is costly to raise the probability because more police need to be hired, but costless to raise the fine, then the desired crime rate can be achieved at the lowest possible cost by reducing the probability and correspondingly raising the fine to the maximum extent that the defendant's wealth allows.[3]

It should be clear, however, that this policy violates both ex post proportionality concepts because the actual fine is neither equal, nor proportional, to the harm caused by the act. Indeed, there is no necessary relationship whatsoever between fines and harms in this case because the fine is determined solely by the offender's wealth rather than by the crime that he or she committed. Nor is it the case that the expected fine equals the harm. In fact, it turns out that the optimal policy involves setting the expected fine *below* the harm. (Thus, for a crime causing harm of $500 the optimal point in Figure 8.1 would in fact be on an iso-crime line that is shifted closer to the origin.) This is true because, as noted, when enforcement is costly, resources should be devoted to apprehension only to the point where the marginal cost of enforcement equals the marginal benefit in terms of harm prevented. Since the cost of enforcement comes entirely from raising the probability of apprehension, it is not cost effective to raise the probability to the point where all inefficient crimes are deterred.

It is the case, however, that under the optimal policy the probability of apprehension should be increasing in the harm from the crime, which implies that the expected fine will be increasing in the harm (given that the actual fine remains fixed at the maximal level). It is only in this very weak sense that proportionality is achieved under the optimal enforcement policy.

The preceding analysis has established that proportionality of punishments to crimes does not generally emerge as a fundamental component of the policies prescribed by the economic model of crime. The importance that society appears to place on proportionality therefore seems to represent an important departure of theory from practice. Another important departure is implicit in the policy prescribing maximal fines, as this obviously implies, given variation in offender wealth, that fines should be individual-specific, with corresponding variation in p as dictated by points along the iso-crime line in Figure 8.1. If we suppose, however, that the probability of apprehension cannot be individualized (principally because the identity and wealth of offenders cannot generally be known prior to apprehension), then it appears that low-wealth individuals will be systematically underdeterred, all else equal, because if caught, they will have less ability to pay fines. The economic model corrects for this by prescribing the use of imprisonment as an additional deterrent for these poor offenders. However, this policy obviously implies a differential treatment of rich and poor defendants who have committed the same crime, with the rich paying high fines and the poor possibly going to prison.

This prescription has led many to ask whether it is acceptable, or indeed constitutional, to engage in such unequal treatment—in effect to allow the rich to "buy" their way out of prison. Although some of this clearly happens, actual practice seems to have placed limits on the implementation of such a policy by setting minimum prison terms for crimes independently of the characteristics of particular defendants. As a result, rich defendants often receive jail terms along with fines that are well below their ability to pay. This effort at equal treatment in the use of imprisonment is likely one of the reasons for the apparent "overuse" of prison in the American criminal justice system.

I suggested that an important institutional factor in establishing proportionality of punishments is the sentencing discretion of judges. Historically, U.S. judges had considerable freedom in determining sentences, but federal sentencing guidelines, enacted in 1987, greatly curtailed that discretion. Under the guidelines, sentences for particular crimes were dictated by the seriousness of the offense and the record of the offender—other factors were not supposed to be considered. The stated goal was to eliminate sentencing differences based on factors such as race that were viewed as irrelevant from a policy perspective. Under the guidelines, the discretion of judges was limited by the specification of sentencing "ranges," which allowed judges only some ability to tailor sentences to the facts of individual cases.

One way to think about this institutional sentencing structure is that the legislative establishment of guidelines is meant to reflect society's priorities regarding the treatment of criminals in a forward-looking sense—that is, before any actual crimes have been committed. At this point, various considerations can influence the policy, but deterrence would seem to be the overriding factor, which is why threats of harsh punishment (such as "three-strikes" laws) sometimes emerge from these deliberations. Talk of harsh punishment is easy at this stage because offenders are only hypothetical wrong-doers who, in any case, will ideally be deterred by the enacted policy. However, judicial sentencing discretion, along with the other forms of discretion in the establishment of actual criminal sentences noted earlier, necessarily offset the credibility of such policies because they are usually dictated by concerns about maintaining proportionality. Thus, a policy devoted to optimal deterrence, such as that dictated by the economic model for example, would have to limit these various forms of ex post discretion. The fact that the guidelines included ranges left some discretion for judges, suggesting that the guidelines were designed with the idea that ex post tailoring of sanctions should not be totally removed from the criminal process. In this way, sentencing policies seemed to strike a balance between ex ante deterrence and ex post proportionality. In 2005, however, the U.S. Supreme Court ruled that the sentencing guidelines were only advisory, which further restricted the ability of legislatures to pre-set punishments, and thereby increased the ability of judges to tailor criminal sentences to the circumstances of individual defendants. In other words, in the current era of declining crime rates, the ability of the legislature to limit discretion has been curtailed, thereby reinforcing the ability of judges to satisfy the proportionality norm, though possibly at the expense of future deterrence.

The theme of this chapter has been that modern day criminal justice policies seem to depart, in some cases rather dramatically, from the policies that the standard economic model of crime prescribes. The norms of proportionality of punishment and equal treatment appear to hold such popular appeal that they override, or at least temper, concerns about optimal deterrence, despite periodic efforts by legislatures to enact get-tough-on-crime policies. It seems that when it comes to law enforcement, society is more concerned about deeply held notions of justice than about minimizing costs.

Notes

1 This reflects what economists call a time inconsistency problem.
2 Technically speaking, the curve is a rectangular hyperbola.
3 If punishment were by prison rather than a fine, it would still be optimal to set the prison term maximally (i.e., to imprison convicts for life). Although prison is costly, it nevertheless saves resources to lower p while correspondingly raising the prison term so as to hold the expected cost of punishment constant because prison is imposed on fewer offenders as p is reduced.

9 Escalating penalties for repeat offenders

It is a common practice in the enforcement of rules in a variety of contexts to impose harsher penalties on repeat violators. Examples include "three-strikes-and-you're-out" laws in criminal sentencing, the issuance of warnings before fines for regulatory infractions, and increasingly long suspensions for violators of drug policies in professional sports leagues. The pervasiveness of the practice suggests that it is an effective enforcement strategy, but it has nevertheless proven surprisingly difficult to demonstrate this result in the context of the standard economic model of crime. The problem is based on the idea that optimal punishments should be structured so that offenders only commit "efficient" crimes, defined to be those for which the gain exceeds the cost. And as we have argued in prior chapters, this outcome is achieved, whether in a criminal or civil context, by setting the expected punishment equal to the harm from the illegal act. According to this solution, there is no basis for increasing the punishment, no matter how many times the offender commits the act; repeat offenders are merely signaling that they value the act more than the cost. From this perspective, repeat crimes are no different (or less desirable) than repeat purchases of an ordinary good.

One might counter that the policy of increasing penalties is primarily directed at offenses that society definitely wants to deter (i.e., the "efficient" level of violations is zero), as epitomized, for example, by crimes to which the three-strikes laws apply. But even here, setting the *initial* punishment at the level of harm (or sufficiently above it to ensure deterrence) would seem to be the optimal policy. If some offenders are undeterred, what is the social gain from threatening to punish them more harshly in the future? While it may be true that long prison sentences are the only way to restrain some truly undeterrable offenders, this conclusion does not seem to offer a satisfying explanation for the pervasiveness of escalating penalties. In this chapter, I offer several possible reasons for the practice, with particular emphasis on two that involve considerations that, while perhaps ubiquitous, are outside of the standard economic model of crime. These are offenses that are committed "accidentally" by some first-timers, and crimes that stigmatize those who have committed them.

One of the basic assumptions of the economic model is that potential offenders are fully informed about the illegality of certain acts. The first explanation I will suggest for escalating penalties therefore concerns the possibility that some offenders are initially ignorant of the fact that a particular act is illegal, and so a lenient punishment for a first violation is a low-cost way of informing offenders about the undesirability of the act. Those who commit a subsequent violation are then assumed to know that the act is illegal and are therefore subject to a harsher penalty. I will show that if the population of "ignorant" offenders is sufficiently high, this escalating punishment scheme is a cost-minimizing enforcement strategy.

It is commonly said that ignorance of the law is no excuse for avoiding punishment, but the reality is that some people are in fact unaware of the illegality of certain acts, especially if the law has recently changed, or if the act is one that people engage in infrequently. Punishing those "innocent" offenders harshly may appear to some to be unjust in the sense that they lacked criminal intent, but it also involves a social cost for which there is no offsetting benefit, given that these offenders were, by virtue of their ignorance, undeterrable. Those factors alone, however, do not necessarily argue for lenient punishments for first-time offenders because if other offenders *were* aware of the illegality of the act, they would be induced to commit the act inefficiently by the low initial penalty. (It would be impossible to distinguish after the fact those who were truly ignorant and only suspend punishment for them.) In this context, I will show that the existence of some informed and some uninformed first-time offenders provides a possible economic basis (depending on the relative proportions) for a punishment scheme that imposes lenient punishments on first-timers and harsh punishments on repeat offenders (all of whom are assumed to be informed about the illegality of their acts).

Consider the following numerical example as an illustration. Suppose that some individuals engage in a certain act that provides them with a private benefit of, say, $800, but that imposes external costs of $1,000. Thus, the act is socially undesirable, and so is made illegal. Further, suppose a punishment is enacted whose dollar cost to the offender would be $1,000, but that would also involve a social cost of $500 for enforcing that punishment. (There may be further fixed enforcement costs independent of the amount of crime committed or the punishments imposed, but those costs are not relevant for this example.) If we assume initially that all those who might engage in this act are both rational and aware of the illegality of the act, as well as the punishment for undertaking it, then according to the standard economic model of crime, all individuals should be deterred from committing it, and the efficient outcome would be achieved. In particular, no net harm would be imposed and no punishment costs incurred. Total social costs, in other words, would be zero.

But suppose that half of the would-be offenders are unaware that the act in question has been declared illegal. In that case, the informed individuals will be deterred from committing the act as in the previous example, but the uninformed will commit the act and will therefore be subject to punishment. The social cost for each of these acts is therefore $1,000+$500 (harm plus enforcement costs), which makes the expected cost on a per offender basis $(.5)(\$1,000+\$500)=\$750$. In a second period, all offenders will be deterred because the initially uninformed offenders will have become informed by virtue of their having been punished for committing the offense in the first period. Thus, the efficient outcome of no crime is achieved in this and all future periods. Total expected costs over the entire time horizon are therefore $750, which is a consequence of the initial ignorance of one half of the population of potential offenders.

Let us now compare the outcome under this "flat" punishment scheme to an escalating scheme in which first-time offenses are subject to zero punishment, though the offender is informed (without cost) that he or she has committed an illegal act. For example, first-timers only receive a "slap on the wrist" but are warned that any subsequent offense will be subject to the optimally-deterring punishment noted above. In this setting, *all* potential offenders will commit the act in the initial period, resulting in per-offender social costs of $1,000, reflecting the harm from the act, but no punishment costs will be incurred. However, all individuals will be deterred from committing the crime in subsequent periods. Thus, the total expected cost over the multi-period time horizon is $1,000, which exceeds the cost of $750 in the prior example. It follows that the cost-minimizing punishment scheme in this example is the flat scheme that threatens punishment of $1,000 for the first and any subsequent offenses.

But now change the example slightly so that the percentage of uniformed individuals is 70 percent rather than one-half. In this case, the expected per-offender cost under the flat scheme rises to $1,050=(.7)(\$1,000+\$500)$, which now exceeds the cost under the proposed escalating scheme. (Note that the escalating scheme is unaffected by the proportions of the two types of offenders because all offenders commit the act in the first period, and then all are deterred in the second period.) Thus, in this example, the escalating scheme is optimal.

These simple examples illustrate that the potential cost savings from enacting an escalating punishment scheme arise from two critical factors: the costliness of imposing punishment, and the existence of a critical proportion of potential offenders who are initially ignorant of the illegality of the act. (The specific threshold for the escalating scheme to be optimal in the above example is $2/3=(\$1,000/\$1,500)$; that is, if more than two-thirds of the population of potential offenders is uninformed, the escalating scheme has lower costs than the flat scheme.) This pair of circumstances would seem to be fairly widely relevant in the context of potentially harmful acts, and so is a broadly applicable explanation for the pervasiveness of escalating schemes.

Finally, it is important to note that the preceding argument for such schemes is not an endorsement of an "ignorance of the law" defense, which in many cases is simply an effort by violators, after the fact, to avoid responsibility. Such claims are clearly not credible, and hence not a good basis for formulating policy. The argument here is instead based on the goal of constructing an optimal response to a perceived "market failure," as embodied by the fact that a known proportion of the population, although rational, lacks the information needed to make efficient decisions when engaged in potentially harmful activities.

I now turn to a second explanation for escalating penalties that relates to the stigma associated with criminal punishment. (The justification here is therefore narrower than the previous one, applying specifically to escalating criminal penalties like three-strikes laws.) The fact that a criminal record reduces an individual's labor market opportunities reflects an employers' rational fear that the individual will be a poor employee or possibly commit crimes on the job. It is also supported by empirical evidence.

The effect of this stigma on deterrence is cross-cutting. For a person with no criminal record, the existence of stigma enhances the deterring ability of criminal punishments in general, which allows a lower threatened punishment to deter someone who is contemplating committing an initial crime. However, the reverse is true for a person who already has a criminal record because his or her legal employment options are impaired. In particular, the opportunity cost of committing *further* crimes is lowered, and so a larger sanction is needed to deter the unwanted act.

To see how these effects translate into an escalating punishment scheme, consider the following example. Suppose that a would-be offender considers committing crimes over a two-period time horizon. A crime yields a gain of $800 in either period, while the best available legal employment promises a gain of $500 for a person with no criminal record, but only $400 for a person with a criminal record. The stigma effect is therefore $100. For purposes of the example, we will assume that detection of the crime in question occurs with certainty, though this not essential for the logic of the argument.

Consider first an offender with no criminal record who is considering committing a first crime in the *second* period. The lowest fine that would just deter him is $300, which is the difference between the gain from crime and the income from legal employment. In contrast, a fine of $400 would be needed to deter an individual with a criminal record. Now consider a would-be offender who is contemplating a first crime in period one. If he expects to be deterred in the second period, his lifetime income over the two periods would be $800+$400=$1,200 if he commits a period-one crime, and $500+$500=$1,000 if he chooses legal employment. The lowest fine that would just deter a first-period crime (assuming it would be a one-time offense) is therefore $200.

Together, these examples show that, in order to achieve complete deterrence of the unwanted act over the two-period time horizon, the optimal fine structure would involve a fine of $200 for a first-time offender in period one, a fine of $300 for a first-time offender in period two, and a fine of $400 for a repeat offender. Thus the stigma effect both *lowers* the minimally deterring fine for a person considering a first-time offense early in his life, and *raises* the fine for an offender with a criminal record.[1]

The preceding explanations for escalating penalty schemes are those that I find most plausible over the widest set of circumstances. However, other explanations have been offered in the literature which may apply to certain specific situations, or which may work in conjunction with the above explanations. I mention some of those explanations now.

The first concerns the possibility, discussed at length in previous chapters (especially Chapter 7), that some offenders are mistakenly apprehended and punished for committing crimes, and that society has a particular aversion to this type of error. (Note that this situation is different from the case of a person who actually committed a crime, albeit accidentally.) Some have argued that an escalating scheme is a response to this problem because repeat offenders are less likely to have been apprehended in error, thereby reducing the risk of wrongful punishment.

Another explanation is based on the idea that potential offenders differ in their propensities to commit a certain crime, due, for example, to different gains or different labor market opportunities (apart from stigma). In this context, it is argued that an escalating penalty scheme may serve as a sorting device to punish more harshly those individuals who signal by their repeated crimes that they are more inclined to commit unwanted acts. This explanation, however, is subject to the caveat noted earlier; namely, that if the optimal punishment is set initially, there is no reason to increase it for repeat offenders. Thus, this explanation applies narrowly to crimes that are definitely undesirable (i.e., the efficient level is zero) and in circumstances where some offenders are undeterrable.

A third explanation for escalating schemes is to offset a so-called "learning by doing" effect, which raises the cost of apprehending experienced offenders. In other words, repeat offenders learn how to commit criminal acts more efficiently or how to better evade detection, and so harsher penalties are needed to deter them. Offsetting this factor is that enforcers often pursue known repeat offenders more vigorously because they are recognized as being more dangerous to society. Thus, the additional deterrence of these offenders is achieved by a greater probability of apprehension rather than by a more severe punishment.

Finally, higher punishments for repeat offenders may be needed for habitual offenders as they get older because, at least as regards imprisonment, the maximum threatened punishment is truncated by their shorter life expectancy. Long prison terms for these "career criminals" incapacitate them before this truncation effect occurs.

Common sense suggests that repeat offenders should be treated differently from first-timers, and actual punishment schemes mirror this view. As this chapter and the preceding one have demonstrated, however, economic theory does not always coincide with common sense or common practice. Sometimes, this is due to departures of the real world from assumptions of the standard model (as exemplified by the arguments in this chapter), while in others it is because actual policy is sometimes based on values, like fairness, not included in the standard economic model (as was the case in the previous chapter). In both instances, however, an expanded version of the economic approach that accounts for these other circumstances or values can often go a long way toward explaining the observed policy.

Note

1 Stigma has no effect on the minimally deterring fine for a person considering a first offense in period two because that person has no "future" job prospects that would be adversely affected by a criminal record.

10 The problem with plea bargaining

Plea bargaining is the process of negotiation between a criminal defendant (or, more particularly, the defendant's lawyer) and the prosecutor, following the defendant's arrest but prior to trial, regarding the conditions under which the defendant would be willing to plead guilty. A successful negotiation usually involves the prosecutor offering the defendant a reduced charge, and hence a shorter sentence, in return for a guilty plea, which thereby saves the state the cost of a trial. The vast majority of guilty verdicts in the United States are obtained in this way—in fact, more than 95% of all convictions in U.S. District Courts in 2015 were by plea—and yet the practice is viewed with skepticism (if not antipathy) by many observers. A correspondingly high percentage of civil cases also settle before trial, but a similar concern is not expressed there; indeed, settlement of civil cases is generally encouraged as a way to ease the caseload crisis. This chapter examines possible reasons for these differing attitudes.

To provide the proper context, we first consider different views of the objectives of the procedural system for criminal cases, of which plea bargaining is a critical component. In an influential article, Frank Easterbrook, a federal judge and law-and-economics scholar, has argued that the structure of criminal procedure can be usefully interpreted as a kind of market system that is aimed at establishing the efficient "price" of crime (Easterbrook, 1983). This perspective is clearly compatible with the economic theory of crime as discussed in preceding chapters, which views criminal penalties as establishing prices for certain socially harmful acts as a way of deterring would-be offenders from committing those acts, or, in the case of "efficient crimes," from committing too many of them. The market analogy would also seem to be congenial to the practice of plea bargaining and the discretion that it affords to prosecutors (and judges) regarding what cases to pursue, and on what charge, because it allows them to make decentralized decisions based on case-specific information. The result, according to Easterbrook, is a pricing system that tailors sentences to crimes, thereby achieving an efficient level of deterrence. Based on this logic, he argues that any efforts to curtail prosecutorial or judicial discretion would only impede the efficient functioning of the system.

In a response to Easterbrook, Stephen Schulhofer argues that it is inappropriate to use a market analogy to describe criminal procedure because, unlike markets, efficiency is not its principal goal. His claim focuses instead on the unfairness in punishments that emerges as a by-product of the unlimited charging discretion of prosecutors and the sentencing discretion of judges, which result in "unwanted disparities in the treatment of similarly situated offenders" (Schulhofer, 1988, p. 80). Besides, he argues that the equilibrating mechanisms needed to establish a market price are lacking, and that the information asymmetries between the parties represent an important potential source of market failure in the system. Such imperfections, he contends, justify the imposition of limits on the discretion of the various participants in terms of their ability to establish criminal punishments—in other words, the "market" for the pricing of crimes needs to be regulated.

Richard Adelstein (1981) offers a compromise view that emphasizes the price-setting function of criminal procedure on one hand, but concedes that the system is subject to market failure because of informational problems on the part of would-be criminals about the "prices" they will face for certain acts on the other. In this perspective, the procedural system is best interpreted as an evolutionary process that involves an interplay between legislatures, which send broad signals about criminal penalties so as to establish optimal deterrence, and prosecutors and courts which seek to individualize punishments to crimes after the fact. As discussed in Chapter 8, however, imperfect detection and concerns about fairness (or proportionality) create an inherent conflict between these ex ante and ex post perspectives, and the overall system needs to constantly evolve to balance those conflicts.

The importance of plea bargaining in the operation of this system has naturally made it the target of considerable scrutiny. The chief concern of critics, however, has not been that it inefficiently prices crime, but rather that innocent defendants might be induced to plead guilty by the promise of a lesser charge. Thus, it again raises the concern, noted in Chapter 8, about the high cost of wrongful criminal punishment. At the same time, the caseload problem has necessitated heavy reliance on the plea bargaining as a practical way to conserve on scarce judicial resources. Supreme Court cases on plea bargaining have emphasized exactly this trade off.

In *Brady v. United States*,[1] for example, the Court conceded the fact that the vast majority of defendants who accept plea bargains are in fact guilty, for otherwise, the justices said, they "would have serious doubts... [about the practice] if the encouragement of guilty pleas by offers of leniency substantially increased the likelihood that defendants, advised by competent counsel, would falsely condemn themselves." The Court went on to note that by avoiding routine trials, "scarce judicial resources are conserved for those cases in which there is a substantial issue of the defendant's guilt." This sorting of the innocent and guilty, however, relies on the discretion of prosecutors to discriminate among cases in this way, a point to which we will return.

A year later, in *Santobello v. New York*,[2] the Court further reaffirmed the practical necessity of plea bargaining as a way of conserving on resources: "When properly administered, [plea bargaining] is to be encouraged. If every criminal were subjected to a full-scale trial, the States and Federal government would need to multiply many times the number of judges and court facilities." The Court's approval of plea bargaining therefore reflected its view that the practice advanced the key objectives of the criminal process. These include conserving on scarce judicial resources and appropriately punishing the guilty, both of which are consistent with the standard economic model of crime, but also of avoiding wrongful punishment of the innocent. As argued in Chapters 7 and 8, this last consideration is a distinguishing feature of criminal, as compared to civil, procedure, and it can help to explain many of the departures of actual criminal practice from the prescriptions of the standard economic model. Despite the court's grudging approval of plea bargaining, the question remains as to how well it advances the above goals. Answering this question requires consideration of specific economic models of the practice.

The standard economic approach to plea bargaining emphasizes the mutual benefits to the defendant and prosecutor of avoiding a trial. The defendant obviously wants to minimize his expected sentence plus the cost of defending himself, but the objectives of the prosecutor are less clear. In theory, she represents the interests of the entire community rather than the individual victim (who is not a formal party to the case), and therefore should pursue the broad policy concerns noted. In reality, however, these lofty goals often give way to more practical budgetary considerations or personal ambitions, such as the prosecutor's desire to maximize her probability of re-election or to seek higher political office.

The earliest economic models of plea bargaining simply viewed the prosecutor as seeking to maximize the expected punishment of offenders, either as a proxy for deterrence or a reputational effect, less the cost of trial; and the defendant as minimizing his expected sentence plus the cost of trial. In this formulation, the punishment (measured in dollar values) is essentially a transfer payment from the defendant to the prosecutor (as it would be in a civil case), and so bargaining between the parties simply divides the mutual gains from avoiding trial costs. For example, if the expected penalty from a trial is worth $10,000 to both parties (the amount of a fine or the dollar value of a prison term), and a trial costs $1,000 to each side, then the defendant will plead guilty to any sentence costing less than $11,000, and the prosecutor will accept any sentence costing more than $9,000. The "settlement range" of $2,000 therefore reflects the joint trial costs. The model predicts that a settlement should always be possible in this case, which conforms with the high frequency of plea bargains. Trials can nevertheless arise in this model if the parties have differing beliefs about the likely outcome of a trial, either because of mutual optimism or private information held by one party about the strength of the case; or if they place different values on the sentence. (The arguments are similar to those offered in Chapter 4 for why some civil cases go to trial.)

A different model of plea bargaining highlights objectives of the prosecutor that are more in line with the social function of criminal procedure, emphasized by the Supreme Court, of sorting innocent and guilty defendants. To illustrate, suppose that innocent defendants have a uniformly lower probability of conviction at trial than guilty defendants, reflecting the fact that there generally will be greater evidence against the latter. Specifically, let the probabilities of conviction for innocent and guilty defendants be .4 and .6, respectively. Let the cost of a conviction to the defendant be $10,000, and let the defendant's cost of trial be $1,000. The overall expected cost of a trial is therefore $7,000 (=.6×$10,000+$1,000) for a guilty defendant, and $5,000 (=.4×$10,000+$1,000) for an innocent defendant. By making a plea offer between these two amounts, the prosecutor can perfectly sort innocent and guilty defendants so that the former all opt for trial and the latter all plead guilty. Although some innocent defendants will be wrongfully convicted at trial, at least some are acquitted, while all guilty defendants are convicted and face certain punishment.

There are, however, two problems with this outcome. First, because trials involve only innocent defendants, any convictions are wrongful, and so the court should acquit them all. Such a strategy, however, would be inconsistent with the prior beliefs the parties held about the outcome of a trial, and so a policy of acquitting all defendants at trial would undermine the choices the parties made at the bargaining stage, thereby overturning the predicted outcome. In order for the prosecutor's sorting strategy to work, therefore, courts must be committed to reaching verdicts based purely on the evidence presented to them, even when they know all convictions obtained in that way would be erroneous.

This criticism turns out to be moot, however, because of the second problem with the model; namely, that it is based on the unrealistic assumption that all guilty defendants have a higher probability of conviction at trial than do all innocent defendants, which is what made perfect sorting possible. More realistically, the evidence against any given defendant, whether innocent or guilty, will vary based on the facts of the case, ranging from low to high (although one reasonably expects that *on average* there will be more evidence against truly guilty defendants). The result of this more realistic assumption, however, is that perfect sorting is no longer possible, and therefore, that some innocent defendants (those with a lot of evidence against them) will nevertheless choose to plead guilty, while some guilty defendants (those with little evidence against them) will opt for trial. The fears of critics that some innocent defendants will wrongfully plead guilty are therefore not unfounded—the only question is how widespread that outcome is, and whether a limitation on plea bargaining would improve the circumstances of those innocent defendants. A comparative perspective can help to shed light on this question.

In contrast to its prevalence in the United States, the practice of plea bargaining has historically been prohibited by the civil law systems of continental Europe. To accommodate the caseload problem, these systems have instead simplified the trial process and weakened the procedural protections of defendants compared to American trials. This raises an interesting question, reminiscent of the debate about the nature of the criminal procedure, regarding the desirability of prosecutorial discretion—specifically, under what conditions will a regime of compulsory prosecution better promote the goals of the criminal justice system as compared to a regime of unlimited plea bargaining?

The answer depends on the specific values that the system seeks to emphasize. Consider first how plea bargaining affects deterrence (i.e., the pricing of crime), given the prominent role that the practice plays in determining actual criminal punishments. The economic theory of crime as discussed in previous chapters envisioned a benevolent enforcement authority with the ability to single-mindedly pursue the goal of optimal deterrence. The enforcer could therefore specify a penalty structure (i.e., a probability of apprehension and a sanction level) and could credibly commit to carrying that policy out. Plea bargaining potentially interferes with that objective by creating an additional stage of sentencing discretion during which objectives besides deterrence—such as fairness, error avoidance, and the self-interest of prosecutors—can play a role.

In particular, there is evidence that prosecutors tend to resist imposing what they perceive to be overly harsh sentences by exercising their discretion, either to drop cases, or to reduce the charge that they choose to pursue. In this way, plea bargaining acts as an impediment to the imposition of the high-penalty, low-probability enforcement schemes that the economic model of crime often prescribes, given that prosecutors will resist the sort of probability scaling of actual punishments that such a scheme requires. Further, the fact that defendants do not have to accept a plea bargain unless it offers a more favorable outcome than the prospect of a trial necessarily reduces their anticipated costs, and hence mitigates the deterring effect of criminal punishment compared to a world where plea bargaining is not allowed.

In contrast, compulsory prosecution gives truly guilty defendants less ability to escape conviction or to negotiate for a more favorable punishment. Consistent with this perspective, continental legal systems typically do not give defendants the right against self-incrimination, thus removing a potential shield for truly guilty defendants.[3] An offsetting factor that enhances deterrence under plea bargaining, as suggested, is that self-interested prosecutors may perceive their personal ambitions as being served by imposing harsh sentences for perpetrators of particularly egregious crimes.

Consider next the goal of avoiding wrongful punishments, which we have argued is a particular concern of the criminal justice system in the

United States. Given the reality that some convictions of innocent defendants are inevitable, it is paradoxically true that plea bargaining actually *lowers* the cost of false convictions by allowing innocent defendants against whom there is substantial evidence to plead guilty to a lesser charge rather than having to face the prospect of a harsher punishment on conviction at trial. Thus, despite the cautions by the Supreme Court, Easterbrook (1983, p. 320) has urged that there is "no reason to prevent [an innocent] defendant from striking a deal that seems advantageous. If there is injustice here, the source is not the plea bargain. It is, rather, that innocent people may be found guilty at trial." Thus, although plea bargains result in certain punishment while a trial holds out hope for acquittal, for some defendants, especially those against whom the evidence is stacked (for whatever reason), the option to plead guilty and avoid a risky trial may nevertheless reduce the expected cost of wrongful conviction compared to compulsory trials.

Taken together, the considerations outlined in this chapter suggest, perhaps paradoxically, "that plea bargaining is more likely to evolve in systems that emphasize the protection of innocent defendants, and systems that stress punishing the guilty are more likely to be able to sustain a regime of compulsory prosecution" (Adelstein and Miceli, 2001, p. 60). Finally, it must be conceded that addressing resource pressures is necessary in any system, and European countries have increasingly had to develop ways to circumvent costly trials, which in some cases have involved allowing a form of plea bargaining to emerge, however thinly disguised, at least for certain classes of crimes. As Adelstein (1998, p. 50) concludes, these systems have come to the inevitable realization "that the search for truth must sometimes be compromised in the name of economy."

Notes

1 397 U.S. 742 (1970).
2 404 U.S. 257 (1971).
3 As argued in Chapter 7, this right makes denials of guilt by truly innocent defendants more believable, but it also benefits the guilty by preventing the court from interpreting their silence as evidence of guilt.

11 The (real) puzzle of blackmail

In the Sherlock Holmes story "The Adventure of Charles Augustus Milverton," Holmes describes the case of

> the Lady Eva Blackwell, the most beautiful debutante of last season. She is to be married in a fortnight to the Earl of Dovencourt. This fiend [Milverton] has several imprudent letters . . . nothing worse—which were written to an impecunious young squire in the country. They would suffice to break off the marriage. Milverton will send the letters unless a large sum of money is paid him.

This scenario describes the prototypical blackmail case: a third party has acquired information that is damaging to one of two other parties who are about to enter into a relationship, whether marital, business, or otherwise. The party in possession of the compromising information seeks payment of money in return for concealing the information from the uninformed party, a request that the victim often agrees to in an effort to avoid jeopardizing the planned relationship. (Going to the law virtually guarantees revelation, and so is not generally a good option—a fact that makes blackmail possible.) In short, the blackmailer and his victim enter into a mutually beneficial transaction to keep the information secret.

The "puzzle" of blackmail is why this transaction is regarded as a crime. Its illegality is puzzling for two reasons. First, the transaction is voluntary in the sense that both parties expect to gain from it—the victim by preserving the planned relationship (which is worth more than the demanded payment), and the blackmailer by being paid. Second, the act of revealing the damaging information would be perfectly legal. What, then, accounts for the illegality of a transaction aimed at keeping it secret?

One argument is that the transaction is not truly voluntary because it involves a threat. In law, contracts are not enforceable when entered into under coercion or duress, as, for example, when someone points a gun at your head and says "your money or your life." By this logic, however, a car dealer, say, could claim that he only lowered his price after a prospective buyer threatened to go across the street to his competitor, but such a plea surely would not be a good legal or economic argument for later requiring the buyer to indemnify the dealer for the discounted price. The average person can of course sense that there is a difference between the "threat" in the current example as compared to that in the prototypical blackmail case, but it would be difficult, and no doubt would sound legalistic, to try to articulate that distinction based purely on different definitions of the word "threat." (Distinguishing them based on economic theory is easier, as will be discussed in Chapter 13, but still would sound pedantic.)

Another argument is that allowing blackmail would encourage the "digging up" of unsavory or embarrassing facts about people for the express purpose of charging them to keep that information quiet. This argument is faulty for two reasons. First, it would imply that blackmail would be legal if the blackmailer could simply prove that he came by the compromising information casually rather than by the expenditure of effort, but this would surely be a losing argument. Second, if gathering such information were truly undesirable, then logically one could also use it as the basis for making acquisition and *disclosure* of unfavorable information about businesses or people illegal. However, such a law would put publications like *Consumer Reports*, most newspapers, and the various online review sites, out of business. Moreover, it is not necessarily the case that the discovery of unfavorable information is socially undesirable; it depends on how the discover intends to use it.

This last point provides the key to the proper economic resolution of the puzzle of blackmail. To see how, it is first necessary to understand the effect that asymmetric information can have on the efficiency of economic exchange, whether that exchange takes place in a formal market setting, or in a non-market setting (like that for the arrangement of marriages). By asymmetric information, I mean a situation in which one party to a proposed exchange has some information that the other doesn't have but would like to. In a market context, that information could involve the quality of the product being offered or the trustworthiness of a potential business partner, and in a marriage context it could represent evidence about the fidelity of a would-be spouse. In a very influential article, the Nobel-prize-winning economist George Akerlof showed that such asymmetric information could lead to serious market failure wherein only low quality products—in his example, used cars—are traded (Akerlof, 1970).

The logic of Akerlof's model is simple. Suppose that sellers of used cars know, based on their experience, whether or not their cars are "lemons," but buyers cannot distinguish by simple inspection between lemons and good cars. As a result, buyers will rationally view all used cars as being of "average" quality, and as a consequence will only be willing to pay a price that represents the average of those cars actually offered for sale. As a result, the market price will overvalue lemons and undervalue good quality cars. In response, therefore, owners of good cars will disproportionately withhold them from the market, thereby causing the average quality of cars in the market to further deteriorate. But this will cause the additional exit of good cars, thereby initiating a cascade that, in the extreme case, results in only lemons being offered for sale. This so-called "adverse selection" problem is an important source of inefficiency in markets where quality matters, with the social loss consisting of the foregone gains from the sale of high quality used cars.

It should be obvious in this setting that sellers of high quality cars have an interest in credibly revealing their types to buyers, while sellers of lemons have a corresponding interest in concealing their types. The latter motive, of course, is the basis for blackmail. To be sure, if sellers of high quality cars could reveal their types credibly and at low cost, thereby allowing them to distinguish themselves from sellers of lemons, the adverse selection problem would largely go away. This will often be difficult to do, however, because the information in question involves proving the *absence* of a defect. (Think of a person buying car insurance trying to convince the insurance company that he or she is not a reckless driver.) In contrast, demonstrating the *presence* of a defect will usually be a much easier matter, but obviously owners of defective products, or bad drivers, will want to keep that information secret.

The application of this logic to the prototypical blackmail case should now be clear. In the context of a proposed marriage or business partnership, one of the parties may be hoping to conceal information about a past indiscretion that, if known by the other party, would alter the terms of the relationship, or possibly cause him or her to break it off altogether. Blackmail occurs when a third party acquires evidence of this information and seeks payment from the victim in return for not revealing it to his or her would-be trading partner. In this setting, the relevant question might be posed as follows: does it make economic sense that the proposed transaction between the blackmailer and his or her victim with intent of *concealing* the compromising information is *illegal*, while the act of *revealing* the same information is *legal*?

When viewed through the lens of the adverse selection problem, the obvious answer is that concealing the information should be illegal because it impedes the efficient operation of the market by perpetuating asymmetric information between the potential trading partners, whereas revelation should be legal because it removes the asymmetry, thereby promoting efficient trade and/or preventing inefficient trade. In other words, the differential legal treatment of transactions aimed at concealment versus revelation makes perfect sense in the context of markets in which asymmetric information is an important source of inefficiency.

This resolution of the puzzle of blackmail—that it is aimed at encouraging third parties who possess valuable information to reveal it rather than conceal it, thereby mitigating adverse selection in markets plagued by asymmetric information—is economically coherent, but it turns out to be an incomplete explanation for the illegality of blackmail. A more careful analysis asks whether this legal preference for revelation is in fact necessary. Specifically, would third parties in possession of valuable information profit more by selling it to those who want the information revealed (the uninformed parties), or to those who want it concealed (the informed parties)? If it is the former, then laws forbidding the latter transaction would be unnecessary, and the preceding explanation would lose some of its force.

To evaluate this argument, consider a simple example based on Akerlof's used car model. Suppose there are two sellers of low quality cars, seller A, who has a reservation price of $350, and seller B, who has a reservation price of $425. Also suppose that buyers are willing to pay $400 for low quality cars. Then, with perfect information, only seller A would be in the market, and that is also the efficient outcome. The net benefit of $50 that seller A receives from selling her car therefore coincides with the social gain.

Now suppose that buyers cannot distinguish between high and low quality cars, and the resulting price of used cars rises to $475, reflecting the average value of all used cars offered for sale, some of which are of high quality. (For example, some owners of high quality cars may be desperate to sell, and so offer their cars even though they are "undervalued.") In this case, both low quality sellers are now willing to offer their cars for sale, yielding a surplus of $125 for seller A (=$475–$350), and a surplus of $50 for seller B (=$475–$425). The two sellers therefore receive an aggregate surplus of $175. The buyers of these two cars, in contrast, each end up suffering a loss of $75 (=$400–$475), for an aggregate loss of $150. (Note that buyers who end up buying high quality cars at the price of $475 enjoy gains, but these transactions are of no interest to us.)

In light of the preceding example, consider the amount that a third party possessor of information about the quality of the cars can profit from selling the information prior to any sales. Suppose first that the third party approaches the two low quality sellers and threatens to reveal their types to would-be buyers. The aggregate amount that the two sellers would pay to keep the information secret is $125, which is the $175 aggregate gain from being able to sell their cars at $475 under the adverse selection outcome, minus the $50 gain that seller A would still be able to receive if information were perfect. Alternatively, the third party could approach the two prospective buyers, who together would pay up to $150 (their aggregate losses) to avoid buying low quality cars. The buyers would thus outbid the sellers by $25. The reason for the difference is that if the information is revealed, seller B would exit the market, thereby avoiding an inefficient transaction. In contrast, when information remains imperfect, seller B inefficiently remains in the market, imposing on society a net loss of $25 (the difference between the value of the low quality car to the buyer and its value to seller B). The extra amount that buyers are willing to pay in this example exactly coincides with this loss.

The conclusion from the preceding example is perfectly general—uninformed buyers are willing to pay more for the information about seller types than low quality sellers are willing to pay to conceal it precisely because disclosure of that information results in a more efficient market outcome. But this conclusion raises the following question: if third parties in possession of information about a seller's type would maximize the value of that information by seeking to sell it to uniformed buyers, why is it necessary to make transactions with informed sellers aimed at concealing that information illegal? This is what I mean by the "real" puzzle of blackmail.

The resolution of the puzzle turns out to depend on the nature of transactions involving information. It is well-established that the production and sale of information presents problems because of its public good qualities. Specifically, once information is produced, it can be used profitably by many individuals without diminishing its quantity (that is, it is inexhaustible). Thus, from a social point of view, information should be widely disseminated so as to maximize its value.

The problem this creates, however, is that potential discoverers of information will have difficulty appropriating its full social value, and therefore will underinvest in its discovery (if they invest at all). This so-called "appropriability problem" is the economic rationale for patents and copyrights (see Chapter 19), which give exclusive rights to innovators and authors to profit from their discoveries or creations. The challenge is to balance the incentives for production of information created by such exclusive rights against the benefits of wide dissemination. This is resolved by limiting the duration of patents and copyrights to a prescribed period of time (20 years for patents and the life of the author plus 70 years for copyrights), after which the information becomes freely available.

What does all of this have to do with blackmail? Consider again the third party in possession of information about seller types in the above example. He is like an inventor who has discovered an idea that has potential commercial value. If he were to try to market the idea without first obtaining a patent, it would be quickly copied by competitors and its value would be dissipated through competition. In effect, the inventor is in the position of having to give his idea away in the process of trying to profit from it. In the used car example, the third party possessor of information about seller types is in the same position if he tries to sell his information to prospective buyers. A buyer would only be willing to pay for the information if he were convinced of its value, which requires the seller to reveal that information. But once the buyer becomes informed, he has no need to pay for the information. In this way, the appropriability problem effectively precludes the third party from transacting with uninformed buyers.

Unlike the inventor, however, the third-party possessor of information has another way to profit from his information—namely, to transact with (blackmail) low quality sellers to keep the information secret.[1] Although we have seen that the information is worth less to sellers than to buyers, the appropriability problem does not impede a transaction aimed at *concealing* the information because the sellers already know it. (In fact, sellers will often seek assurances that the blackmailer will not continue to seek payments for his silence in the future; in the Sherlock Holmes story, the blackmailer commits not to do so by handing over the compromising documents in return for payment.) It follows that, absent laws prohibiting blackmail, possessors of incriminating information will be inclined to deal with informed parties rather than uninformed parties in order to get around the appropriability problem. This conclusion resolves the "real" puzzle of blackmail and justifies its illegality.

As a final point, let's return to the issue of the blackmailer's incentives to acquire the information by which he seeks to profit. In some (perhaps most) cases of attempted blackmail, the relevant information has fallen into the third party's hands casually and without effort; only then does he or she contemplate blackmail. In these cases, the question of whether the information was efficiently acquired is not an issue.

In some few cases, however, a would-be blackmailer may deliberately seek incriminating information with the specific intention of profiting from it. (In the Holmes story, this in fact is the blackmailer's "business.") When that is true, the question of whether the information is socially valuable does arise. This is not a straightforward issue. (See, for example, the discussion of deliberate versus casual acquisition of information in the context of enforceability of contracts in Chapter 13.) On one hand, we have seen that acquisition and disclosure of information can potentially improve the efficiency of markets in which quality is important but unobservable. Even here though, the information is already known to the informed parties, so it seems wasteful for someone else to invest resources in "re-discovering" it. As noted, however, there is often no credible way for high quality sellers to communicate their types to potential trading partners, and so low quality sellers have an incentive to conceal their types and "masquerade" as high quality types. Given this tendency, efforts by third parties to produce and disclose market information is potentially valuable as a way to overcome market failure due to adverse selection. However, the appropriability problem may make it difficult for individuals to profit privately from engaging in this sort of activity. On the other hand, efforts to acquire information purely for concealment—that is, to engage in blackmail—while clearly socially wasteful, may be quite profitable. Thus, the law has rightly made such transactions illegal, which increases the likelihood that the information, if discovered, will be used efficiently.

Note

1 As a thought experiment, imagine an inventor of a new product that would attract customers away from a large corporation. Suppose that the inventor asked the corporation to bribe him *not* to market his product. Would that be considered blackmail? Probably not, although it fits the scenario described.

12 Group punishment

The economic theory of law enforcement as described (and critiqued) in previous chapters emphasized the idea of "individual responsibility," meaning that the principal objective is to apprehend and punish the perpetrator of a criminal act. While this concept seems natural to modern sensibilities, throughout much of human history it has not been uncommon for society to attribute responsibility for wrongdoing to an entire community or group of which the wrongdoer was known to be a member. Examples of such "collective responsibility," or "group punishment," are pervasive in ancient societies, biblical stories, and mythologies. But even in modern times, various forms of group punishment exist, such as when an entire class or fraternity is punished for the misdeeds of a single prankster, a corporation is held vicariously liable for the actions of one of its employees, or an entire country is sanctioned or attacked for the terrorist acts of a small group of its citizens.

The objective of this chapter is to develop an economic perspective on group punishment that seeks to explain (i) the prevalence of the practice in primitive society, (ii) the aversion with which modern people generally view it, and (iii) the lessons we can draw from its surprising persistence in modern times. Our conclusions will be based on the standard economic theory of law enforcement due to Becker (1968), and will involve a simple trade-off, emphasized in earlier chapters, between the net benefits of apprehending and punishing the true offender (whether for deterrence or other purposes), and the costs of wrongfully punishing innocent members of the targeted group. Our chief conclusion will be that the use of group punishment has varied over time and circumstance depending largely on the relative magnitudes of these costs and benefits.

Many scholars have noted that a defining feature of law enforcement in ancient society is its reliance on some form of group punishment. Principally, this reflected the absence of a state or centralized government with the power or ability to apprehend offenders, and so it usually fell to a victim's family or kinship group to retaliate against an injurer. Since detection of the particular offender was often difficult or impossible (in part because the offender's kinship group would generally shield him), retaliation was generally carried out against the entire group that was known to be harboring the guilty individual.

This concept of collective responsibility is reflected in the ancient notion of "pollution," which was the belief that a city or family was partially responsible for the actions of its citizens or ancestors. The most famous example of this idea is the pollution of Thebes that arose as a consequence of Oedipus's murder of his mother, as depicted in Sophocles's play *Oedipus Rex*, but two more modern examples reflect the enduring nature of this concept. The first is found in Samuel Taylor Coleridge's poem, "The Rime of the Ancient Mariner," which symbolizes the collective guilt of a group of sailors for the killing of an albatross by one of them; and the second is the work of Nathaniel Hawthorne, which evokes "the theme that the sins of the father are visited upon the children."[1]

Another notable example of this principle is in the Hammurabi Code of ancient Mesopotamia, which contained a provision that the victim of a robbery, or the kinfolk of a murder victim, if unable to identify the guilty party, could seek restitution from the city in which the robbery or the murder took place. A similar provision remained in English law well into the eighteenth century, when William Blackstone published his *Commentaries on the Laws of England*. This provision obligated residents of a village in which a man was robbed to "make hue and cry after the felon," and if they failed to identify him, the residents were collectively responsible for making good the victim's loss.[2]

Perhaps the greatest source of examples of group punishment comes from the Old Testament. The Genesis stories of Noah's flood and Sodom and Gomorrah dramatically portray the idea that an entire community must face punishment for the sins of a few. The Old Testament also includes a story of "random" punishment, which we will argue is closely related to group punishment. In the story of Jonah, Jonah boards a ship to escape God's command to go to the wicked city of Nineveh to serve as a missionary. To punish Jonah's defiance, God creates a storm that threatens to sink the ship along with its crew. The crew members decide to draw lots to determine who is responsible for God's wrath, and when Jonah is identified as the guilty party, he is thrown overboard and eventually swallowed by a whale. The fact that Jonah's guilt is correctly discovered by this random means is clearly meant to signal to readers that sinners cannot escape the ever-present surveillance of God, which in the absence of an organized state provides an important source of social control.[3] Adam Smith invokes a similar mechanism, in the form of his "impartial spectator," in his treatise on the *Theory of Moral Sentiments*.

Undoubtedly the most egregious example of group punishment in the bible, however, is the New Testament story of King Herod's efforts to locate and kill the messiah, whose coming was foretold to him. After learning of the messiah's supposed birth, Herod first sends the "wise men" to locate the child and report back to him, but when that strategy fails, he orders the slaughter of all male children in the region under the age of two. (This story is an obvious echo of the Old Testament story from Exodus of God's slaughter of all newborns in Egypt as punishment for the pharaoh's refusal to free the Jewish slaves.) Herod's "slaughter of the innocents" portrays, in a dramatic way, the choice between individual and group punishment—and especially of the high cost borne by innocent victims under the latter strategy. Indeed, one can interpret this story as a critique of the Old Testament's reliance on group punishment in favor of a more modern view in which punishment is linked to individual responsibility (especially since Herod's group punishment strategy fails to kill his intended target). As Parisi and Dari-Mattiacci (2004, pp. 502–3) argue, "the collective guilt referred to in the earlier sources was no longer the basis of the communal responsibility for wrongs. An individual's sin did not place any blame on the clan or class to which the wrongdoer belonged."

The culmination of this line of thought is found in the New Testament gospels, in which Jesus, himself an innocent, vicariously accepts responsibility for the sins of others. As a consequence, the guilty are encouraged to confess their sins, rather than to seek refuge, as the only route to redemption. We will argue, however, that vicarious responsibility is truly a variant of group punishment that enlists the recipient of the punishment as a surrogate enforcer. In the current example, that enforcer is God, an omniscient deity who punishes sinners and rewards the penitent.

Roman law provides additional examples of the punishment of individuals other than the actual wrongdoer. The principal concept of wrongdoing in that system of law was the *delict*, which was a sort of tort–crime hybrid for which the wrongdoer was held liable. (The modern distinction between criminal and tort law, as discussed in Chapter 7, was much fuzzier in most ancient legal systems.) However, there also existed various forms of *quasi-delicts*, which represented harms for which someone other than the actual wrongdoer was held responsible. Examples included owners of buildings from which something was thrown or poured so as to harm passersby; ship captains, innkeepers, or stable owners whose employees caused harm or committed fraud; and judges who breached their duty, resulting in harm. The related concept of *noxal* liability held the head of a household (the *paterfamilias*) responsible for harms caused by his sons, slaves, or animals. Finally, an important form of discipline in Roman armies was the practice of "decimation," which involved the random execution of one in ten soldiers in units accused of desertion or mutiny. Interestingly, in his autobiographical novel *A Farewell to Arms*, Ernest Hemingway reported that a similar practice was still being used as a disciplinary device in the Italian army during World War I.

The pervasiveness in ancient societies of group punishment and its close cousins, random punishment and vicarious responsibility, is usually attributed to two features of primitive law enforcement: the importance of vengeance, and the absence of an effective centralized enforcement authority, both of which, it is commonly argued, are no longer relevant today. Nevertheless, numerous examples of group punishment seem to persist. It is instructive to examine some of these modern examples as a way of trying to understand the fundamental factors that underlie the choice of an enforcement strategy.

Perhaps the most common contemporary example of group punishment is the waging of war, or at least the imposition of sanctions, against countries harboring terrorists. There is, of course, ample historical precedent for this tactic. Notable examples include the Greeks laying siege to Troy to avenge the kidnapping of Helen by one of its residents. Union General William T. Sherman's destructive "march to the sea" during the American Civil War; the bombing of German cities by the allies during World War II; and the internment of Japanese-Americans by the U.S. government during that same war. The justification for all of these actions would seem to be that the recipients of the punishment, though not directly guilty, were somehow collaborating (or at least sympathizing) with the actual wrongdoers and hence were partially culpable.

The persistence of group responsibility in modern law is most commonly found in the context of tort law. Examples include various forms of vicarious liability such as *respondeat superior*, under which an employer can be held responsible for the torts committed by its employees; and joint and several liability, under which any one of a group of injurers can be held liable for a victim's entire loss. Liability insurance also represents a kind of group punishment by spreading the cost of accidental harms across an injurer's risk pool.

With the foregoing ancient and modern examples of group punishment in mind, let us turn to a systematic examination of the factors involved in choosing an optimal law enforcement strategy. As noted, the general problem involves the detection and punishment of an individual who has committed some wrongdoing, but whose identity and whereabouts are unknown. Let us suppose, however, that it can be ascertained with certainty that he is a member of an identifiable group of size n (which could be quite large). The problem for the enforcement authority—whether the victim or someone acting on the victim's behalf, such as a government or kinship group—is to formulate a punishment strategy with the objective of maximizing the benefits of punishment less the costs of detection and of imposing the punishment (including the cost of wrongful punishment, if any). The specific question of interest is whether or when group punishment ever emerges as the optimal strategy.

First consider the benefits of punishment. These can come from various sources. The primary motivation in economic theories of criminal law, as discussed at length in previous chapters, is deterrence, or inducing wrongdoers to commit only efficient crimes, but other motives are possible. In ancient societies, the idea of retribution, or "just deserts," based on the talionic dictum of "an eye for an eye," seems to have been the fundamental justification. However, as we argued in Chapter 8, even in modern society there seems to be a strong impulse toward proportionality of punishments, though this is generally recast as serving notions of fairness (i.e., "letting the punishment fit the crime") rather than vengeance. A similar dichotomy exists in the area of tort law, which was largely unknown in primitive society, between the goal of deterring unreasonably risky behavior and of compensating accident victims. Offsetting these benefits are the costs of punishment, which include the cost of identifying the offender, of imposing the punishment, and possibly of wrongfully punishing innocent individuals.

The primary trade-off involved in the choice between individual and group punishment specifically would seem to be that between the certainty of punishing the true offender, and the risk of wrongful punishment. Note in particular that if all members of the group to which the offender is known to belong are punished, then the offender will not be able to avoid punishment. Thus, if the costs of punishment are not deemed to be high, then group punishment may be a desirable strategy, regardless of whether the benefit from imposing punishment is deterrence or vengeance. The New Testament's slaughter of the innocents, for example, reflected Herod's single-minded goal of killing the messiah and his apparent lack of concern for the ancillary carnage (although, as noted, the strategy failed). More modern examples of group punishment also appear to be found in settings where the cost of wrongful punishment is not deemed to be large, at least not by the authority undertaking the strategy. This could be true either because the members of the targeted group are seen as somehow sharing in the guilt for the underlying crime (as in sanctions against countries harboring terrorists, or vicarious liability of a corporation for the actions of its employees), or because the sanction in question is not really viewed as "punishment" but rather as spreading risk (as in the insurance example).

In contrast, in modern criminal law enforcement, which often involves imprisonment and always involves a stigma associated with conviction, there appears to be an especially strong aversion to wrongful punishment. Indeed, the significant safeguards of the rights of criminal defendants in many modern penal systems—such as the high standard of proof for conviction and stringent evidence-collection rules—are reflective of this social value (as emphasized in Chapter 7). Further promoting this reliance on individual punishment are technological advances that have lowered the cost of detection and substantially improved its accuracy (such as fingerprinting and DNA analysis).

I have suggested that there is a link between group punishment and random punishment. In primitive societies where the "science of detection" was largely absent, individual punishment, when it was used, effectively amounted to random punishment, such as in the Roman practice of decimation. Since random punishment is just a scaled-down version of group punishment, however, it follows that if there are constant or increasing returns to scale in the cost of imposing punishment, then group punishment dominates random punishment. To see why, consider first the extreme case where there are no costs of imposing punishment, as was apparently true in the King Herod story. In that case, it makes sense to punish all members of the group rather than a randomly chosen member because the targeted individual is thereby punished with certainty rather than with some probability, and that is all that matters. When punishment is costly, group punishment still dominates random punishment if punishment costs are constant or decreasing on a per-person basis. In this case, if it is desirable to punish one person chosen at random, then it is at least as desirable to punish everyone. On the other hand, random punishment may make sense if per-person punishment costs are increasing. Decimation is a good example of this situation, since the killing of a large number of soldiers eventually reduces the ability of the army to carry out its primary function.

Another situation in which group punishment offers strong advantages over individual punishment is when members of the targeted group are themselves the best detectors of the true offender's identity, and/or are in a good position to deter wrongful behavior in the first place. The tort doctrine of *respondeat superior* and other forms of vicarious liability illustrate these advantages. For example, holding a corporation responsible for the actions of its employees will give it an incentive to monitor their behavior and appropriately sanction wrongdoing. In addition to detection and deterrence, vicarious liability also increases the chances of obtaining compensation for victims, thereby correcting for a situation where the wrongdoer personally lacks the resources to pay compensation. The examples of vicarious liability in Roman law certainly reflect this advantage, as when the wrongdoer was a slave, a minor family member, or an animal. The same advantage obviously applies to corporate liability for wrongdoing by its employees.

It is reasonable to suppose that the size of the group is an important variable when considering the preceding benefits of group versus individual punishment, but the direction of the effect is not obvious. On one hand, it would seem that large groups would be less effective in policing their members, both because it would be easier for individuals to remain anonymous in such groups, and because free rider problems would prevent members of large groups from investing much effort in identifying and reporting bad behavior by other members. According to this logic, Parisi and Dar-Mattiacci (2004, p. 504) have argued that growth in the size of communities over time "might explain the historical evolution towards systems of individual responsibility and in general towards the limitation of the size of the group that was to be held collectively responsible for the wrongs of its members."

On the other hand, small groups, especially close-knit ones, may succeed in inculcating greater group "solidarity" among their members, and so, even though they likely have more knowledge of the actions of individual members, and would therefore find it easier to sanction them for misdeeds, they may be more reluctant to do so. Thus, for example, holding fraternities responsible for the actions of their members may be an ineffective substitute for traditional detection efforts. Another example involves community policing strategies, where the use of group punishment in inner city neighborhoods may be ineffective because it would further instill an "us versus them" mentality among individuals who already view the police with skepticism. In the same vein, some argue that the imposition of harsh sanctions against countries known to harbor terrorists may have the perverse effect of reducing those countries' willingness to aid in the rooting out of terrorists. Taken together, these arguments suggest that group punishment, to the extent that it is effective at all in assisting in the detection of offenders, will tend to work best in "moderately" sized groups and those lacking strong intra-group loyalties.

Finally, Levmore (1995a) describes a revealing case from modern tort law that involved the potential information-revealing function of group punishment. The plaintiff in the case suffered harm as a result of clear malpractice committed by one of several medical professionals during an operation, but because evidence of which one was culpable was unavailable, the court allowed the plaintiff to recover proportionately against all who were present. The fact that none of the defendants revealed the identity of the true injurer reflects the small-group problem noted previously. Levmore therefore speculates as to why the court did not simply raise the threatened sanction on each defendant above the actual harm suffered so that the guilty party would have had an incentive to confess. The likely answer is that such a rule would have been perceived as non-credible given the disproportionality of the punishment if the scheme failed to elicit the desired information. Indeed, it is the intolerance of such disproportionate punishments to modern sensibilities that makes group punishment so objectionable. Apart from the cost of wrongful punishment per se, there is the perception that punishing all members of a particular group might stigmatize them and possibly justify other forms of discrimination. For example, statistical discrimination or profiling based on race, gender, or ethnic background is an example of group punishment that might be justifiable based on narrow economic considerations of imperfect information, but may well be seen as resulting in greater social costs in terms of violation of civil rights. The internment of Japanese-Americans during World War II is a particularly egregious example of this sort of excess.

What the preceding analysis suggests is that group punishment can be justifiable on economic grounds in certain very specific circumstances, but its acceptance has generally declined in favor of individual detection as society has become more "civilized." As Feinberg (1991, p. 67) has observed, this trend has not occurred because "individual responsibility is an eternal law of reason," and it just took time for society to progress to the point where it recognized this truth. Rather, it is because the conditions that made group punishment acceptable or necessary in ancient times are rarely present in the modern world.

Notes

1 Many scholars attribute Hawthorne's invocation of collective guilt to the fact that one of his ancestors was a judge at the Salem witch trials of 1692–3 (see for example, Buell (1986, p. 360)).
2 Blackstone (1766), Book 3, p. 161.
3 See, for example, Wade (2009) and Johnson (2016).

13 When is a contract enforceable?

Contract law provides the legal means by which people enforce promises that they make to one another. Promises come in many varieties, but only some are enforceable by law in the sense that the victim of a broken promise has the right to seek a legal remedy. The key question this chapter will address is, what conditions must be satisfied for a promise to be enforceable? Or, in other words, what constitutes a valid contract? Chapter 14 then addresses a second question; namely, what is the optimal remedy when someone breaks a valid contract?

The benchmark for an enforceable contract is a mutually beneficial transaction, which means that both the buyer and the seller profit from the transfer of the good or service in question. Let's say that person S owns a car that she values at $1,000, but person B values it at $1,500. The value of the car is increased by $500 if S transfers it to B. The exchange is therefore efficient. It is, in addition, *mutually beneficial* if each party receives a share of the "gain from trade." For example, if the price of the car is set at $1,250, then each party receives a gain of $250, or half of the total gain. Mutual benefit, or voluntariness, is the defining characteristic of a "market exchange." Other types of exchanges—like gift-giving or theft—can be efficient in the sense of increasing overall value, but they are not *market exchanges* because only one side benefits.

Contracts are legal devices for facilitating market exchange. In many cases, formal (written) contracts are not needed, particularly when the exchange is instantaneous and information about the nature or quality of the good or service being transferred is perfect. But when an exchange involves a lapse of time between the initial promise and the date of performance, or if there is some uncertainty about quality at the time of exchange, problems can arise later. For example, suppose that in the exchange of a used car the buyer pays with a check that may bounce, or the car turns out to be stolen or to have a hidden defect. Now there is the potential for a dispute between the two parties after the exchange has occurred that may need to be resolved by contract law, assuming that the initial contract was enforceable.

As the preceding example suggests, contract disputes generally arise from an unanticipated change in circumstances that occurs between the time the contract was made and the date of performance, and that change makes one or both of the parties dissatisfied with the original terms. The fact that the change was unanticipated is important, because if it were anticipated, the parties could have explicitly provided for it in the contract. For example, a used car sale might be on an "as is" basis, or it might include a warranty for certain defects. Sometimes, however, even anticipated circumstances are not accounted for in a contract because their likelihood is so remote that it is not worth the trouble of explicitly dealing with them (such as the possibility that gas-powered cars will be declared illegal). In either of these cases, the original contract is said to be "incomplete," and it therefore falls to courts to resolve any dispute that arises owing to that incompleteness.

From an economic perspective, the manner in which courts should resolve such disputes involves answering the hypothetical question: "How would the parties have dealt with this problem if they had been able to bargain over it in a perfectly competitive market setting?" The use of the competitive market paradigm as the norm for contract law is based on the so-called "Invisible Hand Theorem," originally attributed to Adam Smith, which says that when the market is competitive, all gains from trade will be exhausted and the allocation of resources will be efficient. In the real world, of course, the requirements of perfect competition are rarely satisfied, which provides the rationale for courts to intervene and possibly invalidate those contracts that depart from the competitive ideal. The characteristics of a competitive market exchange nevertheless provide the standard against which actual contracts can be compared, and also suggest what remedies would be desirable.

The way that courts assess enforceability in practice is to inquire as to whether a contract includes the following three elements: *offer*, *acceptance*, and *consideration*. These represent an effort to identify mutual benefit. The first two, offer and acceptance, simply indicate that one party, the "promisor," has made a promise which the other party, the "promisee," has accepted. When offer and acceptance are present, there is said to be a "meeting of the minds," but that is not sufficient for the contract to be enforceable. In addition, the promisee must offer consideration in return for the original promise. It is this "return promise" that makes the contract mutual. Consideration usually involves the promisee's offering to make a monetary payment (or a payment in-kind) in return for the delivery of the good or service in question, but it need not take that form. An important alternative example, which serves to illustrate the fundamental nature of consideration, is provided by the famous case of *Hamer v. Sidway*.[1]

The case involved a promise made by an uncle to his nephew which stipulated that if the nephew refrained from drinking and smoking until his twenty-first birthday, the uncle would give him $5,000. The nephew apparently complied with the requirement (i.e., he accepted the uncle's offer), but the uncle's estate (the uncle had died) refused to make the payment on the grounds the original promise lacked consideration. The court, however, ruled that the promise was enforceable because consideration *was* present. In particular, it said that the nephew

> used tobacco, occasionally drank liquor, and he had a legal right to do so. That right he abandoned for a period of years upon the strength of the promise of the [uncle] that for such forebearance he would give him $5,000. We need not speculate on the effort which may have been required to give up the use of those stimulants. It is sufficient that he restricted his lawful freedom of action within certain prescribed limits upon the faith of his uncle's agreement, and now, having fully performed the conditions imposed, it is of no moment whether such performance actually proved a benefit to the promisor, and the court will not inquire into it.

The important principle set forth here is that, while the court will ask whether consideration is *present*, it will not inquire into its *adequacy*. This reflects sound economic reasoning based on the idea that it is the parties to the contract rather than the court who are in the best position to judge whether or not the contract offers a mutual benefit.

The foregoing presumes that the contract was negotiated in a competitive contracting environment. A party seeking to invalidate the contract must demonstrate that it was not. For example, the uncle's estate might have argued that the uncle was not of sound mind when he made the promise, but it would have had to prove that claim to get out of performance. The remainder of this chapter examines two other possible reasons for invalidating a contract based on departures from the competitive paradigm. The first is the possibility that one of the parties did not enter the contract voluntarily—that is, he or she entered under coercion or duress; and the second is that there was incomplete information about some material aspect of the contract at the time it was signed.

On its face, the issue of duress, or involuntariness, seems to be straightforward with regard to enforcement, but some subtleties arise when the logic is extended to cases where a change in the contracting environment limits one of the party's options. Let's begin with an easy example. Suppose that someone approaches a business owner and, in return for a payment of $100 a week, offers assurances that the premises will not be burned down or otherwise vandalized. The owner may well accept the offer, but it should be obvious that the contract would not be enforceable by a court because the business owner accepted the deal under duress, defined here to be a threat of violence.

Now consider the following variation on this example. Suppose a potential car buyer goes to a dealership and offers to buy a car for a price substantially below the sticker price, accompanied by a "threat" to go to a competing dealer if the current dealer refuses. If the dealer gives in, could she not later seek to void the deal by claiming that she accepted it under duress? Simple logic suggests that the answer should be yes based on the previous example, but intuition tells us that the two situations are very different, and economic theory helps to explain why.

In the protection money example, the buyer promises to buy something that he already had a legal right to—namely, the right to be free from harm. Thus, no new value would have been created by the transaction—instead, the business owner's refusal to pay the protection money would have resulted in destruction of value. In contrast, the car-buyer's "threat" in the second example actually promotes competition by forcing sellers to lower their prices to the point where economic profits are eliminated, thereby preventing the exercise of monopoly power and increasing the efficiency of the market.

The preceding examples would present little difficulty for courts, but a less obvious context in which the issue of duress arises involves the problem of "contract modification," or the renegotiation of contract terms prior to performance. Renegotiation is not an uncommon occurrence, and most such changes are carried out without difficulty. But in some cases, one of the parties later regrets having agreed to the change and seeks to have the original terms restored. The question before the court then becomes, under what circumstances is the modified contract enforceable? The traditional legal rule is the *pre-existing duty rule*, which holds that the modified terms are only enforceable if they were accompanied by new consideration. In other words, the modification is itself treated like a separate contract. Consider the application of this rule in two well-known cases of contract modification.

In the first, *Alaska Packers' Assn. v. Domenico*,[2] the defendant hired a crew of fishermen to go on a salmon-fishing expedition off the coast of Alaska. After the ship was at sea, however, the crew refused to fish unless their wage was increased. The defendant agreed, and the crew completed the job, but once back in port, the defendant refused to pay the renegotiated wages, and the plaintiffs sued. The court found for the defendant, holding that the renegotiated wage was *not* supported by new consideration and hence was not enforceable: the fishermen had merely completed the job for which they were originally hired. Thus, according to the pre-existing duty rule, the original wage was restored.

Another case of economic duress, *Goebel v. Linn*,[3] involved a contract that called for an ice company to deliver ice to a brewery during the summer at a pre-arranged price. When the delivery date arrived, however, the ice company requested a higher price, claiming that an unusually warm winter had resulted in a short supply of ice. Lacking an alternative supply, the brewery, which had a stock of beer on hand that would have spoiled for lack of ice, gave in to the demand. However, it later refused to pay the higher price, and the ice company sued. Although it appears that this case also presented a straightforward application of the pre-existing duty rule—after all, the ice company merely delivered the promised ice—the court *upheld* the price increase.

The opposite rulings in the two cases, though difficult to explain based on traditional legal principles, are easily reconciled based on economic theory. In both cases, the price increase was obtained in response to changed circumstances, but the changes had very different economic consequences. In *Alaska Packers'*, the departure of the ship from port substantially enhanced the bargaining power of the fishermen because, once the ship was at sea, it would have been impossible for the ship-owner to hire a replacement crew. The crew's demand for a higher wage therefore did not reflect any change in their cost of performance; it was instead a purely opportunistic attempt to exploit monopoly power given the ship owner's limited options. In contrast, the price increase in *Goebel* reflected a genuine increase in the cost of ice due to the warm winter; in other words, the ice company's supply curve had shifted upward. (Indeed, evidence was presented in the case that if the ice company had not obtained the price increase, it would have risked bankruptcy.)

The courts' opposing rulings in these two cases therefore reflected the fundamental difference between them on economic grounds, and therefore in combination provide the economic basis for a sensible departure from a mechanical application of the pre-existing duty rule. Modern contract law has in fact adopted this approach. For example, Section 89 of the Restatement (Second) of Contracts states that a modification is enforceable if it is "fair and equitable in view of circumstances not anticipated by the parties when the contract was made," where the "fair and equitable" standard requires "an objectively demonstrable reason for seeking modification."[4] Similarly, the Uniform Commercial Code states that for a modification to be enforceable, it must be made in good faith; that is, it must be "motivated by an honest desire to compensate for commercial exigencies."[5]

What these cases reveal is that duress is really about preventing monopoly, or undue bargaining power, in contract settings. (Chapter 16 pursues this aspect of duress further, again in the context of the *Goebel* case.) In both *Alaska Packers'* and *Goebel*, the parties initially bargained on equal footing, but then one party had to make an essential investment that put it at a disadvantage—in *Alaska Packers'* the ship had to leave port, and in *Goebel* the brewery had to produce the beer. This conferred a bargaining advantage on the other party, which allowed it to negotiate more favorable terms. The key difference, which the court recognized, is that the modified terms must be justified by a corresponding change in the contracting environment in order to be legally enforceable.[6]

I now turn to the second departure from a competitive contracting environment, representing situations where one party has more information than the other prior to contracting. This issue is typically dealt with under the contract doctrine of "mistake," which concerns situations in which one or possibly both parties held incorrect beliefs about some material aspect of the contract at the time it was signed. The existence of mistaken beliefs may be a reason for invalidating a contract because it implies that there was no "meeting of the minds," which we noted was a prerequisite for mutual gain. When the mistake is truly mutual, there usually is no difficulty in terminating or redrafting the contract precisely because both parties realize that they misunderstood the nature of the transaction. In this case, a dispute rarely arises.

Most disputes therefore concern cases of *unilateral* mistake—that is, where only one party is (or claims to be) mistaken. Kronman (1978, p. 1) has characterized the essential question in such cases this way:

> if one party to a contract has reason to know that the other party is mistaken about a particular fact, does the knowledgeable party have a duty to speak up or may he remain silent and capitalize on the other party's error?

In other words, is there a duty on the part of the informed party to disclose his or her private knowledge prior to contracting?

The problem of unilateral mistake reflects a situation that economists refer to as "asymmetric information"—that is, where one party to a transaction has superior information about some aspect of the contemplated transaction. (Recall that we encountered this same issue in the previous chapter in the context of cases involving blackmail.) For instance, in the example involving the sale of a used car, the seller/owner may have acquired intimate knowledge about the car—such as its maintenance record or how recently the brakes were replaced—that would be of value to a prospective buyer. In his classic treatment of the used car market, George Akerlof (1970) showed that the existence of asymmetric information of this sort can cause the market to shrink, or in the extreme case, to cease to exist altogether. The reason is that, because buyers are uninformed about the quality of individual used cars, they will view all such cars as being of "average" quality. The price will therefore reflect that average, which will tend to cause owners of high quality cars to withdraw them from the market because they are underpriced. As a result, only those cars at the low end of the quality spectrum—so-called "lemons"—will remain for sale. Economists refer to this problem, which can arise in any market characterized by asymmetric information, as one of "adverse selection."

From an economic perspective, the law of mistake is concerned with correcting the market failure associated with adverse selection. This objective might lead one to suspect that the ideal rule would therefore be to invalidate all contracts in which one party was mistaken, thereby creating an incentive for parties with private information to disclose that information prior to contracting. However, the issue turns out to be more complicated than that because one must also account for the incentives to *discover* socially valuable information in the first place. An efficient disclosure rule therefore needs to balance the benefits of information disclosure against incentives for discovery of that information. Some examples will motivate our analysis of this trade-off.

Consider first a person who purchases an item at a garage sale and subsequently learns, perhaps by watching an episode of "Antiques Roadshow," that the item is extremely valuable—worth much more than the price she paid. Further, suppose that the seller, after seeing the same episode of "Antiques Roadshow," realizes his mistake and sues to have the sale invalidated. What is the appropriate rule? Should the buyer have to return the item, and does it depend on what she knew at the time of purchase (for example, was the mistake mutual)?

As a second example, consider a boy who goes into a baseball card shop and spots a card with a price tag marked $1200. When both he and the clerk interpret this to mean $12.00, the boy eagerly buys the card. However, the actual price was $1,200.00, and the owner therefore sues to have the card returned, citing the doctrine of mistake. Again, should the boy have to return the card?

The final example is the famous case of *Sherwood v. Walker*,[7] which involved a contract for the sale of a cow. The price of cow was set at $80 based on the (apparently) shared belief that the cow was infertile and hence only good for slaughter. Before delivery, however, it was learned that the cow was pregnant, which increased her value to between $750 and $1,000. The seller naturally wanted to invalidate the contract on the grounds of mistake, while the buyer wanted to enforce the original terms. In the resulting suit, the court rescinded the contract based on evidence "tending to show that at the time of the alleged sale it was believed by both the plaintiff and [defendant] that the cow was barren and would not breed." In justifying its decision, the court emphasized the difference between mutual and unilateral mistake:

> It must be considered as well settled that a party who has given an apparent consent to a contract of sale may refuse to execute it, or he may avoid it after it has been completed, if the assent was founded, or the contract made, upon the mistake of a material fact, —such as the subject matter of the sale, the price, or some collateral fact materially inducing the agreement; and this can be done when the mistake is mutual.

A dissenting judge, however, doubted that the mistake was in fact mutual:

> There is no question but that the defendants sold the cow representing her of the breed and quality they believed the cow to be, and that the purchaser so understood it. And the buyer purchased her believing her to be of the breed represented by the sellers, and possessing all the qualities stated, and even more. He believed she would breed. There is no

pretense that the plaintiff bought the cow for beef, and there is nothing in the record indicating that he would have bought her at all only that he thought she could be made to breed. Under the foregoing facts, . . . it is held that because it turned out that the plaintiff was more correct in his judgment as to the quality of the cow than the defendants, . . . the contract may be annulled by the defendants at their pleasure. I know of no law . . . which will justify any such holding.

The majority and dissenting opinions in this case disagreed over the beliefs of the buyer at the time the contract was made—that is, whether or not he suspected that the cow could breed. As a result, therefore, they reached differing conclusions about the enforceability of the contract based on the distinction between mutual and unilateral mistake. Such a debate, however, is not a useful way to approach this or related cases because it requires knowledge about the state of mind of the parties at the time the contract was made—something that the court cannot know or reliably discover after the fact. An economic approach to mistake therefore focuses on a different distinction—namely, that between "purely distributive" and "socially valuable" information. The following example, which closely mirrors the facts of *Sherwood v. Walker*, illustrates this distinction and describes how it can be used to derive a more workable rule for resolving this and similar disputes.

Consider a seller who offers a supposedly infertile cow for sale for $50, the value of such cows for slaughter. Let us assume, however, that in one out of 50 cases involving "infertile" cows, the cow in question is actually fertile, and cow dealers know this percentage (though they obviously don't know which cows are which). Further, suppose that fertile cows are worth $1,000. In the first scenario, we assume that the identity of truly fertile cows emerges naturally after the contract is signed but before delivery, as actually happened in the *Sherwood* case. The question is whether the seller can have the contract rescinded in those cases where the cow turns out to be fertile.

Suppose first that the answer is no—that is, the original contract is enforced. In that case, on the rare occasion where it is revealed that the cow is in fact fertile, the buyer gets a windfall of $950=$1,000−$50. Remember, however, that in 49 out of 50 cases, the buyer gets exactly what he paid for; namely, an infertile cow worth $50. Thus, the buyer's *expected* gain across all transactions equals the *average value* of cows of unknown type, which is $69 = (.02×$1,000) + (.98×$50), less the price of $50. Thus, his net gain on average is $19. The seller, on the other hand, receives $50 regardless of the cow's type, and so the overall (joint) value of the transfer of a cow of unknown type is $69, which is just its expected value.

Now suppose that the original contract is rescinded when the cow turns out to be fertile, as actually happened in the *Sherwood* case. In that situation, it is the seller who realizes the windfall when the cow turns out to be fertile because she can reclaim any cows that turn out to be fertile. Thus, the seller's expected gain is now $69 (based on the same calculation as above), while the buyer's gain is zero; that is, he pays $50 for infertile cows in 49 cases out of 50, and returns the fertile cow in the fiftieth case. Again, the overall value of the cow turns out to be its social value, or $69, which the seller receives in its entirety.

What the preceding examples showed is that the court's enforcement rule *has no effect on the overall value of the cow*, which is equal to its social value under both rules (namely, $69). This is true because, no matter which party gets ownership of the cow, they will put it to its socially optimal use (for beef if it is infertile, and for breeding if it is fertile). The enforcement rule therefore has no effect on the cow's use, but only on the distribution of the gains from the contract, and in particular, who gets fertile cows. When the contract is enforced, the buyer gets to keep them, and when it is not enforced, the seller gets to reclaim them. Thus, we say that the effect of the court's ruling in the current scenario is *purely distributive*.

The reason for the irrelevance of the enforcement rule in the preceding scenario is that the information about the cow's type was assumed to emerge naturally—that is, without the conscious effort on the part of the buyer or seller. Kronman (1978) refers to this as a case where information was "casually acquired" in the sense that no one invested any effort to produce or discover it. This seems to fit the facts of the *Sherwood* case, where no evidence of effort to discover the cow's type was provided. We may conclude, therefore, that the ruling in that case would have had only distributive effects and therefore would not have affected the allocation of resources (i.e., the use of the cow).

But suppose we alter the scenario slightly to allow the buyer, say, to invest effort in "deliberately discovering" the cow's type prior to the time when that information would have come out anyway. Let us suppose, for example, that some buyers of supposedly infertile cows are in fact speculators who seek to profit from the discovery of those cows that are fertile but mistakenly thought to be infertile. In particular, suppose that there is a "test" that these buyers can use to discover (with certainty) which cows are fertile, and that they can keep the result of the test, or even the fact that they undertook it, secret from the seller or anyone else. (If it were known that the buyer conducted the test, the seller would be able to infer the result of the test by the buyer's decision of whether to buy the cow.) The question then becomes, should buyers be allowed to profit from any pre-contractual knowledge that they acquire in this way, or should they have a duty to disclose it?

To answer this question in the context of our example, suppose that the buyer can spend $10 to learn with certainty whether a given cow is fertile or not, and that he can do this secretly before the parties enter into a contract. We can again compute the returns to the buyer and seller under the two enforcement rules. Suppose first that the contract is enforced. By investing the $10, the buyer will expect to discover a fertile cow in one out of 50 cases, and an infertile cow in the other 49. Fertile cows yield a net return of $1,000 minus the price of $50, or $950, while infertile cows yield a net return of zero. (The buyer is thus indifferent between buying and not buying cows discovered to be infertile.) The buyer's overall expected gain is therefore $19=(.02\times\$950)$, which, after subtracting the initial investment of $10, leaves an overall net return of $9. The investment is therefore profitable. As for the seller, his return is $50, either from sale of what turn out to be fertile cows, or retention of infertile cows (depending on whether or not the buyer decides to buy infertile cows). The joint return is therefore $59, which equals the true expected value of the cow, $69, less the investment of $10.

Now consider the outcome when the contract is not enforced; that is, when the seller can reclaim fertile cows. Clearly in this case, the buyer will *not* find it profitable to spend the $10 to learn the cow's type because he knows that the seller will rescind the contract when it becomes public knowledge that the cow is fertile. This conclusion would seem to be inefficient because it prevents discovery of the cow's type before the transaction, but recall that in the current scenario we are assuming that the information would have come out anyway (i.e., "casually"). Thus, the buyer's gain of $9 was purely private in the sense that it had no effect on how the cow would ultimately be used.

To further emphasize this conclusion, note that in the case of non-enforcement, the outcome is the same as in the first scenario where the seller enjoyed a net return of $69 because he got to retain, and breed, any fertile cows. The buyer's expenditure of $10 on the test, while personally profitable, is therefore *socially wasteful*. In other words, the buyer's deliberate (and costly) effort to discover the cow's type prior to sale merely gave him "foreknowledge" while providing no social benefit. What this argument shows is that deliberate acquisition of information is not, in itself, a basis for protecting the investor's right to that information. In fact, when the information generates a purely private benefit but no corresponding social gain, the court should require disclosure so as to discourage the investment. Thus, in the current scenario, non-enforcement is the efficient rule.

Finally, let's consider a third scenario in which the buyer's investment *does* yield a social benefit. Suppose, in particular, that information about the cow's type would never come out but for the buyer's effort. As a result, all cows believed to be infertile would be slaughtered after sale. In this case, discovery of the cow's type prior to sale *would be socially valuable* because it would prevent some truly fertile cows (namely, one in 50) from being slaughtered. Enforcement of the contract in this case gives the buyer a private incentive to invest (the $9 net gain), while yielding a net social return of $59. In contrast, under a rule of non-enforcement, the buyer would not invest in learning the cow's type, and so fertile cows would never be discovered. Thus, all cows would be slaughtered, yielding a net benefit of $50. Clearly in this case, a rule of enforcement (i.e., *no* duty to disclose) is efficient because it results in a more efficient allocation of resources—namely, the discovery and breeding of the one cow in 50 that is fertile but that would be slaughtered but for the buyer's efforts.

Based on the examples given, we can assert the following general conclusions regarding enforceability in cases of mistake: (1) when information is casually acquired, the enforcement rule is purely distributive and therefore has no effect on efficiency; (2) when information is deliberately acquired but that information is mere foreknowledge (purely distributive), there should be a duty to disclose private information prior to contracting; (3) when information is deliberately acquired and that information is socially valuable, there should be no duty to disclose information prior to contracting. Let's now apply these rules to our various examples.

As suggested, the actual facts of the *Sherwood v. Walker* case seem to conform to the first scenario, suggesting that the court's ruling had no efficiency consequences. Of course, it is possible, and the dissenting judge's comments provide some evidence of the fact, that the buyer was a speculator who may have known that the cow was potentially fertile. If true, the case would fall under scenario two, and we would conclude that the court's ruling to rescind the contract was probably correct.

As for the antique case, the correct ruling would seem to depend upon whether the buyer of the item was an antiques expert, or was just lucky. This difference matters because becoming an expert on antiques (or cows) is a costly endeavor, and represents a form of deliberate acquisition of information, whereas if the buyer was just lucky, it is a case of casual acquisition. Assuming the buyer was an expert puts the case in scenario two or three, though scenario three seems more likely because items offered at garage sales probably would have ended up being thrown away or hidden away in an attic if not for the buyer's astute purchase. In this case, the efficient rule is therefore to enforce the contract.

The baseball card case also seems to fall into either scenario two or three, assuming the boy was a baseball card expert, a status he had no doubt attained by deliberate effort. Here, however, scenario two seems to be the more likely one given the virtual certainty that the owner of the store knew the true value of the card in question. Thus, there is little danger that the card would have been undervalued but for the boy's purchase. This suggests that the correct ruling in this case would have been to return the card to the store owner.

As a final example, consider the famous case of *Laidlaw v. Organ*,[8] which involved a contract for the sale of tobacco from a man named Laidlaw to a tobacco buyer named Organ. The contract was set during the British blockade of New Orleans during the War of 1812, and so the price of tobacco was depressed. Prior to finalizing the contract, however, Organ learned of the signing of the Treaty of Ghent, which ended the war, and he therefore knew that the price would soon rise substantially, allowing him to make a large profit at the expense of the uninformed seller. When the information became public, Laidlaw therefore tried to get out of the contract, but the Supreme Court apparently upheld the original terms.

Opinions on this case differ, depending on the assumptions one makes. For example, Posner (2003, p. 111) seems to endorse the court's ruling based on the need to create incentives for people to obtain socially valuable information (our scenario three). Cooter and Ulen (1988, p. 26), however, suggest that the information in question (the end of the war) was purely distributive in the sense that it allowed Organ to profit at Laidlaw's expense, but produced no social value, given that the information was certain to become widely known soon after Organ learned it (scenario one or two). Finally, Kronman (1978, p. 15) speculates on whether Organ acquired the information casually or as a result of deliberate effort, "for example, by cultivating a network of valuable commercial 'friendships'." The facts of the case make it unclear.

These differing views illustrate the sort of factors a court would have to take into account in applying the above rules. The case illustrates the complexity of the mistake doctrine, but the proposed rules at least provide an objective basis for reaching a decision that does not rely on the state of mind of the parties at the time the contract was made.

Notes

1 124 N.Y. 538, 27 N.E. 256 (1891).
2 117 F. 99 (9th Cir. 1902).
3 47 Mich. 489, 11 N.W. 284 (1882).
4 Restatement (Second) of Contracts (1981), § 89, Comment b
5 U.C.C., § 2–209:61, citing *Roth Steel Products v. Sharon Steel Corp.*, 705 F. 2d 134 (1983).
6 Although the price increase for the ice in *Goedel* was upheld, the court presumably would *not* have allowed a price increase that exceeded the increase in costs.
7 66 Mich. 568, 33 N.W. 919 (Mich. 1887).
8 15 U.S. (2 Wheat.) 178 (1815).

14 Efficient breach theory

Chapter 13 examined the first fundamental question of contract law, namely, what contracts are enforceable? This chapter turns to a second question: what is the optimal remedy when a party breaches a valid contract? Should the court require that party to carry out the contract as promised, or should it allow him or her to get out of performance by paying money damages to the other party? Are there ever circumstances in which it should excuse performance without any penalty? The economic theory of contract law seeks to answer these questions based on the objective of maximizing the gains from exchange. The idea behind "efficient breach theory" is that it is desirable not to perform those contracts for which the cost of performance turns out to exceed the benefit of performance. From this perspective, the purpose of legal remedies for breach is to create incentives for promisors to breach only in those circumstances where this is true.

To illustrate the logic of the argument, consider a contract that calls for a seller (the promisor) to produce and deliver a good to a buyer (the promisee) at some specified date. Let $50,000 be the gross value of the good to the buyer, and let the negotiated price be $40,000, which is payable on delivery. Thus, the buyer's expected gain from the contract is $10,000 (the buyer's surplus). Let us suppose, however, that the possibility of breach arises because the cost of performance is uncertain at the time the contract is made, reflecting unavoidable uncertainties in the production process. Obviously, the *expected costs* must have been less than $40,000 at the time the contract was made, for otherwise the seller would not have anticipated a profit from the deal, but if *actual costs* turn out to be larger than $50,000, it is efficient to breach the contract. To be specific, suppose the realized cost of performance is $55,000. In that case it is efficient for the seller not to produce and deliver the good because the cost of the resources needed to complete production exceeds the value of production; in other words, performance would entail a net social loss of $5,000 and hence is inefficient. The general principle is that breach is efficient if

Cost of Performance > Benefit of Performance. (1)

It is important to note that the contract price is not relevant for this condition. Although breach prevents the seller from incurring a loss of $15,000 in this case (=$55,000–$40,000), it also deprives the buyer of a gain of $10,000 (=$50,000–40,000). What matters for efficiency is that the seller's loss exceeds the buyer's gain by $5,000, thus resulting in a net *social* loss, which justifies non-performance. Suppose instead that the realized cost of performance had turned out to be $45,000. In that case the seller would still incur a loss of $5,000 from performing, but since that loss is less than the buyer's foregone gain of $10,000, performance remains efficient. The point is that the efficiency of breach depends only on whether there exists a net social gain from performance, not on how that gain is distributed between the two parties (as determined by the contract price).

As an illustration of this principle, recall the case of *Goebel v. Linn* from the previous chapter, which involved a contract between a brewery and an ice company calling for the latter to deliver a quantity of ice at a certain date. The actual cost of the ice at the time of delivery, however, depended on how cold the winter turned out to be, which neither party could know at the time the terms of the contract were set. As events unfolded, however, the cost of ice exceeded the contract price, but the parties were able to negotiate a new and higher price at which the ice company was willing to make delivery. This suggests that performance was efficient in the above sense, for otherwise, the parties could not have agreed on a new price. Of course, the brewery later sued to have the original price reinstated. Alternatively, it could have sued for breach of the original contract in an effort to obtain delivery at the original price. The fact that it didn't suggests that it viewed the available remedy as being inferior to renegotiating the price, a point to which we will return.

Efficient breach theory is concerned not only with the conditions under which breach is efficient (as given by condition (1) above), but also whether actual remedies achieve this ideal. We focus initially on a money damage remedy, meaning that the breaching party has the option to perform the contract as written, or to pay damages in lieu of performance. The question is what amount of damages (if any) induces the seller to breach only when that is the efficient action; that is, only when (1) holds.

In the example of cost uncertainty, the seller decides whether or not to breach the contract once the actual cost is realized. At that point, she will breach if her cost of breach, consisting of the damage payment, is less than her net loss from performance. (Obviously, the seller will never breach if she expects a positive profit from performance.) The loss from performance is the excess of the realized cost of performance above the contract price. Thus, we can write the condition for the seller to breach as

Damages < Cost of Performance – Price, (2)

which *does* depend on the price. Comparing this condition to the condition for efficient breach in (1), we find that the two coincide if

$$Damages = Benefit\ of\ Performance - Price. \tag{3}$$

That is, the seller's breach decision will be efficient if the amount of damages is set equal to the buyer's net benefit from performance. In other words, efficient breach requires that damages must equal the buyer's surplus. In the example, damages should therefore be set at $10,000. Given the contract price of $40,000, condition (2) implies that the seller will breach for any cost of performance above $50,000, which is the efficient threshold.

The analysis so far has been purely normative in the sense that it specifies the efficient remedy for breach. The next step is to compare that measure to the measure that courts employ. The most common measure is referred to as "expectation damages," which is defined to be an amount of money that leaves the victim of breach (the buyer in this case) as well off as if the contract had been performed. In other words, it fully compensates the buyer for the cost of breach, which equals his foregone expected benefit from the contract. This amount, of course, is just the buyer's surplus, *which is exactly the measure that we computed in (3)*. It follows that expectation damages—the measure most commonly used by courts—gives promisors exactly the right incentives to breach efficiently.

On reflection, this conclusion should not be too surprising. Because the expectation damage measure is intended to fully compensate victims of breach, the breaching party is forced to internalize the cost of the breach and therefore makes the socially efficient decision. In this sense, the expectation damage measure resembles strict liability in torts, where breach of contract is interpreted to be the "accident," with the promisor (seller) playing the role of the "injurer" and the promisee (buyer) playing the role of the "victim." Based on this analogy, we can see that breach of contract is just another example of an externality, and the efficient damage remedy is simply a form of Pigovian tax aimed at internalizing it.

We now turn to an extension of efficient breach theory that concerns the possibility that parties to a contract sometimes can (or must) make investments in advance of performance that are aimed at increasing its value. For example, in the beer case, the brewery had to choose the amount of beer to brew before taking delivery of ice. While such investments, referred to as "reliance," are socially productive, they must often be made in advance of the performance decision; and, if they involve non-salvageable expenditures, there is a risk that those expenditures will be lost in the event of breach. For example, if the ice company failed to deliver the ice, the brewery's stock of beer would have spoiled. In this situation, the efficient choice of reliance should therefore account for the uncertainty of performance.

To illustrate this point, consider the two extremes. If performance is certain, the buyer should choose the level of reliance that promises the highest possible profit. In contrast, if breach is certain, the buyer should invest in zero reliance because the entire investment would be lost. When performance is uncertain, the buyer should therefore invest an intermediate level of reliance, with the amount of the investment increasing in proportion to the probability that performance will occur.

The buyer's actual choice of reliance, however, will depend on the amount of damages he expects to receive in the event of breach. Thus, if we are concerned about creating incentives for efficient reliance *and* breach, the measure of damages may need to be adjusted. As a benchmark, let's first consider the buyer's incentives under the expectation measure, which, recall, fully compensates the buyer for his losses in the event of breach and therefore leaves him indifferent between breach and performance. While this made expectation damages desirable with respect to breach, it turns out to give the buyer an incentive to *overinvest in reliance*. The reason is easy to see. Since the buyer expects to be fully compensated for breach, he will behave as if performance were certain, and therefore will invest in the level of reliance that is appropriate for that outcome. But we argued that when performance is uncertain, the buyer should curtail his reliance correspondingly so as to reduce the unrecoverable loss in the event of breach. In the brewery example, under expectation damages the brewer would brew the amount of beer that would be optimal if delivery of ice were certain, rather than reducing it in proportion to the probability of breach.

Continuing the analogy of expectation damages to strict liability, it is the case that expectation damages induces the buyer to overinvest in reliance for that same reason that strict liability resulted in accident victims investing too little care in the context of the bilateral-care model discussed in Chapter 5. We argued there that, because victims expected to be fully compensated for their losses under strict liability, they had no incentive to take care to reduce the accident risk. The same logic applies here with respect to buyers, who, because they expect to be fully compensated under expectation damages, behave as if there were no risk of breach and therefore over-rely.

We argued that the solution to this bilateral-care incentive problem in the tort context was the negligence rule, which created efficient incentives for both injurers and victims by virtue of its threshold character. Although there is no exact analogy to a negligence rule in contract law, we suggested in Chapter 5 that there is a doctrine that accomplishes the same objective, also by establishing a threshold of behavior for one of the parties. This is the rule articulated in the famous case of *Hadley v. Baxendale*.[1]

The case concerned a contract between a mill operator and a transport company calling for the latter to transport the broken crank shaft of the mill back to the manufacturer to have a new one built. However, when the return of the shaft was delayed due to the transport company's admitted negligence, the mill owner sued for the lost profit during the period of the delay. The court denied the request, holding that the mill was only entitled to the losses that could "reasonably be supposed to have been in the contemplation of both parties, at the time they made the contract, as the probable result of the breach of it." In other words, the amount of damages was limited to that amount which could reasonably have been foreseen at the time of breach. (Apparently, in those days it was standard practice for mills to have spare shafts on hand.)

The significance of this ruling is that it limited damages based on a threshold of behavior for one of the parties according to a "reasonableness standard," which we previously equated with efficient behavior. This implies, particularly, that reasonably foreseeable reliance can be equated with *efficient* reliance, and that the *Hadley v. Baxendale* rule therefore limits damages to that amount which would have arisen from the promisee's efficient reliance rather than from his actual reliance. Regarding incentives, the effect of this rule is that promisees will be discouraged from over-relying because any losses they suffer as a result of that excessive reliance will be uncompensated.

Let's say, for example, that the brewery in the *Goebel* case had brewed a quantity of beer based on the expectation that the delivery of ice was certain. Under the *Hadley v. Baxendale* rule the court would have nevertheless limited the amount of the brewery's damages to the lost profit from the quantity of beer that the brewery *should* have brewed, given the positive possibility of breach. As for the ice company, its incentives for breach would be unaffected by this limitation because it still would expect to pay "full" damages, given its belief that in equilibrium the brewery will choose efficient reliance. Thus, the limited expectation damage measure prescribed by the *Hadley* case, like the negligence rule in tort law, achieves efficient bilateral incentives.

The *Hadley* court also addressed the possibility that some promisees will have unavoidably high reliance. For example, the mill in *Hadley* clearly did not have a spare shaft to install while the broken one was being repaired, thus requiring it to shut down until the new one was delivered. In situations like this, it is desirable for promisees to communicate their particular circumstances to promisors so they can expend additional efforts to avoid breach, thereby mitigating the loss.[2] If promisees make such a communication, then the damages in the event of breach "would be the amount of injury which would ordinarily follow from breach of contract under these special circumstances so known and communicated." However, if they fail to communicate any special circumstances, the damages would be limited to the "injury which would arise generally, and in the great multitude of cases not affected by any special circumstances." In other words, the rule limits the ability of promisees to recover so-called "consequential damages," defined to be damages in excess of what would be reasonably anticipated. In the *Hadley* case, the mill did not inform the transport company that it would have to shut down as a result of the broken shaft, and so the court denied recovery for the lost profits.

The economic theory of efficient breach as described so far is based on making the efficient choice between performance and breach in the face of uncertainty, but what about circumstances in which the changed circumstances make performance physically impossible? Suppose, for example, that a performer falls ill on the date of a scheduled appearance, or a factory burns down before it can take delivery of a custom-made machine. While payment of damages by the breaching party may still be possible, it can no longer be justified as a means of inducing efficient breach (assuming the circumstances rendering performance impossible were not under the promisor's control). In these cases, the criterion for determining the optimal remedy is instead to ask how the risk of the unavoidable circumstance can best be absorbed. The relevant economic consideration here is therefore *optimal risk sharing*, which may lead to a different answer than that prescribed by efficient breach theory.

Economists generally assume that people are averse to risk, which means that they prefer certain (predictable) outcomes—whether in the form of gains or losses—to unpredictable ones. This explains why people buy homeowners, car, or health insurance. The existence of competitive insurance markets allows risk-averse people to shift unavoidable risk to risk-neutral insurance companies, who, through risk pooling and diversification, can bear it at lower cost.

Remedies for breach of contract, in addition to providing incentives for breach and reliance, also necessarily assign the risk of uncertain performance to one or the other of the parties. Under expectation damages, for example, which fully compensates promisees for their losses, the risk of that loss is fully assigned to the promisor. In effect, the promisor insures the promisee against non-performance. Conversely, if the promisor's breach were excused without damages, the risk would be assigned to the promisee, who thereby becomes the insurer of the promisor's expected profit from the contract.[3] The contract doctrine of "impossibility" corresponds to this latter outcome. Physical impossibility, or the inability of the promisor to perform the contract as promised, however, is not necessarily grounds for discharge without penalty—from a risk-sharing perspective it depends on which party is the superior risk bearer.

As an example, consider a contract for the excavation of a foundation for a building. Suppose that in the process of digging the contractor encounters large boulders whose removal requires a larger, more expensive machine. Who should bear the extra cost? The contractor may have better knowledge of the likelihood of such obstacles by virtue of past experience, and could build that cost into the originally quoted price, which is a form of self-insurance. In that case, we would say that the promisor is the superior risk-bearer, and the original contract should be enforced. Alternatively, the owner of the property may have better knowledge of local soil conditions, which he should have communicated to the contractor. In that case, the landowner is the superior risk-bearer, and he should bear the extra cost of complying with the contract terms. What these examples illustrate is that as a general proposition, the determination of which party to a contract is the better risk-bearer will depend on the specific circumstances of the case, and therefore, no general rule can be articulated.

The final issue we address in our discussion of efficient breach is the remedy of "specific performance," which is an order by the court that the party seeking to breach a contract must carry it out as written (assuming such performance is physically possible) rather than being allowed to pay damages. The idea of a contract as an enforceable promise suggests that this should be a more prevalent remedy, but in practice it is limited to contracts for which money damages may not be a good substitute for performance, such as contracts for the sale of land or for "unique" goods.

Despite the possible appeal of an order of specific performance on moral grounds ("people should keep their promises"), from an economic perspective it seems contrary to the theory of efficient breach. In particular, it would seem to promote excessive performance. This turns out not to be true, however, provided that the parties are able to renegotiate the terms of the contract in the presence of unforeseen circumstances. As an example, consider a contract for the sale of a parcel of land for which a buyer has agreed to pay $100,000. Suppose that before the transaction is completed another buyer arrives and offers $120,000. Under a money damage remedy, the seller would breach the contract and pay damages equal to the original buyer's expectation interest, which in this case is the difference between his valuation of the land, say $110,000, and the price. The damages would therefore set at $10,000, which the seller will gladly pay and then sell to the new buyer for $120,000, netting the seller a gain of $10,000. The outcome is efficient because the new buyer values the land more than the original buyer.

Now consider the outcome under a specific performance remedy. One possibility is that, after the initial transaction is completed based on the court's order, the original buyer turns around and resells the land to the new buyer for a net gain of $10,000. But suppose that the original buyer is unaware of the new offer. In that case, the seller could offer the first buyer some amount of money greater than $10,000 (the original buyer's expected surplus), but less than $20,000 (the premium offered by the second buyer) to cancel the original contract, and then turn around and sell the land to the new buyer. Either way, the land ends up with its higher valuing user.

How would a specific performance remedy have worked in the brewery example, where non-performance is due to unexpectedly high costs? Recall that the value of performance to the brewery was $50,000 and the price of performance was $40,000. If the ice company's cost of performance turned out to be $55,000, breach is efficient, and we know that that outcome would be achieved by a money damage remedy of $10,000. Under specific performance, the ice company would stand to lose $15,000 if it were compelled to perform, and so it would be willing to pay any amount less than that to be allowed to breach. At the same time, the brewery would accept any amount greater than $10,000, its surplus from performance, to permit breach. Thus, there is room for a bargain whereby the ice company would pay the brewery some amount between $10,000 and $15,000 to cancel the contract.

The key point of these examples is that under either remedy—money damages or specific performance—the efficient outcome can be achieved. The only difference is how that outcome arises. Under money damages, the court dictates the amount of compensation that the original buyer will receive in the event of breach, whereas under specific performance, the buyer is able to participate in the determination of the terms of a breach, either by bargaining directly with the new buyer (as in the first example), or by bargaining with the seller for a buyout (as in the second). It follows that specific performance and money damages are, in theory, equally capable of reaching the efficient outcome in breach of contract cases, a conclusion that is assured by the Coase Theorem. In light of these examples, the only argument against specific performance on efficiency grounds is the possibility of high transaction costs of renegotiating the original contract. But these costs have to be weighed against the litigation costs involved in the court's determination of a damage remedy under money damages, and it is far from obvious that the latter cost will generally be lower.

There is, however, another important consideration that favors specific performance: when the court might have difficulty in accurately measuring the promisee's value of performance, possibly resulting in an inefficient breach decision. This risk is probably slight in the case of commercial contracts like that between the brewery and the ice company, where the lost profits of the brewery are relatively easy to observe or estimate. In other cases, however, the promisee's value may be much harder to measure.

As an illustration, consider the well-known case of *Peevyhouse v. Garland Coal & Mining Co.*,[4] which involved a contract between the Peevyhouses, the owners of a farm that sat on top of a coal deposit, and the Garland Mining Company. The contract called for the mining company to conduct a strip mining operation, after which it agreed to restore the land to its pre-mining condition. However, when it came time to do the remedial work, the mining company reneged on its agreement, arguing that the cost of the work, estimated at $29,000, greatly exceeded the market value of the remediation, which was put at a mere $300. The court agreed with the mining company and allowed the breach, for which they awarded the Peevyhouses compensation of $300, the market value of the restorative work. It seems likely, however, that the Peevyhouses attached substantial value to their land above its market value—referred to as its "subjective value"—which means that performance of the contract was probably worth considerably more to them than the $300 market value. By setting damages at market value, the court therefore underestimated the true cost of breach, thereby creating a risk of excessive breach.

Recognition of this problem provides an argument in favor of specific performance when subjective value is thought to be an important component of the value of performance. The reason is that specific performance removes the need for the court to measure this value, instead putting the responsibility for determining whether the contract will be performed back in the hands of the parties. If Coasian bargaining is possible, the outcome will be efficient, as the examples illustrated. Offsetting this, however, is the possibility that such bargaining is costly, which then raises the concern that specific performance will result in excessive performance.

This trade-off reveals that the choice between specific performance and money damages exactly mirrors that between property rules and liability rules, as discussed in Chapter 3. Property rules (like specific performance) rely on bargaining between the parties to a dispute, and therefore assure a mutually beneficial outcome on the condition that bargaining is possible. Liability rules, in contrast, substitute a court-determined transaction for a negotiated one, thereby overcoming impediments to bargaining, but at the risk of court error in measuring damages, which is especially high when subjective value is involved.

The fact that the actual use of specific performance is generally limited to the transfer of goods that tend to have idiosyncratic or hard-to-measure value—like land or unique goods—seems to conform to this conclusion. Some economists, however, have urged wider use of specific performance based on the argument that money damages involve higher litigation costs (because of the need for the court to measure the promisee's damages), coupled with the belief that renegotiation between contractors should not ordinarily involve high transaction costs because, after all, the parties have already demonstrated an ability to bargain. Ultimately, of course, this is an empirical question.

Notes

1 9 Exch. 341 (1854).
2 The idea of mitigating damages is related to the concept of "compensating precaution," as discussed in Chapter 6.
3 The assignment of risk therefore obviously affects the incentives for breach when it is under the promisor's control. As we saw, under expectation damages, the promisee over-relies on performance precisely because he is fully insured against breach. Under zero damages, the promisor will breach too often because she is insured against a loss. These situations reflect the general conflict between risk-sharing and incentives (or moral hazard).
4 382 P.2d 109, *cert. denied*, 375 U.S. 906 (Okla. 1962).

15 A question of title
Rules for protecting the ownership of land

Chapters 2 and 3 examined, in a fairly abstract way, the basic economic principles underlying the definition, enforcement, and exchange of property rights. This chapter turns explicitly to the protection of property rights in land. In an ideal world of perfect information, the mere possession of land would be a sufficient guarantee of legitimate ownership, or "clear title." It would, in particular, be an indication that all previous transfers of the property, back to the initial establishment of ownership, had been consensual, thereby making the current possessor the "rightful owner." In the real world, however, there is no such guarantee; prospective buyers always face the risk that at some time in the past there was a break in the chain, and a claim may therefore be asserted on behalf of a previously defrauded owner—someone who in the past lost ownership through fraud, error, or theft. In the face of this uncertainty, the goal of an optimal system of property rights is to minimize the risk of such nonconsensual transfers.

The first point to make about such a system is that it is generally not optimal to *completely* eliminate the risk of error. This is true for the same reason that is not optimal to completely eliminate crime or pollution—namely, that it would be too costly to do so. It is instead optimal to invest in determining the legitimacy of ownership rights only up to the point where the last dollar spent on increased security yields one additional dollar of benefits. One implication of this proposal is that the security of ownership will vary in direct proportion to the value of the property in question. For low-valued property, owners will invest little or nothing in security beyond mere possession, and would-be buyers will generally be satisfied with that evidence. As property becomes more valuable, however, buyers will want additional evidence that the possessor is the true owner before entering into a transaction. Thus, for example, a person seeking to buy a watch from a friend will generally not worry about whether the seller is the true owner if the watch is a cheap Timex, but he may worry if it is a Rolex. When property becomes extremely valuable, like cars, art, or land, evidence of ownership in the form of a certificate title, or in the case of art, solid provenance, is usually a prerequisite for any legitimate transaction.

A further implication of the preceding analysis is that, even with optimal investment in the security of ownership, disputes will occasionally arise. Regarding land ownership in particular, a claimant may emerge seeking restoration of his or her legitimate title. When that happens, the law confronts a fundamental question: whose claim to ownership should the law protect; the original owner who was wrongfully deprived of title (i.e., the "last rightful owner"), or the current possessor, assuming that he or she acquired the property in a legitimate transfer (i.e., the "innocent possessor")?[1] The two types of title systems that have historically been used for land transfer in common law countries (including the United States) give different answers to that question.

The predominant system in the United States, called the *recording system*, is based on the maintenance of a public record of land transactions that prospective buyers consult for evidence that the current occupant of a piece of land is the legitimate owner. In this context, "legitimacy" is based on the best available evidence that the land in question has been conveyed by consensual means all the way back to the time when it was first converted to private property. However, this string of transactions does not definitively establish title. For example, if a fraudulent conveyance occurred somewhere in the past, if there was an error in the definition of a boundary, or if any other flaw exists, the title is compromised, and a previous rightful owner can assert a claim of full or partial ownership. Additionally, because lawyers' opinions can sometimes differ on the validity of title, or they can overlook or misinterpret evidence, prospective buyers usually search the record anew with each transfer. It nevertheless remains true that clear title cannot be established with complete certainty. As a result, many landowners purchase title insurance (and mortgage companies usually require it), which provides owners with monetary compensation in the event that a valid claim is asserted and they have to surrender ownership to the last rightful owner.

The other major land title system, called *land registration*, is the predominant system in England and has had some limited use in the United States. Under this system, a landowner registers title with the government at the time of purchase, at which point there is a judicial search of the record. If no outstanding claims are found, the court certifies that the current owner holds good title against most future claims. Then, if a claimant comes forward, he or she can usually at most seek compensation to be paid from a public fund that is financed by land registration fees. Thus, the current possessor retains ownership and the claimant receives monetary compensation. The outcome thus reverses that under the recording system. The question is whether there is an economic basis for choosing between these two different solutions to the ownership question.

The economic criterion for assessing the relative efficiency of the two systems is to ask which maximizes the value of land. This amounts to asking who values the land more, the current possessor or the claimant. From the possessor's perspective, the value of the land is the minimum amount of wealth he or she would be willing to accept in return for it in a consensual transaction, called the possessor's *reservation price*. Note that this will generally exceed the property's *market value*, which is defined to be the maximum amount that someone would pay to acquire it. This is a reflection of what economists call the possessor's "subjective value," which is the amount that the latter values the land in excess of its market value. (We encountered this concept in the previous chapter in the context of measuring the damages from breach of contract.) Justice Oliver Wendell Holmes colorfully expressed the idea behind subjective value when he observed that "A thing which you have enjoyed and used as your own for a long time, whether property or opinion, takes root in your being and cannot be torn away without your resenting the act and trying to defend yourself" (Holmes, 1897, p. 477). This description is especially relevant for occupation of land, to which most people develop a special attachment that grows with the duration of that occupation.

In contrast, a claimant is by definition not in possession of the land and may never have been, suggesting that his or her subjective value is probably small or zero. Thus, the measure of the claimant's value is probably closely approximated by the property's market value. This difference between the valuations of the two parties suggests that the current possessor would strictly prefer retaining title to receiving market-value compensation, whereas the claimant would probably be indifferent between the two options. The objective of maximizing the value of the land would therefore seem to favor leaving the land in the hands of the possessor, as under the registration system.

This conclusion needs to be qualified, however. If the land is awarded to the claimant, the displaced owner can always seek to buy it back, and if she truly values the land more than the claimant, she should be able to do so. Consider, for example, a parcel of land with a market value of $100,000, but which the current owner values at $150,000, where the extra $50,000 reflects her subjective value. Suppose a claimant arrives and is awarded title, while the owner receives compensation equal to the market value. Assuming the parties can bargain, the possessor would be willing to pay up to $150,000 to re-acquire title, whereas the claimant would probably be willing to accept any amount above $100,000. Thus, there is room for a mutually beneficial transaction that restores the land to the possessor.

This outcome is just a consequence of the Coase Theorem, which in the current context implies that land will end up with the higher valuing owner regardless of how the title system initially assigns it. The only effect of the assignment is distributional—as the example illustrates, if the claimant receives title she can bargain for a share of the original owner's subjective value, whereas if the possessor retains title he keeps all her subjective value.

Another factor in assessing the efficiency of a land title system concerns the incentives it creates for land improvement. In this respect, security of possession is important, apart from considerations of subjective value, because it gives investors confidence that they can make long-term investments without fear of losing possession. This factor also seems to favor land registration. A dramatic example of this benefit was the adoption of a land registration system (called the Torrens System) by Cook County, Illinois following the Great Chicago Fire of 1871, which destroyed all land records. The need for quick rebuilding placed a high premium on land development, and local officials recognized that the traditional system of land recording would have impeded such investments because of developers' fears that previous owners would come forward and assert title claims for years to come. In contrast, the registration system provided possessors with stronger property rights and hence speeded redevelopment of the city.

The adoption of land registration in Cook County, and its co-existence alongside the recording system over the next century in that county, provided a unique natural experiment for assessing the relative merits of the two title systems. A recent study exploiting that fact found that landowners in Cook County in fact sorted themselves into the competing systems in exactly the predicted way: that is, higher risk owners opted for the registration system, and lower risk owners opting for the recording system. (The choice of the recording system by low-risk owners reflected its lower administrative cost.) The declining use and eventual repeal of the registration system by the county in the late twentieth century reflected the lessening need for the extra security that the system had offered as the effects of the fire, and hence the risk of past claims, faded.

The Cook County example portrays the importance of secure title for thinking about economic development more generally. The economist Hernando de Soto has argued, for example, that an important impediment to economic growth in South America and other developing countries throughout the twentieth century and beyond has been the lack of a well-functioning capital market, which would allow entrepreneurs to transform their primary asset, land, into financial capital. The problem, he claims, is not insufficient wealth, but the absence of strong institutions for protecting land title, which has prevented landowners from using their land as collateral for obtaining loans (de Soto, 2000). Although most countries have informal systems for resolving disputes over land claims, more formal government-backed systems that operate efficiently are necessary if banks are to use land as security for loans. Empirical studies showing the positive impact of secure title on land development in under-developed countries provide support for this argument.

The discussion to this point has emphasized that avoiding non-consensual transfers of land should be an important goal of an optimal land title system. The doctrine of adverse possession, which exists in all 50 states, therefore poses a particularly difficult challenge to this logic. Adverse possession is sometimes described as "legal theft" of land because it allows a person to claim full title to another person's land, without even the need to pay compensation, provided that the claimant occupies the land for a statutorily set period of time, typically between 15 and 20 years. (Some other conditions also have to be met, such as occupying the land continuously and, in some states, paying taxes on it.) How can this doctrine be justified as part of an efficient property rights system?

Some have defended it as preventing landowners from "sleeping on their rights"—that is, from inefficiently leaving their land idle or unused. This is not a good argument, however, because the timing of development is a crucial decision given the irreversibilities inherent in land investment, and retaining the option to develop in the future is sometimes more valuable than developing it today. Also, letting farmland lie fallow, or leaving it as a hayfield or wood lot, can be an important agricultural practice. Another common argument for adverse possession is based on the standard justification for statutes of limitations generally. As time passes, evidence of title deteriorates, thereby making it costlier to establish clear title. This is a better argument, but in the era of modern record-keeping, it too is a fairly weak justification for allowing the expropriation of the current owner's title, especially without compensation.

A different economic argument for adverse possession relies on a more subtle understanding of the uncertainty of ownership as discussed in connection with the determination of title. Recall that the issue there was the risk that current owners might face claims from previous owners who were wrongfully displaced. One way to strengthen the current owner's rights is therefore to extinguish any claims filed after a set period of time has elapsed, with the strength of the current owner's rights increasing as the length of the statute is shortened. It follows that a statutory length of zero would provide the current owner with the greatest degree of protection from the time of purchase going forward, which is effectively what land registration does. But if this represents the highest degree of title protection, why is it not the optimal solution? What could be the economic advantage of allowing past claims for any finite period of time (as adverse possession does)?

The answer is that the preceding argument only considers ownership risk in a "backward looking" way. That is, it asks what statute length provides the *current possessor* with the maximum protection against past claims, to which the answer is zero. But we get a different answer if we recognize that the current owner is himself subject to the risk of losing title in the future—whether to a squatter, boundary encroacher, or as a result of fraud or error—especially if he is an absentee landowner who is leaving his land fallow or is waiting for the optimal time to develop. From this perspective, the current owner would like an unlimited length of time to be able to recognize such infringements and correct them. In other words, it would be better if no adverse possessors could *ever* acquire title. This logic argues for an infinitely long statute length.

Taken together, these arguments suggest the following trade-off: the current owner as the potential *victim of a past claim* would like a statute length of zero, whereas the owner as a potential *future claimant* would like an infinite statute length. The optimal length—the one that minimizes the combined costs—balances these two considerations. Of course, there is no way to come up with a specific number here—as noted, actual lengths vary by state. The point is that the law has settled on an intermediate length, thus reflecting the trade-off.

A final issue, closely related to adverse possession, is the so-called "mistaken improver problem," which arises when an individual invests in improvement of a piece of land that turns out to be owned by someone else. Most often this happens accidentally, as when the location of a boundary is uncertain or a title turns out to be defective. If the conditions for adverse possession are satisfied, the improver can simply wait for the statutory period to run and then claim title. The question is how the law should deal with this problem if the encroachment is discovered *before* the statutory period has elapsed. What should the penalty be on the improver (if anything)?

Note first that some mistaken improvements will be unavoidable as a consequence of the principle established previously, that in a world of uncertainty, it is not efficient for putative landowners to determine their ownership rights with certainty. Some good faith mistakes will therefore occur, just as some accidents occur even when injurers take efficient care. The role of the law in this context is to establish remedies for victims of mistaken improvement that create incentives for would-be improvers to invest efficiently in determining ownership prior to making irreversible investments (in other words, to optimally avoid mistaken improvement). Ideally, the rules should also be designed to deter "intentional" improvers of another's land, a question that we will address later.

The law of mistaken improvement dates back at least to the Roman "law of accession," which held that materials affixed to land become the property of the owner of the land. The mistaken improver could at most seek compensation for the resulting increase in the land's value. English common law incorporated this rule, but curtailed the right of improvers to seek compensation. In the United States, most states have enacted so-called "betterment acts" which provided for more generous remedies. A common rule, for example, gives owners of mistakenly improved land the option either to retain the land and pay for the improvements, or to require the improver to buy the land at its unimproved value. It turns out that this "owner's option" rule gives improvers efficient incentives to avoid making mistakes.

To illustrate, consider someone (the "improver") who wishes to improve a piece of land that he thinks he owns but may in fact be owned by a neighboring landowner (the "neighbor"). Let the market value of the improved land after the improvement be $10,000, regardless of who the owner is. However, if the neighbor is in fact the owner, he may place a higher value on the land in its unimproved state, possibly reflecting his subjective value. (Suppose, for example, that the improvement requires cutting down an old tree that the neighbor highly values.) Let us suppose in particular that there are two types of neighbors: those who value the unimproved land at $8,000 and those who value it at $12,000, and that there is an equal probability of each type. If the neighbor is of the low-type, the improvement is efficient, whereas if he is of the high-type, it is not efficient.

Now, in a world of certain ownership and low transaction costs, the Coase Theorem ensures that the efficient outcome will arise regardless of who actually owns the land. Specifically, the land will be improved if the neighbor is the low-type (which would require the improver to buy the land if he is not the owner), and it will not be improved if the neighbor is the high-type (which would require the neighbor to buy the land if the improver is the owner). One requirement for this outcome, however, is that property rights must be well defined, and in the current situation we are hypothesizing that they are not. Thus, Coasian bargaining cannot proceed until the true owner is ascertained, which requires a costly investment.

Let us therefore suppose that a survey can be undertaken by the improver at a cost of $500 which determines with certainty who owns the land. Let us further suppose that if the improver conducts the survey, any bargaining necessary to reach the efficient outcome will proceed costlessly. Given this hypothesized outcome, the first question is whether it is efficient for the improver to conduct a survey before investing, and the second is whether the "buyer's option" rule replicates this outcome.

Considering the efficiency question first, suppose that the improver goes ahead with the improvement without a survey. The value of the land in that case is fixed at $10,000 regardless of ownership (i.e., the improvement cannot be reversed). However, if the improver surveys first, we assume that the land will be used efficiently regardless of ownership. Specifically, the improvement will occur if the neighbor is a low-type, and it will not occur if the neighbor is a high-type. The expected value of the land in this case is $(.5) \times (\$12,000) + (.5) \times (\$10,000) = \$11,000$. It is therefore efficient for the improver to conduct the survey because the expected increase in value of the land from doing so exceeds the cost of the survey. Specifically,

$$\$11,000 - \$10,000 = \$1,000 > \$500.$$

Economists refer to the left-hand side of this inequality as the "value of information" because it reflects the gain from learning with certainty who the true owner is before investing, while the right-hand side is the cost of information.

The preceding analysis has established that it is socially optimal to conduct a survey in this example. The next question concerns the improver's actual incentives under the "owner's option" remedy. Suppose first that the improver proceeds without a survey and a mistake is discovered—that is, the neighbor turns out to be the true owner. Which option the neighbor chooses will depend on whether she is a high- or low-value type. If she is a high-value type, she will compel the improver to buy the land from her at $12,000, which is her value of the land in its unimproved state. Since the market value of the land is $10,000, the improver suffers a loss of $2,000 in this case. Conversely, if the neighbor is a low-value type, she will be indifferent between retaining the land and paying the improver $2,000 (the difference between the market value of the improved land and her valuation of the land in its unimproved state), and demanding compensation of $8,000. In either case, the improver receives a net benefit of $2,000. Given an equal likelihood of the two types, the improver's net gain is $(.5)(-\$2,000) + (.5)(\$2,000)=0$.

Suppose alternatively that the improver conducts a survey before going ahead with the investment. If he discovers that he is not the owner, he will buy the land from a low-value type for $8,000 and improve it, yielding a gain of $2,000. Conversely, he will not buy it from a high-value type, yielding a gain of zero. His expected gain is therefore $(.5)(\$2,000) + (.5)(\$0) = \$1,000$. Since the survey costs $500, the improver is better off conducting the survey as it promises a net gain of $500 compared to an expected return of zero without the survey. The improver's calculation in this case coincides exactly with the social condition for a survey above. Thus, we conclude that the owner's option remedy is efficient. (One caveat to this conclusion is that we assumed the low-type neighbor would sell the land for her true valuation of $8,000. In fact, if the neighbor succeeds in negotiating a higher price—theoretically, it could be anywhere up to $10,000—then the value of the survey would be diminished by a factor of .5 for every $1 increase in the price the neighbor is able to negotiate. Thus, to the extent that the neighbor is a good negotiator, the owner's option rule may lead to an inefficiently low number of surveys.)[3]

Finally consider the issue of intent. The question here is whether the law provides sufficient deterrence of would-be improvers who knowingly improve another's land in an effort to by-pass the market. The answer is yes, given that the preceding analysis of the buyer's option remedy did not depend in any way on what the improver knew or did not know before deciding whether to conduct a survey prior to investing. (In other words, the results were not contingent on whether the improver truly was mistaken.) Thus, the prescribed rule gives the right incentives regarding the survey decision to innocent and opportunistic improvers alike, thereby relieving the court of the need to inquire into the improver's state of mind (which is never a reliable way to learn the truth).

Intent may, however, bear on the likelihood that a "mistaken" improvement will be discovered at all, or at least that it will be discovered before the conditions for adverse possession have been met, which is a pre-requisite for the above rule to be invoked. (For example, an intentional improver may only proceed if he is confident that the "mistake" will not be easily discovered.) In his study of adverse possession cases, Helmholz (1983) found that when courts have evidence that a person intentionally encroached on another's land, they are reluctant to award title, even if the statutory period for adverse possession has elapsed. In this sense, intent does matter, and from an economic perspective it should, precisely because intent implies efforts to avoid detection, which reduces the efficacy of the law in correcting genuine mistakes.

Notes

1 It is obvious that the law should not protect one who gained possession by fraud.
2 There are, of course, exceptions to this claim. For example, a claimant might be the heir to an estate that was lost long ago, but for which he or she has developed substantial sentimental value based on family lore.
3 The example focused on the case where the improver is not the true owner. The rule also gives the correct incentives when the improver turns out to be the owner. In the case of no survey, the improver's return is fixed at $10,000, whereas in the case of a survey, the improver will go ahead with the improvement if the neighbor is the low-valuer, and will sell the land if the neighbor is the high-valuer, yielding a net return of $(.5)(\$10,000) + (.5)(\$12,000) - \$500 = \$11,000 - \$500 > \$10,000$. The condition for the survey again replicates the social condition (though with the same caveat as in the text, this time regarding the bargaining ability of the high-type neighbor).

16 Holdups and holdouts

The "holdup" and "holdout" problems are familiar phrases to economists and legal scholars, but their exact meaning and the relationship between them (if any) are not clear. The similarity of the terms has led some commentators to use them interchangeably, but in fact they arise in quite distinct contexts, and the commonly proposed "solutions" are outwardly very different. It turns out, however, that the similarity of their names does in fact reflect an underlying commonality. Demonstrating that relationship, and examining the legal and economic responses to the two problems in light of their similarity, are the purposes of this chapter.

As it is most commonly described, the holdup problem refers to contracting situations in which one or both of the parties to a contract would like to make transaction-specific investments (that is, to invest in "reliance" based on the promise of performance) prior to trade that would enhance the joint value of the contract. However, because they cannot sign a completely enforceable contingent contract, they fear losing a portion of the return on those investments in subsequent bargaining. As a result, they underinvest.

The case of *Goebel v. Linn*,[1] which we first encountered in Chapter 13, offers a somewhat anachronistic, though nevertheless classic, illustration of this problem. Recall that in this case, the defendant was a brewery that had contracted with an ice company to supply ice during the summer months to ensure that the brewery's stock of beer didn't spoil. (The case predated the development of artificial refrigeration, so breweries had to rely on a supply of natural ice cut from ponds during the winter and stored in insulated icehouses.) The contract called for the delivery of ice according to a pre-set price schedule, but because of an unusually warm winter, the market price of ice had risen well above the contract price, and the ice company refused to make delivery at that price. Fearing loss of its beer, the brewery agreed to a price increase above that provided for in the contract, and the transaction was completed. Later, however, the brewery regretted its decision and reneged on paying the higher price. In the ensuing lawsuit brought by the ice company, the court upheld the price increase on the grounds that economic circumstances had changed in an unexpected way, and the increase was needed to ensure the economic viability of the ice company. (The brewery could have sought damages for breach of the original contract when the ice company initially refused to make delivery at the pre-set price, but it did not pursue that remedy, apparently because the ice company did not have sufficient resources to pay the damages; see Chapter 14.)

For our purposes, the important point is that the brewer's need to invest in the production of beer *before* the cost of ice was (or could have been) known left it vulnerable to being held up—that is, induced to agree to a higher price—by the ice company later on. If the brewery could have anticipated the higher price it would have had to pay, it likely would have scaled back on its beer production in response to the upward shift in its supply curve.[2]

In contrast to the preceding description of the holdup problem, the hold*out* problem typically describes a situation in which a private land developer or a governmental entity seeks to assemble a large number of contiguous and independently-owned parcels of land for purposes of undertaking a large scale project such as a highway or urban redevelopment plan. However, once individual owners become aware of the scope of the project, coupled with the fact that each of their parcels is essential to its successful completion, they will often refuse to sell for "reasonable" prices, holding out instead for a larger share of the eventual profits. While there does not seem to be a consensus among scholars on the real source of the holdout problem—it has variously been attributed to monopoly, high transaction costs, an "anti-commons" problem, or asymmetric information—both economists and lawyers (and certainly developers) have long recognized that it poses a serious threat to completion of otherwise beneficial projects.

A classic holdout problem was at the center of the controversial Supreme Court case of *Kelo v. City of New London*,[3] which authorized the use of eminent domain by the City of New London, Connecticut, to acquire the land needed for a large scale redevelopment project aimed at revitalizing the city's waterfront area. Although the local development authority initially had attempted to acquire the necessary land through market purchases, a small group of owners refused to sell, and so the city sought to use its power of eminent domain to forcibly acquire their land. In a 5–4 ruling, the U.S. Supreme Court upheld a previous State Supreme Court ruling granting the city's request. The Court argued that although the primary beneficiaries of the project were private entities (real estate developers and a large pharmaceutical company), the overall redevelopment plan promised sufficient spillover benefits to the public in terms of new jobs and enhanced tax revenues that it met the public use requirement of the Fifth Amendment. As a result, the remaining holdouts were forced to sell. (See the further discussion of this case, and the public use requirement of the Fifth Amendment, in the next chapter.)

As a final illustration, consider the well-known case of *Boomer v. Atlantic Cement Co.*,[4] which we previously encountered in Chapter 3 in the context of the choice between property rules and liability rules. The case is especially interesting in the current context because it has been interpreted by different authors as involving either a holdup or a holdout problem. The case involved a nuisance suit brought by several residents living near a cement plant operated by the defendants. The plaintiffs sought to have the plant shut down due to the noise and dust that it caused, but the court rejected the request for an injunction and instead ordered the plant to pay permanent damages, thereby allowing it to continue operating. (In other words, the court opted for a liability rule rather than a property rule.) The court's reasoning was based on the anticipated loss of over $45 million in assets and 300 jobs if the plant had been forced to shut down, compared to the estimated damages of only $185,000 that its continued operation would have imposed on the plaintiffs. Given these facts, allowing the plant to continue to operate apparently was the efficient decision.

Victor Goldberg's (1985) analysis of the *Boomer* case viewed it through the lens of the hold*up* problem based on the argument that, once the plant was built, granting the neighboring residents, as a group, the right to shut it down would have given them substantial bargaining power in any subsequent negotiations with the plant over its right to pollute. Thus, while the issuance of an injunction may or may not have resulted in the plant's closing given its high value relative to the external costs it imposed, such a decision would, in any case, have precipitated costly bargaining that likely would have had a chilling effect on future entrepreneurs contemplating similar investments, suggesting that from a social perspective too few such plants would be built. Goldberg thus argues that the damage remedy was appropriate because it did not allow the residents to hold up the plant in this way after it was built.

William Fischel (1995, pp. 75–77) reached the same conclusion regarding the court's decision in *Boomer*—namely, that a damage remedy was the appropriate choice—but he justified the decision instead as overcoming a hold*out* problem. As he saw it, the problem with an injunction in this case is that it would have required the cement company to negotiate with each of several plaintiffs, any one of whom could have enforced the injunction ordering the factory to shut down. In other words, the company would have had to "assemble" pollution rights from the plaintiffs. The court's issuance of a damage remedy instead effectively allowed the cement company to forcibly purchase ("take") the pollution rights in return for the court-determined compensation, thereby eliminating the threat of holdouts.

The preceding cases, and especially the *Boomer* case, provide a point of departure for developing an economic framework that allows us to identify the similarities and differences between the holdup and holdout problems. Let's begin with the holdup problem.

In its starkest terms, the holdup problem involves two parties, one who wishes to undertake some productive activity (for example, brewing beer or operating a factory), and another who is contracted to supply an essential input to the production process (ice or pollution rights). The producer, however, has to make an initial investment (deciding how much beer to brew or how much to invest in the factory) *before* the price of the essential input can be determined. (It doesn't matter if this is because the price is uncertain at the time of the investment, or because the parties simply cannot write enforceable contracts.) Importantly, the initial investment is irreversible in the sense that at least some of the costs expended will be lost if the essential input is not supplied and the planned production therefore fails to take place. For example, if the ice is not delivered, the beer will spoil before it can be sold.

One might argue that the producer should therefore wait until the price of the input is known before making the initial investment, but sometimes this will not be possible for technological reasons, such as the time needed for the production process to be carried out or for the factory to be built. Alternatively, the input supplier may simply refuse to honor the original price once the investment is in place. In either case, the producer is eventually put at a bargaining disadvantage with the input supplier, who, at the time of delivery, can therefore demand a price up to the variable profits from going forward (that is, the profits exclusive of the costs of the sunk investment), also called the "quasi-rents." This is the sense in which the supplier is said to "hold up" the producer.

As an example, suppose the gross return from a venture is $1,000, but this requires an initial non-salvageable investment of $500, and the later purchase of an input whose opportunity cost is $300. Thus, the overall project promises a net economic benefit of $200. However, once the $500 investment is in place, the variable profit (quasi-rent) from purchase of the input is $700 (=$1,000–$300) because the initial investment is not recoverable if the project doesn't go forward. If we suppose that bargaining over the price of the input therefore divides the quasi-rent evenly, the resulting price will be $650 [=$300+($1,000–$300)/2]. Now, however, the producer's overall return from the project, including the initial investment, is negative (=$1,000–$500–$650=–$150). The producer will nevertheless pay the price because his net loss of $150 is less than his loss of $500 if he does not go forward.

Of course, producers can rationally anticipate this problem before making their initial investments, and in this example, the producer would possibly fail to initiate the project, resulting in a foregone social benefit of $200. More generally, projects susceptible to the holdup problem will be underprovided. For example, if the brewery brews less beer in the first place, it is less vulnerable to a later holdup threat by the ice company. Because of the resulting loss of profits, however, it is in the parties' mutual interests to develop legally enforceable ways to avoid the holdup problem. I will discuss some ways in which they do this in practice.

Turning to the holdout problem, it typically arises when a buyer (either public or private—it doesn't matter) wishes to assemble several (two or more) contiguous parcels of land for purposes of undertaking an investment project. The key elements of the problem are, first, that there is a complementarity between the parcels to be assembled, which makes them collectively more valuable to the prospective buyer than to the individual owners (in other words, there is a kind of scale economy); and second, the buyer values *individual* parcels less than their current owners do. The first requirement implies that assembly is efficient, while the second implies that partial assembly is not.

In this setting, suppose the buyer seeks to acquire the parcels by sequentially negotiating with the individual owners. At first, the sellers may be unaware of the nature of the project, and so initial purchases will proceed smoothly. It is important to emphasize here that a true holdout problem cannot arise in single-parcel purchases—that is, in the absence of complementarities among parcels. Although individual owners can always refuse to sell for what the buyer might believe is a reasonable offer, if the buyer truly values that particular parcel more than the seller, the latter should eventually be willing to accept a price that makes both parties better off. The determination of the price is simply a bargaining problem.

A true holdout problem only arises after one or more parcels have already been acquired and later sellers realize the overall scope of the project. At that point, the buyer is committed to the project because, as noted previously, the already-assembled properties are not especially valuable to him (or at least they are less valuable to him than they were to the sellers). This realization confers a significant bargaining advantage on the later sellers because they know the buyer will suffer a substantial loss if he falls short of acquiring most or all of the remaining parcels. In the extreme case where the project cannot proceed without acquiring all parcels first, each seller can hold out for a price that reflects the *entire* expected surplus from the project. Another way to say this is that the transactions are interdependent. Clearly, this situation will prevent the completion of many projects (resulting, for example, in the proverbial "highway to nowhere"), and will discourage others from being initiated at all.

To illustrate, suppose again that the gross value of the project in question is $1,000, but this requires assembly of two contiguous parcels, each valued at $400 by their owners. (For this example, assume that the parcels are individually worthless to the buyer.) Thus, if both parcels are acquired, the project yields a net return of $200. Now suppose that the buyer succeeds in acquiring the first parcel for its opportunity cost, $400. Since purchase of the second parcel is necessary to complete the project and the first parcel alone is worthless, the variable profit from acquiring that second parcel (the quasi-rent) is $600 (=$1,000–$400), which we again assume the parties split. Thus, the second parcel will sell for $700 [=$400+($1,000–$400)/2].[5] But the return on the overall project is now negative (–$100=$1,000–$400–$700), which, because the buyer anticipates it, will discourage him from initiating assembly in the first place. (The example understates the severity of the problem because both sellers will want to be the last to sell, thereby exacerbating the likelihood of delay or incomplete assembly.)

The preceding archetypal examples reveal the following similarities between the holdup and holdout problems:

(1) The project in question requires an up-front, non-salvageable investment (a sunk expenditure of some kind) that commits the investor to the project.
(2) The project requires the purchase of an additional input (inputs) that is (are) essential to the completion of the project.
(3) The price(s) of the essential input (inputs) cannot be credibly determined prior to the initial investment, but is (are) determined by bargaining after that investment is in place.

The effect of the up-front investment is that it reduces the buyer's bargaining power in the subsequent negotiation with the input supplier(s), the anticipation of which creates a disincentive for the buyer to initiate the project in the first place. As a result, both the holdup and holdout problems potentially result in the undersupply of valuable projects, as the examples have illustrated, absent some legal or contractual remedy.

Commonly proposed remedies for the two problems, like their superficial descriptions, are outwardly quite different. The large literature on the holdup problem, for example, focuses on two types of remedies: long-term contracts between producers and suppliers, and vertical integration (or merger) of producers and suppliers. Proposed solutions to the holdout problem, in contrast, include eminent domain (forced sales) for projects that satisfy the Fifth Amendment's "public use" requirement, and option contracts that give assemblers the right to purchase land at pre-set prices (referred to as "call options"). Private land assemblers can also sometimes avoid the holdout problem by disguising the scope of the project, for example by using secret ("dummy") buying agents, but such a solution is not realistically available to public assemblers because of their need to operate in the open. However, the *Kelo* ruling has, in the opinion of some commentators, sufficiently blurred the distinction between private and public projects that eminent domain may effectively be available for most large scale developments, public or private. (A flurry of state laws passed in the wake of the case has, however, sought to limit its use for urban redevelopment projects like that in *Kelo*.)

The discussion of the common features of the holdup and holdout problems reveals that the various remedies all share a crucial feature. As emphasized, the inefficiency in both cases stems from the ability of the "input" supplier to bargain over the price of the input *after* the buyer has committed resources to the project. The key to eliminating this inefficiency, therefore, is to remove the supplier's ability to bargain at that point in time. For example, in the case of the holdup problem, long term contracts or vertical integration each foreclose ex post negotiation over the price of the essential input, either by committing the parties to a legally enforceable price before any investments are made under a contract, or by consolidating the investment and input-delivery decisions into the hands of a single decision-maker (the residual claimant) under vertical integration. The choice between the two depends on the relative transaction costs of writing and enforcing contracts versus vertically integrating.

To illustrate how a contract works to resolve the holdup problem, return to the previous example and note that under ex ante negotiations, the price of the input would be determined based on the *overall* surplus from its purchase (including the cost of the initial investment) rather than on the quasi-rent. That surplus, recall, is $200. Thus, assuming as before that this is split evenly, the contractually-set price of the input will be $400 [=$300+($200/2)], which is substantially less than the spot price of $650 under ex post negotiations. In this case, the buyer expects a positive surplus of $100 from the project (=$1,000–$500–$400), and so it goes forward.

As for the holdout problem, eminent domain (when permitted) allows the buyer to force sales of the needed land at prices objectively set by the court rather than by negotiations with the sellers. In our example, both sellers would therefore receive compensation of $400, and the project would be profitable. (This assumes, of course, that the court is able to accurately measure the owners' true opportunity costs, which is not assured. Indeed, as noted in Chapter 3, this measurement problem is the chief drawback of using a liability rule.) Option contracts involve negotiations between the buyer and sellers over the price of any future potential sales, but crucially, those negotiations all occur *before the buyer has made any purchases*. In our assembly example, the price of both (all) parcels would therefore be negotiated before the assembler has acquired any parcels. In the example, equal division of the $200 surplus from the overall project would therefore result in a price of $466.67 [=$400+($200/3)] for each seller, and the overall project would promise a positive return of $66.66 for the buyer.

The commonality of these solutions is further epitomized by the court's use of a damage remedy (liability rule) rather than an injunction (property rule) in the *Boomer* case. The holdup aspect of the case was therefore resolved by the inability of the plaintiffs to negotiate with the plant over terms that would allow the plant to continue operating, and the holdout aspect was resolved by effectively allowing the plant to "take" the pollution rights from the residents at prices set by the court. In both cases, ex post negotiation was therefore foreclosed. The interpretation of the court's ruling in this case—whether it was a response to a holdup or a holdout problem—turns out to be a moot issue. The important point is that, under either interpretation, the ruling was correct from an economic perspective because it overcame the key inefficiency that the two problems share.

Notes

1 47 Mich. 489, 11 N.W. 284 (1882).
2 It doesn't matter if the price increase is necessitated by a genuine cost increase, as in this case, or is an effort by the seller to extract a larger share of the profits from the transaction. In either case, the brewery would rationally cut back on its production.
3 125 S.Ct. 2655, 545 U.S. 469 (2005).
4 26 N.Y.2d 219, 309 N.Y.S.2d 312, 257 N.E.2d 870 (Court of Appeals of N.Y. 1970).
5 The buyer may be able to resell the parcel to the original owner if he fails to get the second, but he probably would not be able to get $400 since that owner knows the single parcel is worthless to the buyer. If he could get, say, $200, the quasi-rent becomes $1,000−$400−$200=$400, in which case the second parcel would sell for $600 (=$400+$400/2).

17 Eminent domain and the paradox of public use

The previous chapter focused on the distinction between the holdup and holdout problems as different, but related, sources of inefficiency in the development of certain productive activities. This chapter continues to highlight the holdout problem, but now in relation to another potential source of market failure—namely, the free rider problem. The purpose of the comparison will be to elucidate the meaning of the public use requirement of the Fifth Amendment Takings Clause, which has been at the center of controversy over the appropriate scope of the government's eminent domain power. The debate was revitalized by the Supreme Court's ruling in *Kelo v. New London*,[1] but that case was only the latest skirmish in a long-standing debate about when the government should be able to take private property without the owner's consent.

According to the Fifth Amendment, private property can only be taken for "public use," and provided that "just compensation" is paid.[2] The Constitution provides no further guidance on the meaning of these phrases, so it has been left to courts and legal scholars to define them. It is a fairly settled issue that just compensation is equal to the "fair market value" of the property in question, but it is commonly acknowledged that this measure tends to systematically undercompensate owners compared to what they would have demanded in a consensual sale. As it turns out, it is this undercompensation that makes the public use requirement so important and contentious because it defines those circumstances in which the government can use eminent domain to acquire private property.

As argued in the previous chapter, the use of eminent domain is a justifiable response to the holdout problem associated with land assembly. In the absence of eminent domain, socially beneficial government projects requiring the assembly of land, such as highways, airports, and parks would tend to be underprovided. In cases like these, where the land is targeted for a truly "public" project (a project that meets the traditional economic definition of a public good), the use of eminent domain, while unpopular, is not particularly controversial. It is when the land is to be used as part of a largely private development project, such ase urban renewal, that it raises questions. In what sense, critics ask, is such a development a "public use," considering that much (if not most) of the benefits will accrue to private parties? This question was at the center of the controversy over the *Kelo* case, where the assembled land was to be used as part of a large scale urban revitalization project that, while initiated by the city, principally benefited a large pharmaceutical company and other developers. The Supreme Court discovered the public use in the spillover benefits to the public in the form of jobs and enhanced tax revenues, but one could counter that, because such external benefits arise to varying degrees from any economic development project, invoking them as the source of public use essentially renders the requirement meaningless as a limitation on the scope of eminent domain.

Of course, this debate about the meaning of public use did not newly arise with the *Kelo* case. In *Berman v. Parker* the Supreme Court allowed the use of eminent domain to acquire blighted properties as part of a redevelopment plan for Washington, D.C.[3] As in *Kelo*, the Court justified the takings as serving a legitimate public interest in the form of the revitalization plan. Likewise, in *Poletown Neighborhood Council v. City of Detroit*,[4] the Michigan Supreme Court allowed the city of Detroit to condemn an entire ethnic neighborhood in order to clear the way for a General Motors assembly plant. Once again, the Court justified its ruling based on the jobs and tax revenues that the project would generate. Other recent cases have authorized the use of eminent domain to prevent a professional football team from being relocated to a different city,[5] and to reduce the degree of market power in a certain concentrated land market.[6] Dating back to the nineteenth century, courts routinely allowed the use of eminent domain to facilitate the development of railroads, canals, water powered mills, and mines, all in the interest of promoting economic development.

The point of these examples of what many would call "private takings" is not to suggest that they represent improper uses of eminent domain. Rather, it is to demonstrate the resulting incoherence of the public use restriction. The remainder of this chapter asks whether economic theory can be used to restore some substance to it, and in the process, provide a sounder basis for defining the proper scope of eminent domain.

I will argue that the crux of the problem in discovering an appropriate meaning of public use stems from its apparent congruence with the economic concept of "public goods." In economic theory, a public good has a specific meaning: it refers to those goods having the dual characteristics that once they are provided, one person's consumption does not reduce the quantity available for consumption by others (called inexhaustibility), nor can consumption be denied to anyone, whether they have paid for the good or not (called non-excludability). Because of these characteristics, but especially the second (also referred to as the free-rider problem), ordinary market provision of public goods is generally not feasible because suppliers would be unable to recoup the cost of provision. Thus, it is generally left to the government to provide them. The classic example of a public good is national defense (or, on a local scale, police protection), given that once an army (or police force) is assembled, everyone will benefit from the enhanced safety. Another example is a public (i.e., free access) highway system, which benefits everyone, even if they choose not to use it, because it promotes commerce and economic growth.

As suggested, use of eminent domain to provide true public goods (national defense or a highway system) is uncontroversial because they satisfy the plain meaning of the public use requirement. But what about the use of eminent domain to assemble the land needed for a railroad that is operated as a private enterprise? Surely that will also promote economic development, but here the case for public use is less clear because use of the railroad is not free—railroads can deny access to non-payers and so are not public goods, but few would deny that they generate spillover benefits to non-users. Thus, does construction of a railroad qualify as a public use? By similar reasoning, would construction of a limited access highway (a toll road), as opposed to a freeway, qualify? These questions illustrate the difficulty in using the theory of public goods to offer a coherent definition of public use.

One way to begin to untangle this issue is to use the distinction, first proposed by Thomas Merrill (1986), between the "means" and the "ends" of a governmental project. The means approach concerns the manner in which the needed land (and other inputs) will be acquired, and the ends approach concerns the specific use to which those inputs will be put. The key question regarding the public use requirement is whether it should involve an analysis of means or ends. As suggested, the literal interpretation of public use implies that it should depend on the ends—that is, will the project provide a public good, or serve a public purpose? The preceding discussion raised some doubts about that logic, however. On the other hand, the actual exercise of eminent domain, because it involves the coercive taking of land needed for the project, literally concerns the means by which the land is acquired. But since the manner of acquisition is theoretically independent of the use to which the land will be put, how does this interpretation relate to public use? To get a handle on this question, it will be necessary to examine in more detail the relationship between the free rider problem associated with public good provision, and the holdout problem associated with land assembly.

As noted, the free rider problem arises because of the non-excludability of public goods, which allows non-payers to consume those goods once they are available. A simple example illustrates the problem this creates. Consider two neighboring businesses, A and B, each owning assets worth $200. Both are vulnerable to theft, however, which, if uncontrolled, costs each of them $100, or half of their assets. Let us say that A hires a security guard at a cost of $120 that will prevent all thefts from A, but suppose that it also cuts B's thefts in half (a spillover benefit). A's net return would thus be $200–$120=$80, while B's return would be $200–$50=$150. B thus free rides on A's security guard. The same would be true in reverse if B were to hire a security guard. Finally, suppose that A and B can jointly hired a guard at a total cost of $150 and thereby deter all thefts from both businesses. Assuming equal cost sharing, the net return for each from jointly hiring the guard would be $200−$75=$125. Table 17.1 summarizes the returns from the various cases, where each business chooses between two strategies: "contribute" and "not contribute" to the cost of a security guard.

The jointly optimal outcome is clearly for both to contribute (i.e., to jointly hire the guard) because it yields the highest combined profit ($250). It turns out, however, that this is not the equilibrium outcome of this game. To see what the parties will actually do, consider first business A's optimal strategy. If it expects business B to contribute (the left-hand column in the table), then its best strategy is *not* to contribute because that strategy yields a return of $150 as compared to $125. (Thus, A is a free rider.) Likewise, if A expects B not to contribute, it is best for A also not to contribute because that strategy yields a return of $100 as compared to $80. Thus, no matter what A expects B to do, it is best for A not to contribute. (We say that A has a "dominant strategy" of not contributing.) Because the returns are symmetric, B will also choose not to contribute regardless of A's action. The unique Nash equilibrium for this game is therefore for neither business to contribute to the hiring of a security guard, which results in a suboptimal outcome.

Some readers will recognize this interaction as an example of a prisoner's dilemma game, which is characterized by this sort of divergence between the dominant strategy Nash equilibrium and the jointly optimal outcome. In the current example, the reason for the divergence is the free rider problem, which allows both businesses to benefit when either one hires the security guard. Since both businesses are unwilling to unilaterally incur the cost of the guard in this setting, neither does, and the inefficient outcome emerges. This is the essence of the market failure associated with public goods, which, recall, are characterized by this sort of benefit spillover. As a result, public goods will tend to be underprovided by the private market. One may object that this problem could be avoidable by cooperative behavior by the two businesses, but that logic would not be persuasive in settings involving larger numbers of individuals, as would be true, for example, with the

Table 17.1 Payoffs for the security guard example

		Business B Contribute	Business B Not contribute
Business A	Contribute	A: $125 B: $125	A: $80 B: $150
	Not contribute	A: $150 B: $80	A: $100 B: $100

establishment of a city police force purely by means of the voluntary contributions from all property owners who would benefit.

The usual solution to the free rider problem is therefore to give the government, acting as an agent of all property owners, the responsibility for providing public goods, such as police protection, so that it can use its tax powers to force all those who receive benefits to contribute to the cost. In this sense, "forced purchase" replaces market transactions as the mechanism for providing public goods. While this solution overcomes the free rider problem, it introduces another potential source of inefficiency, owing to the inability of the government to observe the amount that each consumer (taxpayer) values the public good. Thus, individual tax contributions cannot be matched to benefits, resulting in some consumers overpaying and some underpaying.

For example, taxes are usually assessed on some readily observable characteristic of taxpayers, such as their income or the value of their property, rather than on their unobservable valuation of the good in question. Not only does this prevent matching of individual contributions to benefits (really just a fairness issue), it potentially prevents the efficient overall level of the public good from being produced, because that calculation depends on an accurate aggregation of the individual valuations. For these reasons, government provision of public goods financed by taxes is an imperfect substitute for market provision. Still, it is normally better than not providing the good at all.

To summarize the argument to this point, the "ends" approach conceives of the public use requirement as a response to the free rider problem associated with the provision of public goods. The preceding example, however, showed that the proper solution to this problem is for the government to use its tax powers to force consumers to contribute to the provision of public goods—that is, to *force the purchase* of public goods.

Let's now turn to the "means" approach, which concerns the manner in which the inputs needed to undertake the government project in question are acquired. In the case of large scale projects involving land assembly, this raises the holdout problem, the nature of which was described in detail in the preceding chapter. For present purposes, the key issue is that the existence of holdouts, like the presence of free riders, endangers the completion of socially beneficial projects, though for a different reason. In the case of free riders, the inefficiency stemmed from the spillover of benefits from a public good to non-payers, causing a *demand-side* failure. In the case of holdouts, in contrast, the problem is one of monopoly on the part of sellers once they realize that their properties are essential to completion of the project. Thus, they seek prices in excess of their true valuations, resulting in a *supply-side* failure.

The solution to the holdout problem proposed in the previous chapter was to implement a liability rule, which allowed the purchaser to acquire the land at a price set by the court—in other words, to allow a *forced sale* of the land. This approach solves the problem because it deprives the owner of the ability to negotiate over the price (as is permitted under property rules). Of course, that is precisely what eminent domain, a form of liability rule, achieves. As with tax financing on the demand side, however, this solution is imperfect because, like any transaction involving liability rules, it is susceptible to errors in the court's assessment of the owner's valuation. Indeed, as we have noted, the accepted meaning of just compensation—fair market value—almost certainly undercompensates landowners because it deprives them of their subjective value (the amount they value their land in excess of its market value). As a result, there is a risk of excessive assembly.

In his analysis of the public use requirement for eminent domain, Merrill argues that courts have nearly always framed the issue in terms of ends: that is, they focus on whether the targeted land will be used for a public purpose. While this test is easily satisfied when the project in question is a public good in the classic economic sense, such as a highway or park it is more problematic when the project is largely private, as was the case in *Kelo*. In these "private takings" cases, courts nevertheless struggle to discover some public benefit, however strained the argument is. In particular, they usually point to the spillover benefits in the form of jobs, taxes, or elimination of urban blight that will arise as a by-product of the project.

The problem with the ends approach to public use is not that it inappropriately permits the use of eminent domain in cases like *Kelo*—it may or may not. Rather, by focusing on ends rather than means it identifies the wrong market failure as the appropriate justification for forced sales. As the preceding discussion of the free rider and holdout problems has revealed, these are separable problems that require different solutions: the free rider problem arises in the presence of a demand-side failure that justifies the use of taxation (forced purchase), while the holdout problem is a supply-side failure that justifies the use of eminent domain (forced sale). By framing the public use issue in terms of ends rather than means, the court conflates these two problems and thereby confuses the issue.

The preceding point is illustrated by Table 17.2, which shows the four possible scenarios that can arise when a transaction may be plagued by the

Table 17.2 Framework for determining the appropriate rule for the government in facilitating efficient transactions

		Holdout problem?	
		No	Yes
Free rider problem?	No	Category I: No tax financing No eminent domain	Category II: No tax financing Eminent domain allowed
	Yes	Category III: Tax financing No eminent domain	Category IV: Tax financing Eminent domain allowed

free rider problem, the holdout problem, or both. In Category I, shown in the upper left cell, neither problem is present, so neither tax financing (forced purchase) nor eminent domain (forced sale) is necessary to achieve an efficient exchange. This is the case of ordinary market transactions, whether between two private parties or between the government and a private party. According to the Invisible Hand Theorem, consensual exchange will lead to an efficient outcome in this case without the need for coercion on either the demand or supply side of the market. Thus, neither forced purchases nor forced sales are justified.

At the other extreme is Category IV (lower right cell), which shows the case where both a free rider and holdout problem are present. This situation represents the prototypical case where the government needs to assemble land for purposes of producing a public good like a highway. Here, the use of eminent domain is justified to overcome the holdout problem associated with assembly, and tax financing is justified to overcome the free rider problem. The public use debate does not ordinarily arise in the context of these types of transactions because the use of eminent domain is uncontroversial. Thus, the particular theory used to justify its use, whether based on the means or the ends approach, is immaterial. (Some commentators have in fact argued that Category IV is the only one in which eminent domain *should* be allowed.)

Consider next Category III (lower left cell), which involves a free rider problem but no holdout problem. As indicated, taxation is appropriate here but use of eminent domain is not. An example of this situation might be the provision of police protection by a local government, which, as the previous example showed, is a public good in the sense that all residents enjoy the benefits of a reduced crime rate. Thus, using taxation to finance the cost of hiring police officers, buying cars, and building a police station is justified to overcome the free rider problem. However, it would not be appropriate for the government to use eminent domain to conscript the officers, or to take the cars, or even to acquire the parcel of land needed for the station (assuming that it is small enough not to require assembly of multiple parcels). Instead, the government should have to acquire these inputs by ordinary market transactions, just as a private security firm would. According to this framework, an effort by the city to use eminent domain to acquire the land in this case would not be justifiable on economic grounds. That doesn't mean that cities don't sometimes try to do that; the fact is, however, that the legal costs of pursuing such a strategy are usually an adequate deterrent of such overreach.

Finally, consider the situation in Category II (upper right cell), where a holdout problem is present but a free rider problem is not. Most economic redevelopment cases, like *Kelo*, *Berman*, and *Poletown*, fall into this category—that is, they involve private developers, often acting under the authority of a local government, who face a holdout threat. Thus, the use of eminent domain is justified on economic grounds to overcome the holdouts, but use of tax financing would not be (although one could argue that some subsidization might be appropriate to account for the spillover benefits.)

As noted, courts have tended to follow this prescription by allowing the use of eminent domain in cases like this, but rather than appealing to an argument based on *means* (the need to overcome holdouts), they rely on arguments based on *ends*, for example by emphasizing the public benefits that will arise from the project. It is easy to understand why they do this: the plain meaning of the public use requirement suggests that eminent domain is intended to facilitate the provision of public goods, and so should be limited to such cases. Thus, when the benefits from the project in question are largely private, the court, in seeking to justify the use of eminent domain, needs to find some public benefit or purpose.

Economic theory, however, reveals that this is misguided logic: the proper justification for use of eminent domain in *Kelo* and similar cases is the presence of a holdout problem. The existence of any spillover benefits is beside the point; if anything, it justifies subsidization of the project but is irrelevant to the takings question per se. The bottom line is that, according to the logic underlying Table 17.2, the decision in *Kelo* was correct, but the justification the Court relied on, which was based on a consideration of ends rather than means, was not. This conflation of means and ends in an effort to satisfy the plain meaning of the public use requirement of the Fifth Amendment is what I mean by the "paradox of public use."

It is interesting to note that the difficulty courts have had in justifying the use of eminent domain for private projects like that in *Kelo* is strangely at odds with the pervasiveness of what amount to "private takings" in other areas of law. Three cases that we have already encountered in other contexts will both illustrate the point and reveal the general applicability of the framework in Table 17.2. The first is the now familiar case of *Boomer v. Atlantic Cement Co.*,[7] which, recall, involved a nuisance suit filed by neighbors of a cement plant whose pollution caused them harm. Although the residents sought an injunction to have the plant shut down, the court allowed the plant to remain in operation as long as it paid damages to the residents. The court's use of a damage remedy (liability rule) rather than an injunction (property rule) in this case essentially authorized a private taking by the plant of the plaintiffs' right to be free from noise and pollution.

In terms of Table 17.2, the *Boomer* case falls into Category II because the plant, if forced to shut down, would have had to negotiate with all of the residents to lift the injunction. In other words, the plant would have faced a holdout problem based on its need to assemble pollution rights from the residents. (Recall that this was one of the interpretations of the case in the previous chapter.) Thus, based on the logic underlying Table 17.2, use of a forced transfer of the pollution rights by means of a liability rule was an appropriate remedy.

The second case is *Spur Industries v. Del E. Webb Development Co.*,[8] which involved a land developer who, when his activities encroached upon a pre-existing cattle feed lot, sought to have the lot shut down because of its foul odors. The court granted the developer's request, but required the

Eminent domain and paradox of public use   135

developer to pay the lot's relocation costs. In effect, the court allowed the developer to "take" the feed lot's land in return for monetary compensation. Consequently, the remedy in this case, like that in *Boomer*, falls into Category II in Table 17.2.

An important difference between this case and *Boomer*, however, is that there appears to be no assembly problem here—if the feed lot's right to operate had been protected by a property rule rather than by a liability rule, the developer presumably could have entered into negotiations with the owner of the lot to purchase his land in a market transaction, and there is nothing in this case to suggest that such a transaction would have been problematic. Thus, it appears that a better remedy may have been for the court to have protected the feed lot's right with a property rule. In other words, one could argue that, because there was no holdout problem, the court should have treated this case as if it belonged in Category I rather than Category II by rejecting the developer's request for relief.

The final illustrative case is *Peevyhouse v. Garland Coal and Mining Co.*,[9] which was a breach of contract case brought by the plaintiffs, owners of a tract of undeveloped land, when a strip mining company refused to honor its contractual obligation to restore the land to its pre-mining state after completing its operations. The mining company's logic was that the $29,000 cost of restoration far exceeded the market value of the restorations, which amounted to a mere $300. The court agreed with the mining company and allowed the breach in return for a damage payment of $300. Again, one can interpret the court's ruling in this case as effectively allowing the mining company to "take" the plaintiff's land in return for its market value.

Notice, however, that owing to the small numbers involved in this dispute, and the obvious absence of an assembly problem, this case is more like *Spur* than *Boomer*, and therefore would have been more appropriately classified as falling into Category I than Category II in Table 17.2. It follows that the proper remedy would have been to enforce the contract as written—that is, to protect the plaintiff's performance right with a property rule rather than a liability rule—thereby encouraging the parties to resolve the dispute through bargaining rather than by court order. As we argued in Chapter 14, this logic is in fact part of a larger critique of the routine use of monetary damages for breach of contract, owing to the absence of impediments to bargaining in most such settings.

The *Boomer*, *Spur*, and *Peevyhouse* cases, whether rightly or wrongly decided, nevertheless illustrate the point that liability rules are routinely used, and with little controversy, throughout the common law. It is this observation that makes the public use debate seem a bit overwrought from an economic perspective, given the ready availability of a perfectly good justification for using eminent domain in cases where a genuine holdout problem exists. Of course, nuisance and breach-of-contract cases do not ordinarily raise Constitutional issues, which in the public use context impose additional constraints on the remedies and arguments that judges can use in reaching their decisions. It is almost certainly this legal difference that explains the paradox of public use.

Notes

1 125 S.Ct. 2655, 545 U.S. 469 (2005).
2 The complete clause reads: "nor shall private property be taken for public use, without just compensation."
3 348 U.S. 26 (1954).
4 304 N.W.2d 455 (Mich. 1981).
5 *City of Oakland v. Oakland Raiders*, 183 Cal. Rptr. 391 (Ct. App. 1982).
6 *Hawaii Housing Authority v. Midkiff*, 467 U.S. 229 (1984).
7 26 N.Y.2d 219, 309 N.Y.S.2d 312, 257 N.E.2d 870 (Court of Appeals of N.Y. 1970).
8 494 P.2d 700 (1972).
9 382 P.2d 109, *cert.* denied, 375 U.S. 906 (1962).

18 Regulatory takings and the compensation question

The previous chapter focused on the public use limitation of the government's power to seize private property under the Takings Clause of the Fifth Amendment. Another equally contentious debate, also tied to eminent domain, is the question of whether government regulations of private property that limit its use without actually taking title ever rise to the level of a taking for which compensation is due. Such regulations are pervasive; examples include land-use zoning, environmental and safety regulations, historic landmark designations, and rules requiring accommodations for the disabled. From a purely economic perspective, regulations that reduce the value of land are not fundamentally different from outright seizures—the difference is one of degree rather than kind. This perspective reflects the commonly accepted idea, articulated in Chapter 2, that property is not a monolithic entity but rather is a bundle of rights or entitlements, each of which has a separate value. Thus, the deprivation of any subset of those rights reduces the overall value of the property proportionately. If a physical taking of the entire piece of property requires full compensation, then why shouldn't a partial taking require partial compensation?

This question presents something of a puzzle in light of the very different legal treatment by courts of full versus partial takings. Whereas compensation is virtually assured for the former, it has rarely been awarded for the latter. Indeed, courts have historically granted governments broad police powers to enact regulations in the public interest without the need to compensate owners at all for the resulting loss in value. In only a few cases have courts found that some "threshold" has been crossed, in which case the action in question has risen to the level of a "regulatory taking" for which compensation is due. The question is where the dividing line is between non-compensable and compensable regulations; that is what I mean by the "compensation question."

There exists a considerable body of case law and scholarship (by both economists and legal scholars) seeking to answer this question. The purpose of the current chapter is to try to make sense of the proposals that have emerged from this effort. The issue poses an interesting challenge for a positive economic theory of law because of the apparent disconnect between the all-or-nothing way that courts have treated full versus partial takings, and the economic view that they represent points on a continuum. A brief review of the key legal and scholarly arguments will illustrate, without attempting to be exhaustive, the variety of answers that have been proposed to the compensation question, and will set the stage for a resolution of the issue.

Nearly all courts have agreed that any regulation that involves some sort of physical invasion of the owner's property, however slight, triggers compensation. For example, in *Loretto v. Teleprompter*,[1] the Supreme Court held that a taking had occurred when a state law allowed a cable television company to affix wires and other equipment to the plaintiff's building. In *U.S. v. Causby*,[2] the Court extended the definition of a physical invasion to include the airspace up to 100 feet above the petitioner's property when it ruled that airplane flights over that property, which caused the death of some of the landowner's chickens, were compensable takings. Although the *physical invasion test* is well-established in law, it has little relevance for the vast majority of regulations that involve no physical contact with the targeted land. We therefore turn to other tests that have been proposed for these situations.

The case of *Mugler v. Kansas* concerned a prohibition law passed by the state of Kansas, pursuant to an amendment to the state constitution, that prevented the operation of breweries.[3] The owner of a brewery sued, claiming a taking of his property, but the Supreme Court denied the claim on the grounds that the state had the right, under its police powers, to regulate without compensation those activities that it deemed "to be injurious to the health, morals, or safety of the community." This ruling, referred to as the *noxious use doctrine*, focused on the government's responsibility to protect the public from harm (however that is defined), and held that when it regulates for this purpose, no compensation is due. The impact of the regulation on the landowner apparently was of no relevance under this doctrine.

That view changed dramatically in 1922 when the Supreme Court issued its ruling in the famous case of *Pennsylvania Coal v. Mahon*.[4] The case concerned a law passed by the State of Pennsylvania aimed at protecting surface owners from cave-ins (subsidence) caused by underground coal mining. The law specifically required coal companies to leave sufficient coal in the ground to support the surface, but the Pennsylvania Coal Company sued, claiming a taking of its mining rights. (Under a common legal arrangement, reflecting the idea of property as a bundle of rights, the coal companies had sold surface rights while retaining subsurface mining rights.) Although the case seemed to present a clear example of a noncompensable regulation under the noxious use doctrine, the Court ruled that compensation was due.

Writing for the majority, Justice Oliver Wendell Holmes began by acknowledging the government's right to impose some regulations without compensation, for otherwise, the ability of the government to function would be greatly impeded. However, he went on to argue that there must be a limit to that power so as not to impose an excessive burden on private property owners. He said, in particular, that if the government's regulatory powers were unrestrained, it would overreach until "at last, private property disappear[ed]." He further noted that a relevant basis for this limit is the impact of the regulation on the landowner: "One fact for consideration in determining such limits is the extent of the diminution [in value of the land]. When it reaches a certain magnitude, in most if not all cases there must be an exercise of eminent domain and compensation to sustain the act." In other words, "if regulation goes too far, it will be recognized as a taking." Unfortunately, the Court offered no further guidance on how to apply this so-called *diminution of value test*. It did not say what amount of diminution qualified as going too far, instead leaving the determination to be done on a case-by-case basis.

Many observers have described the *Pennsylvania Coal* case as a watershed in regulatory takings law in recognition of its apparent departure from the noxious use doctrine. Indeed, Justice Louis Brandeis, in his dissenting opinion, pointed out that

> Every restriction upon the use of property imposed in the exercise of the police power deprives the owner of some right theretofore enjoyed, and is, in that sense, an abridgement by the States of rights in property without making compensation. But restriction imposed to protect public health, safety or morals from dangers is not a taking. The restriction here in question is merely the prohibition of a noxious use.

We will return to the seeming irreconcilability of the Holmes and Brandeis opinions later.

The next key case, *Penn Central Transportation Co. v. City of New York*,[5] arose out of the city's decision to designate Grand Central Terminal as an historic landmark, which severely limited allowable alterations of the building. Thus, when the city turned down a proposal by the building's owner to erect a multi-storied office building above the terminal, the owner sued, claiming a taking of its development rights. In deciding against compensation, the Supreme Court cited the following factors as being relevant: (1) the character of the government action, (2) the extent of the diminution of value suffered by the owners, and (3) whether or not the regulation interfered with the plaintiff's "investment-backed expectations." The first two factors reflected the noxious use doctrine and diminution of value tests, respectively, while the third added the idea that the owners' loss must be based on reasonable expectations, backed up by actual investments. In other words, owners could not claim a loss based on future uses that they never would have contemplated, or that would not have been allowed by law. In his dissenting opinion, Justice Rehnquist added a fourth consideration when he argued that a taking does not occur if a regulation "secures an average reciprocity of advantage" across all landowners. This idea reflects the argument that some regulations, like zoning, are so pervasive that all landowners suffer from them, but also benefit from them, thereby spreading the costs and benefits equally. In this sense, monetary compensation is not needed because any losses are, in principle, compensated for by offsetting benefits. We will return to this point in the discussion of Richard Epstein's view of the compensation question.

The final legal test for compensation I will mention emerged from the case of *Lucas v. South Carolina Coastal Council*,[6] which involved a land developer, David Lucas, who owned two undeveloped parcels of land on the South Carolina shore. Developing the parcels at some future date seemed to be a reasonable expectation given that neighboring parcels had already been developed, but before Lucas could begin his development, the South Carolina state legislature passed a law banning future coastal development in an effort to control beach erosion. Lucas sued the state seeking compensation for his nearly total loss in value. The South Carolina Supreme Court ruled against compensation based on the stated purpose of the law as preventing harm to the public—the old noxious use doctrine, but the U.S. Supreme Court reversed the decision in light of the nearly complete diminution of value suffered by Lucas. However, the Court left open the possibility that the state could still avoid paying compensation if it could demonstrate that the action prohibited by the regulation constituted a nuisance under the state's common law. The new element is that this standard, called the *nuisance exception*, provided an objective basis—namely, the state's nuisance law—for defining a noxious use.

In addition to these legal tests for compensation, several other tests have been proposed in the scholarly literature. I will only describe a few. The first, referred to as the *harm-benefit rule*, says that no compensation should be due for regulations that prevent a landowner from imposing a harm on others (for example, a regulation preventing pollution), but compensation should be paid for government actions that compel a landowner to bestow a benefit on the public (for example, a regulation preventing development in order to preserve open space). The logic behind this rule is that, on the one hand, landowners have no legal right to impose harm on others (and so a rule preventing such harm is not a taking); but on the other, the public should be required to pay for any benefits that it receives rather than burdening one or a few individuals with that cost. Several authors have proposed variants of this rule, reflecting its intuitive appeal. The problem, however, is that from an economic perspective, a prevented harm can always be re-defined as a benefit, and a foregone benefit can be re-defined as a harm. As the logic of the Coase Theorem demonstrates, the initial assignment of property rights (i.e., the initial "entitlement point") is irrelevant with regard to the efficient assignment of those rights.

Recall, in particular, that in the rancher-farmer dispute discussed in Chapter 2, the rancher can be either the "injurer" or the "victim," depending on how property rights are initially assigned, but that issue has no bearing on the efficient size of the rancher's herd or the number of acres the farmer should cultivate. The initial point only affects the distribution of wealth, which in the current context determines whether compensation is due.[7] What is needed, therefore, is a meaningful delineation of property rights that defines "neutral" conduct, which would then serve as a baseline for determining whether compensation should be paid for a given government action.

William Fischel (1995) proposed such a baseline in the form of what he called the "normal behavior standard." According to this standard, no compensation would be due for regulations that prevent landowners from engaging in below-normal behavior, but compensation would be due for regulations requiring them to undertake above-normal behavior, where "normal behavior" would be defined by community standards based on what landowners can reasonably expect to be allowed to do with their land. (It is therefore similar to the nuisance exception.) This "reasonableness standard" thereby establishes an entitlement point that defines the difference between harms and benefits (or between injurers and victims).

For example, a landowner in a residential neighborhood could not reasonably expect to build a factory on his or her land because it would constitute below-normal behavior, and so a zoning ordinance preventing such a use would not be a taking. Conversely, a law requiring an individual owner to leave part of his or her land vacant to provide open space for all other residents in the neighborhood compels above-normal behavior, and so it would be a compensable taking. What makes this distinction an economically sensible one, according to Fischel, is that it saves on the transaction costs of achieving an efficient land use pattern because most people will voluntarily comply with normal behavior (the zero compensation point), thus minimizing the administrative costs of preventing externalities on one hand, and providing public goods on the other.

The final test I will mention is the standard proposed by Frank Michelman in his highly influential article on the compensation question. Like Fischel, Michelman recognized the importance of minimizing the transaction costs (which he called "settlement costs") of paying compensation, but he noted that this consideration must be balanced against the cost of *not* paying compensation—what he termed "demoralization costs." He defined these costs to be

> the total of (1) the dollar value necessary to offset disutilities which accrue to losers and their sympathizers from the realization that no compensation is offered, and (2) the present capitalized value of lost production . . . caused by demoralization of uncompensated losers, their sympathizers, and other observers disturbed by the thought that they themselves may be subjected to similar treatment on some other occasion.
>
> (Michelman, 1967, p. 1214)

142 *Regulatory takings and compensation*

Michelman argued that if the settlement costs exceed these demoralization costs, compensation should not be paid, but if the reverse is true, it should be.

The preceding catalog of tests for answering the compensation question suggests a serious lack of consensus among courts and scholars; indeed, one observer has referred to this area of law as "incoherent" (Rubenfeld, 1993, p. 1080). The challenge for a positive economic theory of regulatory takings is to offer a perspective that synthesizes the conflicting views within a consistent framework. The basis for such a framework will be a threshold approach along the lines discussed in Chapter 4. Recall that the focus there was on negligence law and the due care standard, but I also argued that threshold rules are pervasive in the law, including, as one example, the law of regulatory takings. Here I will develop that example in detail, and then apply it to the actual law as described previously.

Recall that the economic justification for threshold rules was their ability to achieve efficient outcomes in so-called bilateral care situations—that is, situations in which two parties make choices that jointly determine some outcome. In the accident context, for example, potential injurers and victims made choices of care that determined the probability that they will become involved in an accident. In that context we argued that a properly structured negligence rule would induce the parties, acting independently, to choose the efficient levels of care, which were defined to be the levels that minimized expected accident costs.

In the current context, the two parties that may come into conflict will be a landowner and a government regulator. The landowner's decision concerns whether to make an irreversible investment in his land that would enhance its value if developed, but that may also produce an external cost. The regulator's decision is whether to impose a restriction on the allowable uses of the land, which, if imposed, would prevent the external cost but would also deprive the owner of the returns from his proposed development. A key aspect of the situation is that the landowner must make his investment decision *before* it is known with certainty whether the regulator will impose the regulation. (In this sense, the situation involves a sequential choice problem, like that examined in Chapter 6.) This is not a restrictive assumption, however, because the threat of regulation is ever-present, reflecting the possibility of changing standards about what types of activities are socially valuable. The situation that gave rise to the *Lucas* case provides a prototypical example of this scenario. Recall that the landowner there had planned to develop his beachfront lots for residential use, as many other owners had already done, but before he could proceed, the state banned all future development because of fears of excessive beach erosion and loss of undisturbed beachfront land.

In this setting, the legal question is whether compensation should be paid if the regulator imposes the regulation. The economic question concerns the efficient actions of the two parties. First, should the landowner invest in the land, knowing there is a chance that subsequent development will be prohibited and the investment lost? Second, given the landowner's investment, should the regulator act to prevent development? The confluence of the legal and economic questions involves structuring a compensation rule that induces both parties to act efficiently.

To see why the compensation rule matters, suppose that compensation was always paid when regulations preventing development are enacted. In that case, landowners would have no incentive to account for the possible external costs that their actions might have, and so would likely over-invest in activities that might impose such costs. In this case, compensation creates a moral hazard problem for landowners by insuring them against any loss in their investment decisions. Regulators, on the other hand, would have a strong incentive to regulate only when it is efficient to do so because they would have to pay for any losses incurred by landowner. (This assumes that regulators are motivated at least in part by budgetary concerns.)

If, on the other hand, compensation was never paid, the results would be reversed: landowners would invest efficiently because they would recognize the possibility that development may not be efficient due to the externality and so would be prohibited, whereas regulators would have a tendency to over-regulate because there would be no cost of doing so. An all-or-nothing compensation rule therefore involves a trade-off between efficient investment and efficient regulation, thus providing an example of what we referred to in Chapter 4 as the "paradox of compensation."

One resolution of this paradox is to adopt a threshold rule that, like negligence, conditions the payment of compensation on whether one of the parties complied with a "due standard" of behavior. In the current context, one version of such a rule would take the following form: if the regulator imposes a regulation inefficiently (specifically, if it over-regulates), full compensation for the lost value suffered by the landowner would be due, whereas if the regulator imposes the regulation efficiently, no compensation would be due. Under this rule, a regulator who cares about budgetary considerations will refrain from over-regulation so as to avoid having to pay compensation. In this sense, the "threat" of compensation acts to deter excessive regulation, just as the threat of liability under negligence induces injurers to be careful. At the same time, landowners will not overinvest in activities that may be regulated because they anticipate that regulators will only enact efficient regulations, and that when a regulation is enacted, no compensation will be due. In the Nash equilibrium, therefore, both parties act efficiently and no compensation is actually paid. The outcome is therefore analytically the same as in the bilateral care accident setting with a properly structured negligence rule, where both parties invest in efficient care and the victim is not compensated.

One may question the practicality of this rule based on the difficulty courts would have in distinguishing between efficient and inefficient regulations. This is a valid concern, but as discussed in Chapter 5, courts routinely have to make similar calculations in tort cases (specifically, by applying the Hand test) to determine whether or not an injurer is negligent. Further, a re-examination of the various tests for compensation in regulatory takings cases shows that courts are already implementing what amount to threshold rules along the lines of the one proposed here. In this sense, the proposed rule offers a positive theory of the law in this area.

Most obviously, the rule resembles the diminution of value test from *Pennsylvania Coal* in the sense that it establishes a threshold for determining when a regulation "goes too far"; namely, when it is *inefficient*. Less obviously, the rule also provides a standard for applying the noxious use doctrine from *Mugler*. Recall that the Court defined a "noxious use" to be one that is "injurious to health, morals, or safety of the community." In contrast to this vague and all-encompassing standard, the efficient threshold rule would define a noxious use to be one that is *efficiently regulated* (and hence requiring no compensation). Note that, according to this interpretation, the diminution of value test and the noxious use doctrine are really two sides of the same coin: the diminution of value test describes the side of the threshold where the regulation fails to comply with the due standard of efficiency, and so compensation is due, while the noxious use doctrine describes the side where the regulation does comply, and so compensation is not due.

Seen in this light, the Court's ruling in *Pennsylvania Coal* no longer appears to be the sharp break in the law that it has often been portrayed as. Instead, it is just another way of articulating the same rule that it had previously announced in *Mugler*. The difference is that the regulation was found to be efficient in *Mugler*, so the Court characterized its ruling of no compensation in keeping with that factual scenario, whereas the regulation in *Pennsylvania Coal* was found to be inefficient, so the Court's reasoning highlighted that scenario.

By similar logic, the disagreement between Holmes and Brandeis in *Pennsylvania Coal* may now be characterized, in light of the proposed rule, as being a disagreement over *facts* rather than *law*. To illustrate this point, let us suppose that both Holmes and Brandeis were approaching the case from the perspective of the efficient threshold rule—that is, they were applying the same legal standard. However, Holmes believed that the benefit to society of the law in question in terms of its protection of surface owners against cave-ins was outweighed by the lost value of coal to the mining companies. In other words, the regulation was inefficiently imposed. In contrast, Brandeis believed that the reverse was true and the regulation was efficiently imposed. As a result, the judges reached opposite conclusions regarding the compensation question, even though they agreed (according to this interpretation) about the applicable law. The point is no different than if two judges differed regarding a finding of negligence under the Hand test.

An interesting revival of this same debate arose 65 years after *Pennsylvania Coal* had been decided when the Supreme Court confronted the case of *Keystone Bituminous Coal Assn. v. DeBenedictus*.[8] The case is striking because the factual scenario is virtually identical to that in *Pennsylvania Coal*. Specifically, it involved a suit brought by an association of coal companies seeking compensation for a law passed by the State of Pennsylvania requiring coal companies to leave sufficient coal in the ground to protect surface owners against cave-ins. Despite the similarity of facts, however, the Court this time found against the coal companies—that is, no compensation was required. The obvious question is whether *Keystone* "overturned" *Pennsylvania Coal*.

In endeavoring to distinguish the two cases, the *Keystone* Court pointed out that the number of surface owners had greatly increased since the time of *Pennsylvania Coal*, when only a few owners were involved. This in fact is a crucial point. If the value of the surface land had increased during the intervening years, then the social benefit of a regulation aimed at preserving that value would also have increased. At the same time, the decline in the value of coal as a source of energy between 1922 and 1987 had reduced the cost side of the calculation. Thus, a regulation that was, by Holmes's reckoning, inefficient in 1922 may very well have become efficient by 1987. Seen in this perspective, the decisions in the two cases are perfectly compatible, reflecting a change in factual circumstances rather than a departure from established law.

Yet another test for compensation, the nuisance exception from *Lucas*, can be interpreted in light of the proposed threshold rule. Recall that this exception allowed the government to avoid paying compensation for a regulation, despite its impact on the landowner, if the regulation prevented an activity that would be classified as a common law nuisance. The key point here is that a nuisance is most commonly defined to be conduct that is unreasonably harmful; that is, for which "a reasonable person would conclude that the amount of the harm done outweighs the benefit served by the conduct" (Keeton, et al., 1984, p. 630). Thus, the nuisance exception would prescribe that no compensation should be paid precisely in those cases where the regulation is inefficiently imposed, just as the proposed rule does.

The final issue I want to address is how the efficient threshold rule relates to Richard Epstein's views on the compensation question (Epstein, 1985). Epstein's perspective on the regulatory takings issue, and on takings law in general, begins with the Lockean notion that the government should not stand in a preferred position compared to private citizens in its dealings with them. "Government" in this perspective is nothing more than the vehicle by which citizens act collectively. Thus, if and when the government wrongfully deprives a citizen of his or her property, it should have to pay compensation for the resulting loss, just as any citizen would have to pay under the law of torts for damaging another citizen's property. In contrast, if the government (representing all citizens) prevents one citizen from harming others—as when it prevents citizens from creating a nuisance—it should not have to pay compensation based on the right that all citizens have to be free from nuisances caused by their fellow citizens. In Epstein's view, therefore, the principal protection of landowner rights, and hence the basis for takings law, should be the law of nuisance. This logic suggests that, to the extent that nuisance law provides an efficient standard for the proposed threshold rule, as we have just argued, that rule is consistent with Epstein's view.

The congruence is not perfect, however, as illustrated by the case of *Miller v. Schoene*.[9] The case involved a law passed by the State of Virginia that allowed government officials to cut down cedar trees growing within two miles of an apple orchard when it was discovered that the cedar trees harbored a virus that was harmful to apple trees. The owner of the cedar trees sued claiming a taking, but the Supreme Court denied compensation on the grounds that apple growing was a valuable industry and deserved state protection.

If we suppose that the regulation in this case was efficient—that is, the value of protecting the apple trees exceeded the value of the cedar trees—then the finding of no compensation in this case was compatible with the efficient threshold rule. Specifically, no compensation was due because the regulation was efficiently imposed. Epstein's view, however, is that unless the state could show that the cedar trees were a nuisance under the state's common law, it should be required to pay compensation. Nuisance law and economic efficiency often converge to the same outcome (as exemplified by above cost-benefit test), but not always. When they differ, Epstein argues that the standard for compensation should be dictated by nuisance law, whereas the efficient threshold rule prescribes that it should be based on efficiency. Fundamentally, this reflects a different normative perspective on the appropriate function of the just compensation requirement of the takings clause. While Epstein acknowledges that efficiency is an appropriate norm for deciding whether to *enact* a government regulation, he objects to its exclusive use in deciding on the compensation question. This is a valid point of view that focuses on the role of compensation in protecting certain assignments of property rights—namely, those prescribed by nuisance law. The efficient threshold rule, in comparison, emphasizes the function of compensation in creating incentives for efficient behavior by landowners and regulators (specifically, in overcoming the paradox of compensation). The fact that landowners are not compensated in an efficient equilibrium is a distributional question that is of secondary importance in this view.

Epstein does, however, recognize that government-imposed restrictions on landowner rights do not always require *monetary* compensation because the just compensation requirement can also be satisfied by "in-kind" compensation. The situations to which this argument applies are widely imposed regulations like land-use zoning that affect all landowners equally. Thus, as noted earlier, all landowners are equally burdened, but also equally benefitted by the regulations; and if the regulations are efficiently imposed, aggregate gains should outweigh aggregate losses, resulting in a net gain on average.

Note that this logic reflects the "average reciprocity of advantage" enjoyed by all landowners arising from broad government actions, and therefore argues against claims of compensation by individual landowners. For example, a zoning ordinance that prevented a landowner from opening a gas station in a residential area would not give rise to a valid taking claim because, although the owner could claim a loss due to the regulation, that loss would only be measured relative to a background in which all other landowners are complying with the regulation. In other words, the plaintiff's "loss" would be calculated based on his unilateral departure from an efficient land use configuration. In fact, the enactment of the regulation, if efficient, raises everyone's property value compared to an unregulated market in which individuals are free to impose costs on their neighbors. It is in this sense that all citizens receive in-kind compensation for the regulation, and so the denial of monetary compensation for individual claims is economically justified.

Further, as Michelman recognized, a rule denying compensation in this case also reflects a fundamental notion of fairness:

> [a] decision not to compensate is not unfair as long as the disappointed claimant ought to be able to appreciate how such decisions might fit into a consistent practice which holds forth a lesser long run risk to people like him than would any consistent practice which is naturally suggested by the opposite decision.
>
> (Michelman, 1967, p. 1223)

This reflects the perspective, shared by Epstein, that the eminent domain clause is at least as much about fairness as it is about efficiency, but that in-kind compensation can often be seen as satisfying the fairness requirement.

Notes

1 458 U.S. 419 (1982).
2 328 U.S. 256 (1946).
3 123 U.S. 623 (1887).
4 260 U.S. 393 (1922).
5 438 U.S. 104 (1978).
6 505 U.S. 1003 (1992).
7 In this sense, the harm-benefit rule merely begs the compensation question.
8 480 U.S. 470 (1987).
9 276 U.S. 272 (1928).

19 Fair use
Fair or foul?

Copyright law is designed to protect the rights of authors, musicians, artists, and producers of any creative work. Like patents, copyright law is motivated by the trade-off between the social benefits of allowing wide availability of the protected work, both for direct consumption and for the creation of derivative works, and the need to give creators an incentive to produce such works in the first place. In the case of both patents and copyrights, the fundamental problem of enforcing property rights in intellectual property arises from the public good nature of information, which derives from the fact that once an idea or invention is created, it can be costlessly used by anyone. Thus, in a competitive market with free entry, any potential profits from the creative work will be bid away, which leaves little economic incentive for the originator to undertake the up-front investment necessary to produce it. Some legal protection in the form of monopoly control is therefore necessary to overcome this "appropriability problem." In the case of both patents and copyrights, that protection involves granting the producer exclusive property rights over the creation for a set period of time—for patents it is 20 years, and for copyrights it is the author's life plus 70 years.

Copyright law differs from patent law, however, in some important respects. First, it does not preclude independent discovery of an idea, only copies of the original creative work. The likely reason is that independent creation of an identical artistic, musical, or literary work is a remote possibility. Second, copyright protects the *expression* of an idea, not the idea itself. This also makes sense given that a particular idea can often be expressed in a multitude of ways, each constituting a unique creative work. Several of Shakespeare's plays, for example, were re-tellings of earlier stories, and there are many contemporary expressions of Shakespearian themes (think of *Romeo and Juliet* and *West Side Story*). All such derivative works are permissible under modern copyright law.

This last point relates to the *scope* of copyright protection, as opposed to its duration. The relevant question here is, exactly what types of uses would constitute an infringement of copyright protection of the original creation? This is where the "fair use" doctrine comes in. Under copyright law, fair use allows limited uses of a copyrighted work, without the holder's consent, for purposes of criticism, scholarship, news reporting, and education. The economic rationale usually offered for allowing these unauthorized uses is that they are socially beneficial in the sense that the gain from the use exceeds the cost to the copyright holder, which means that a mutual benefit is possible, but the transaction costs involved in obtaining actual consent from the copyright holder would be high. In other words, there is market failure preventing the mutually beneficial exchange of the property rights in question, which justifies the coercive transfer of at least some portion of those rights. The crucial question therefore concerns where the "limit" of these allowed uses should be set. The following economic model offers some answers, which we will then apply to the examination of several fair use cases.

The analysis is based on a simple model of the market for "differentiated products," meaning products that come in multiple varieties, or qualities. Most consumer goods are of this sort, with different companies offering varieties that are imperfect substitutes for each other. Think of soft drinks or cell phones, for example. We can apply this idea to the current context by defining a "quality index," denoted q, that ranges from zero to one, with the original work put at $q=1$ (the highest quality level), and lesser quality (i.e., more differentiated) copies being associated with correspondingly lower values of q. This situation represents the supply side of the market.

On the demand side, we suppose that consumers can also be arrayed along this product spectrum according to their most-preferred quality (product variety), ranging from those who place the highest value on the original itself at $q=1$, to those who would be satisfied with correspondingly lower quality versions (less exact copies). Figure 19.1 shows this situation schematically.

In an efficient equilibrium, each consumer would "locate" along this continuum at his or her most-preferred, or ideal, quality. This outcome, however, presupposes both that the original exists, and that a competitive market emerges for the production and sale of copies of varying quality at all other levels of q. Specifically, competing firms enter to fulfill the demand for all possible market niches. This characterizes the situation in most product markets. As argued, however, such an outcome is not likely to happen for ideas or other forms of intellectual property due to the appropriability problem, which prevents the creator from recovering the cost of his or her

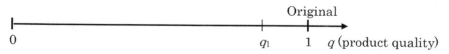

Figure 19.1 Index of product quality

150 *Fair use*

initial investment if unlimited entry of competing suppliers (or unlimited copying) is allowed. In other words, production of the original *and* free entry of copiers are incompatible with each other.

As a possible remedy for this, consider the opposite extreme in which the creator is given exclusive control over sale of the original work, meaning that copying is completely forbidden (that is, only $q=1$ is available). In this setting, potential consumers are forced to choose between buying the original and not consuming the good at all. The resulting equilibrium will involve a threshold, shown by q_1 in Figure 19.1, which separates consumers from non-consumers. Specifically, consumers whose ideal quality of the good exceeds q_1 will buy the original, while those whose ideal quality is below q_1 will not enter the market.[1] In this outcome, those buyers who enter the market (i.e., those with $q \geq q_1$) will all be clustered at $q=1$, so only those whose ideal quality coincides with $q=1$ will be fully satisfied, while all consumers whose ideal varieties are below q_1 stay out of the market altogether. As a result, significant consumption benefits are foregone. This is the consequence of complete copyright protection.

In an effort to improve on the previous two extremes—i.e., free entry of copiers, resulting in non-production of the original, and no copying at all—suppose that some copying is allowed as long as the copies are not "too close" to the original, where proximity will be measured here in terms of the index q. Specifically, let q_f represent the threshold for allowable copying—the fair use standard—such that copies with $q < q_f$ are permitted without the copyright holder's consent, but those with $q > q_f$ are not. In this sense, we will interpret fair use as a threshold test (see Chapter 5). Consumers whose ideal varieties lie in the allowed copying range will now be able to consume exactly that quality by making legal copies, whereas those whose ideal varieties exceed the threshold (i.e., that lie between q_f and $q=1$) will have to be satisfied with either making a copy of quality q_f, buying the original, or staying out of the market.

Referring to Figure 19.1, suppose that q_f is set below q_1, the threshold separating buyers and non-buyers in the no-copying case. In this setting, we might be tempted to conclude that legal copying is completely *harmless* to the creator because only those consumers who were not previously in the market will make legal copies. This is not necessarily true, however. To see why, note that some individuals whose ideal quality is larger than, but close to, the legal threshold, q_f, will now find it optimal to make copies of quality q_f rather than buying the original or not entering the market. Thus, there will be a clustering of consumers at the threshold, q_f, and this cluster may include some consumers who would have bought the original if copying were totally prohibited (i.e., some consumers to the right of q_1). The extent of this *harmful copying* will clearly be larger the closer is q_f to q_1. If q_f is set equal to or above q_1, as shown in Figure 19.2, then it will certainly be true that some permissible copying will be harmful to the creator. Ultimately, the equilibrium in this case will involve the following sorting of consumers: those whose most-preferred quality is less than q_f

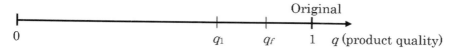

Figure 19.2 The case where copying is definitely harmful to the creator

will make legal copies; those whose most-preferred quality is slightly above q_f will make copies of quality q_f; and those whose most-preferred quality is close to $q=1$ will buy the original. Finally, some consumers whose most-preferred quality is mid-way between q_f and $q=1$ may remain out of the market—the number of these consumers will be greater the further away from $q=1$ that q_f is set.

It should be clear that consumers as a group are better off as the threshold for legal copying is raised, taking as given existence of the original. (In the extreme, when $q_f=1$, all consumers get their ideal quality.) However, the profits of creators will correspondingly decrease, thereby weakening their incentives to produce the original. As a result, the optimal fair use threshold, q_f^*, should be chosen to balance these factors. An implication of this conclusion is that the fair use standard should never be set in the range where copying is non-harmful to creators, for otherwise, additional consumer benefits can be obtained by raising the threshold without reducing creators' profits at all. The optimal fair use standard should therefore always be set in the range where copyright holders perceive it as allowing harmful uses. (This point will be relevant in our discussion of the fair use cases that follow.)

It is also the case that the optimal threshold will be dependent on the technology of copying, though perhaps not in an obvious way. Let's say that the technology of copying improves in the sense that copies become cheaper, of better quality, or both. Copies therefore become increasingly close substitutes for the original, which argues for a more permissive standard (i.e., a larger q_f^*) as the benefits of copying increase, all else equal. But on the other hand, the resulting loss of customers for the original further erodes the profits of the creator, which argues for a stricter standard (i.e., a smaller q_f^*). Improvements in copying technology therefore affect both the costs and benefits of fair use, so the net effect of such improvements on the optimal standard is ambiguous.

Finally, a factor not yet considered is that certain unauthorized uses of the copyrighted work may benefit the creator by increasing demand for the original. Examples include air play of recorded music and quotations in book reviews (even unfavorable ones). Unauthorized uses of this sort provide a form of advertising for the original work, and so unlike copies in the above model, which we regarded strictly as substitutes for the work, these uses are also complements to it. This factor clearly works in the direction of a more permissive fair use standard for qualified uses.

With the foregoing analysis in hand, we now turn to the law of fair use. The Copyright Act specifies the following factors as being relevant for determining fair use:[2] (a) the purpose and character of the use (for example, whether it is for commercial or educational purposes); (b) the nature of the original work; (c) the amount of material used in relation to the original; and (d) the effect of the use on the value of the copyright. Factors (a) and (d) clearly relate to the impact of the use on the profits of the creator, while factor (c) conforms to the above model's interpretation of fair use as a threshold test based on how close the copies are to the original. (It is not clear how factor (b) relates to the proposed framework.) In light of these factors, and the conclusions of the above economic model, I now discuss several fair use cases.

The first case is *Williams & Wilkins Co. v. United States*,[3] which concerned a claim by a publisher of medical journals that the unauthorized photocopying of articles by government libraries was an infringement of its copyright. In finding that the use was fair, the court emphasized the limited number of copies made, the fact that the copies were for the advancement of scientific knowledge rather than for commercial use, and that the plaintiffs offered little evidence of detrimental financial effects. These conclusions suggest that the use in question was clearly welfare-enhancing in the sense described earlier, while having little if any harmful effect on the copyright holder. Thus, it appears that the court properly found it to be well within the permissible range, as established by the model outlined previously.

The next two cases involve suits brought by copyrights holders, not against actual infringers, but against companies manufacturing technologies that potentially facilitated infringement. The claim was that the manufacturers in question thereby engaged in "contributory infringement," as opposed to "direct infringement" by those who used the technology. (The difficulty of identifying actual infringers is one reason for this strategy; another is the deeper pockets of the contributory infringers.) In *Sony Corp. of America v. Universal City Studios*,[4] the Supreme Court held that video recording of television programs for later viewing was itself not an infringement of copyright law, and hence was a fair use. The Court noted that such copying provided a clear benefit to consumers (the ability to "time-shift" programs); that it was non-commercial in nature; and that it imposed little harm on copyright holders. Again, these conclusions reflect the above economic standard. Nor did the Court find that the actual defendants in the case, manufacturers of the recording equipment used by the alleged infringers, were contributory infringers because the technology had substantial non-infringing uses.

In both of the preceding cases, the court judged that the challenged uses enhanced consumer welfare without substantially hurting the copyright holders, which raises the question of why the latter challenged the uses. In other words, why did the court and the copyright holder apparently disagree about the degree of harm suffered by the latter? It was clear in both cases that infringing uses of the copying technology *were* possible: photocopying of published works can substitute for purchase of the original, and video-recording of television programs can reduce television studio profits by allowing users to fast-forward through commercials. In the *Williams & Wilkins* case, the offsetting benefits were external to the publisher (advancement of scientific knowledge), and so it is clear why it sought a legal remedy. However, in the *Sony* case, video-recording technology also seemed to offer substantial profit-making opportunities for copyright holders through the sale of pre-recording material. Thus, the fact that the television studios brought suit in this case apparently reflected their misjudgment about the relative harm versus benefit of the technology in question. Indeed, as events turned out, the court was more correct because the studios actually stood to benefit a great deal from it.

In contrast to the *Sony* case, a court found that the internet file-sharing service offered by Napster was contributory infringement.[5] Although this technology also had non-infringing uses, the court held that it did not meet the fair use standard because the principal use of the technology directly reduced the demand for the copyright holder's product, and that the resulting harm to the copyright holder more than outweighed any offsetting benefits. In addition, the court found that Napster had actual knowledge of some users' infringing behavior.

Finally, a court recently held that the searchable Google Books database, which contains the full text of public domain books (those for which the copyright has expired) and excerpts from some copyrighted books, was fair use.[6] The court emphasized the significant public benefits that arise from the wide availability of such works, and it further noted that the rights of copyright holders would not be seriously infringed because demand for the excerpted works may well be enhanced by the service. This reflects the complementarity of certain uses to the copyright holder's product, as described earlier.

The lesson from these cases is that courts continually need to revisit the scope of fair use in the face of technological changes that lower the cost and raise the quality of potentially infringing uses. The fact that this will have offsetting effects on the optimal threshold will likely make the fair use standard a moving target. The economic framework offered in this chapter nevertheless provides a consistent approach for balancing the relevant costs and benefits in the face of such changes, and the case review suggests that the courts seem to be following that approach.

Notes

1 How close q_1 will be to $q=1$ depends on how steeply a consumer's satisfaction declines away from his or her ideal qualities.
2 17 U.S.C. §107.
3 487 F.2d 1345 (1973).
4 464 U.S. 417 (1984.
5 *A&M Records, Inc. v. Napster, Inc.*, 239 F.3d 1004 (9th Cir. 2001).
6 *Authors' Guild v. Google*, 721 F.3d 132 (2nd Cir. 2013).

20 Lawsuits for sale?

Nearly all parties involved in the litigation process—by which I mean the use of the court system to resolve legal disputes between private parties—are infrequent participants and hence rely on lawyers for advice. Clients and their lawyers thus enter into contractual arrangements that dictate the means by which the lawyer will be compensated. Generally, defense lawyers are paid on an hourly basis, but in the United States the principal arrangement under which plaintiffs in tort cases engage lawyers is on a contingency basis, which typically specifies that the lawyers will cover all out-of-pocket costs incurred during the course of the litigation in return for a share of any recovery (usually a third), whether obtained by settlement or trial. (In some cases, the percentage recovery is different for settlements and trial judgments, but we will ignore that complication hereafter.) The lawyer is thus paid only if the plaintiff succeeds in recovering some money, which is the sense in which the arrangement is "contingent" on the outcome of the case.[1]

The three principal arguments advanced in favor of contingent fee contracts are, first, that they provide lawyers an incentive to work hard for their clients by giving them a stake in the outcome of the case; second, that they share the risk of an uncertain trial outcome between the plaintiff and the lawyer; and third, that they give poor plaintiffs access to the legal system by allowing the lawyer in effect to loan the plaintiff the cost of pursuing the claim, which the latter is only obligated to pay back in the event of a positive outcome. This chapter evaluates these claims, and in the process proposes an alternative arrangement that involves the "sale" of lawsuits from plaintiffs to lawyers. The idea of selling lawsuits, which are valuable assets, is not a new one, but it has generally been viewed with considerable skepticism within the legal community. The analysis here will suggest that much (though not all) of that skepticism may be unfounded. The methodology that I will employ in developing this argument is the economic theory of contracts, referred to as *principal-agent theory*.

In general terms, principal-agent theory is concerned with deriving the optimal contractual arrangement between an employer (the principal) and an employee (the agent) under the assumption that the employer cannot easily monitor the employee's efforts, and hence cannot condition compensation on that effort. Instead, the agent typically is paid, at least in part, based on some observable measure of output, such as the recovery from a lawsuit. The benchmark for evaluating the efficiency of any particular contractual arrangement is a situation in which the employer and the employee are one and the same person, for in that case, the "employee" necessarily internalizes the full benefits and costs of his or her effort and therefore chooses the efficient level of effort. The question is how closely actual contracts can duplicate this outcome.

It will be useful in evaluating legal contracts to relate them to the prototypical example of a principal-agent relationship—namely, that between a landowner and a tenant-farmer hired to cultivate his land. Output in this case is assumed to depend on the farmer's (unobservable) effort but also on random factors such as the weather. It is because of this randomness that the landowner cannot perfectly infer the farmer's effort from the harvest, and so cannot condition payment directly on effort. (For example, even if the farmer works hard, the harvest may turn out to be poor because of lack of rainfall.) A very common contractual arrangement in this setting throughout history has been a "sharecropping contract," which literally calls for the harvest to be divided between the farmer and the landowner. In what follows, I will compare and contrast this contract with the contingent fee contract in law, which is also a kind of "share" contract.

In the lawyer-client setting it is certainly the case that most clients either cannot observe, or cannot properly evaluate, the lawyer's effort. Thus, as in the agricultural context, an unfavorable outcome need not reflect lack of effort by the lawyer—it could also be due to an adverse legal precedent or an unsympathetic judge or jury. It is therefore not surprising that a sharing arrangement has also arisen there as the principal means of compensating plaintiffs' lawyers. Against this theoretical backdrop, let us turn to a more detailed examination of the claimed merits of the share contract in both law and agriculture.

Consider first the problem of giving the agent (the lawyer or farmer) an incentive to exert effort, referred to as a *moral hazard* or *agency problem*. Consider, in particular, a lawyer who takes on a case under a contingency contract that promises her one-third of any recovery, but obligates her to bear all of the litigation costs. The lawyer will clearly have an incentive to exert *some* effort, but less than what is jointly optimal for the two parties (i.e., less effort than what a combined lawyer-client would choose) because she incurs the full marginal cost of effort but only receives a third of the marginal benefit. If the sharing rate were increased, however, the lawyer's effort would correspondingly rise, and would converge to the efficient level when the rate approaches one—that is, when the lawyer retains the full amount of the recovery.

Of course, this would not be an acceptable arrangement for the client (principal), but suppose the lawyer offers to "buy" the claim from the plaintiff up front, in return for a fixed payment. Under this type of arrangement, the lawyer effectively becomes the client and would therefore devote optimal effort to the case (i.e., the moral hazard problem would be solved), while at the same time, the plaintiff would be compensated by the up-front fee, which would presumably reflect the expected value of the lawsuit as assessed by the lawyer in an initial consultation. Both parties would therefore be happy and the efficient outcome (in terms of effort at least) would be achieved.

The corresponding arrangement in the agricultural setting would be for the landowner to sell the land to the farmer, or, what would be more likely, to rent it out to the farmer for the duration of the growing season. Then the farmer would be in the same position as the lawyer in the sense that he would retain the entire harvest and hence would choose the efficient level of effort. The two contracts—sale of the lawsuit and rental of the land—are therefore equivalent from an economic perspective (which shows that the idea of selling lawsuits is not an outlandish scheme after all).

Having established the efficiency of such an arrangement with regard to lawyer/farmer effort, we next consider how it would fare with regard to risk-sharing, or the allocation of uncertainty associated with the random factors affecting output. Note first that sale or rental contracts, as just described, assign all of the risk to the agent—the lawyer or the farmer. In the lawsuit context, one supposes that this is probably optimal because, as between the lawyer and the client, the lawyer will nearly always be the better risk-bearer.[2] This is true because lawyers can diversify the risk across their entire caseload, something that infrequent plaintiffs cannot do. Risk-sharing and moral hazard considerations therefore both seem to work in the direction of allowing plaintiffs to sell their suits to lawyers.

The conclusion is probably different in the agricultural context because there is no reason to believe that the farmer is the better risk-bearer. Indeed, it is often assumed that landowners are risk-neutral while farmers are risk-averse. (Landowners, for example, can diversify their holdings geographically, which can mitigate random output fluctuations, whereas farmers cannot.) In this case, optimal risk-sharing would seem to call for all or most of the risk to be shifted to the landowner in the form of a fixed (hourly) wage contract. Such a contract, however, would provide no incentive for farmers to work hard. Thus, in the agricultural setting it is often argued that a share contract strikes an optimal balance between risk-sharing and incentives.

Consider finally the limited-wealth argument, which asserts that contingent fee contracts give low-income plaintiffs access to the legal system. This factor also seems to work in the direction of allowing the sale of lawsuits because plaintiffs would receive the full expected value of their lawsuits up-front. Such an arrangement would have the further social benefit of promoting optimal deterrence because injurers would not expect to be able to avoid responsibility for the harms they caused merely because their victims sometimes lack the resources necessary to pursue their claims.

The opposite conclusion would again seem to be true in the agricultural setting. Generally, one supposes that it is tenant-farmers who lack the resources needed to buy or rent land up-front, and so a rental contract would not be a good arrangement for addressing the liquidity problem. In contrast, a sharecropping contract allows wealth-constrained farmers to effectively "borrow" the land during the growing season, with the harvest serving as collateral.

The preceding arguments have provided an economic rationale for the prevalence of share contracts in agriculture as a means of balancing incentives (moral hazard) against risk-sharing and wealth-constraints. In the lawyer-client context, however, all three factors seem to work in the direction of allowing plaintiffs to sell their lawsuits. In view of this conclusion, the skepticism with which such proposals have historically been viewed by the legal community presents something of a puzzle. In an effort to unravel it, we next turn to the consideration of some factors that are unique to the legal context; namely, potential conflicts of interest between lawyers and clients during the litigation process. We particularly focus on conflicts that might arise regarding the plaintiff's filing decision, and the decision of whether to settle the case or take it to trial. In the absence of any conflict of interest, these decisions should be made based on a comparison of the full expected value of the case to the cost of filing suit, and to the defendant's settlement offer, respectively. Realistically, however, both decisions will also depend on the contractual arrangement between the plaintiff and his or her lawyer, and on the allocation of decision-making authority between the two parties.

Consider first the settlement-trial decision, which we discussed in a general sense in Chapter 4. Conflicts of interest aside, settlement will occur if the defendant's maximum offer is at least as large as the plaintiff's expected value of taking the case to trial. Suppose, for example, a case has an expected recovery at trial of $75,000 but would entail litigation (trial) costs of $20,000. The case therefore has an expected value at trial of $55,000, and so any offer by the defendant in excess of that amount should result in a settlement, and this is what would happen if the interests of the plaintiff and lawyer were perfectly aligned.

The situation may be different, however, under a contingency arrangement that promises the lawyer one-third of any recovery. Assume in this case that the lawyer would bear the full trial costs of $20,000.[3] The lawyer's expected return from going to trial is therefore $5,000 (=$75,000/3–$20,000), while the plaintiff's expected return is $50,000 (=(2/3)($75,000)). Given these returns, consider the incentives of the parties to accept a settlement offer, assuming that settling is costless for both parties and that the contingency rate is the same (that is, the lawyer gets one-third and the plaintiff two-thirds from any accepted settlement offer). Note that the lawyer would like to accept any settlement offer greater than $15,000, since his return from settling would be $5,000 (or more), while the plaintiff would like to accept any offer greater than $75,000, since her share would be

$50,000 (or more). In comparison, we have seen that if there were no conflict, the case would settle for any amount above $55,000. Thus, the lawyer will want to settle too often, and the plaintiff will want to go to trial too often. The actual resolution of this conflict will therefore depend on which party ultimately controls the decision. In theory, the law vests control with the plaintiff, but in practice the lawyer will often exercise considerable influence.

Note that the source of the divergence in interests between the two parties in this example again stems from the fact that the lawyer receives only a third of the proceeds from a trial while incurring the full costs. The conflict would therefore not arise under an arrangement that allowed the lawyer to buy the case up-front because the lawyer would in essence become the plaintiff in all future proceedings. In view of this conclusion, concerns about conflicts of interest in the settlement-trial decision would seem to provide further support for the idea of allowing the sale of lawsuits.

Consider next the plaintiff's filing decision. This raises the oft-stated concern that contingent fees may encourage the filing of frivolous lawsuits, which are defined to be suits with little or no legal merit (or, more precisely, with a negative expected value at trial). Historically, this concern is embodied in the common law doctrines of *champerty* and *maintenance*, which have traditionally prohibited third parties from acquiring a financial stake in a lawsuit in return for supporting or otherwise promoting the furtherance of that suit. On first glance, this criticism of contingent fees seems well-founded in the sense that plaintiffs appear to have nothing to lose by filing a lawsuit under such an arrangement. The reason is that, if the suit turns out to produce a positive recovery, the plaintiff retains two-thirds of it, whereas if it results in no recovery, the plaintiff owes nothing. Thus, because the plaintiff incurs no up-front costs from filing the suit and can only reap a positive gain, she has no reason not to proceed with it, regardless of its merits.

This argument, however, ignores the screening function of lawyers at the filing stage. Specifically, lawyers will only accept cases that promise them a profit, and so they will presumably refuse cases with little or no chance of producing a positive recovery. Indeed, since lawyers only receive a third of any recovery under standard contingency contracts but bear all of the costs, they may actually turn down some cases that are in fact meritorious.

To illustrate this last point, consider a case with a gross value at trial of $30,000 and total trial costs of $20,000, all of which will be incurred by the lawyer. From a social perspective, the case therefore has a positive net value of $10,000 and thus has legal merit. However, the expected return for the lawyer under a one-third contingency rate contract is –$10,000 (=$30,000/3–$20,000), so he would not accept the case. This logic suggests that contingent fees not only will not encourage excessive litigation, they may inhibit the filing of some meritorious suits. Notice again that this conclusion is a consequence of the fact that the contingency rate is less than the lawyer's share of total trial costs. In contrast, a rule that allows plaintiffs to sell their lawsuits to lawyers up-front will not distort the filing decision at all because the lawyer will only buy the case if it has merit (i.e., a positive expected value), and from that point forward he internalizes the full costs and benefits.

The preceding arguments regarding potential conflicts of interest between plaintiffs and lawyers in the pre-trial period have further reinforced the economic case for allowing plaintiffs to sell their lawsuits. This conclusion only makes it all the more puzzling that such arrangements remain illegal or at least unethical in most countries. In fact, our analysis suggests that we should rephrase the question: why are lawyers allowed to have a *partial* stake in a case (at least in the United States) but not to buy it outright? I offer two possible answers.

The first is based on the existence of asymmetric information between plaintiffs and lawyers regarding the merits of a case. Although lawyers have considerably more expertise than clients regarding the legal aspects of a case, clients may have private information about the facts, which are equally important in achieving a favorable result at trial. (For example, in a tort case, the plaintiff/victim *knows* whether she was contributorily negligent.) At the filing stage, the prospect that plaintiffs will be able to sell their suits in return for a guaranteed up-front payment may disproportionately encourage those plaintiffs who know they have weak cases to seek to file suit in hopes of reaping a windfall while incurring no risk. If lawyers lack sufficient information at this early stage to be able to fully evaluate the actual prospects of a case, the screening function will operate imperfectly. The result is a potential adverse selection problem that benefits plaintiffs with weak cases at the expense of those with strong cases. (Specifically, the "price" for suits will reflect the average quality of suits as perceived at the filing date, which will allow some frivolous suits to go forward.) In contrast, a rule requiring plaintiffs to retain a partial stake in the eventual outcome of their cases may discourage the weakest plaintiffs from filing suit because their payoffs will depend on the actual strengths of their cases.

Another argument against the outright sale of lawsuits is that such a contract would presumably discourage plaintiffs from fully participating in the lawsuit up to its conclusion. Again, because of plaintiffs' intimate knowledge of the facts of their cases, it is usually essential for the success of the suit that they be ready and willing to supply inputs (such as testimony) throughout the litigation process. Up-front sale removes any incentive for plaintiffs to provide these inputs. In other words, it creates a moral hazard problem for plaintiffs, which is the counterpart of the moral hazard problem for lawyers under a fixed fee arrangement. In the presence of this "double moral hazard problem" (which is a version of the bilateral care problem we examined in Chapter 5), a partial contingency rate ensures that both parties retain some stake in the final outcome of the case and therefore have an incentive to participate until it is resolved. Although neither party will invest the fully efficient level of effort, it is almost certainly in their joint interests for both to participate at some level throughout the litigation process, and a contingency (share) arrangement may be the best practical means of promoting that outcome. Finally, incentive issues aside, it is almost certainly a better tactic, especially in a jury trial, for the true plaintiff to remain the "face" of the case rather than for it simply to be seen as an investment opportunity for the lawyer.

Notes

1. A contingent contract need not, however, compute the lawyer's compensation as a percentage of the recovery. It could alternatively specify a fixed payment, or an hourly fee, conditional on winning.
2. A case where the client may be the better risk bearer is a large company that is sued frequently because it can pass the costs on to its customers. Such companies, however, will usually have in-house lawyers.
3. For simplicity, we ignore any time costs the plaintiff would incur by going to trial. The existence of such cost, however, would not change our qualitative conclusions.

Bibliographic essay

This essay provides a guide to the literature for each chapter so as to allow interested readers to pursue specific topics in more detail. The bibliography that follows provides the details for the cited references.

Chapter 1

Most scholars date the origin of law and economics as a coherent sub-field of both economics and law to the paper on social cost by Coase (1960), although an economic perspective on law predates that, as exemplified by the classic article by Holmes (1897). The seminal work that first demonstrated the breadth of the field was the treatise by Posner, first published in 1973 and now in its ninth edition (Posner, 2014). Several survey and textbook treatments are now also available, including Cooter and Ulen (1988), Friedman (2000), Mercuro and Medema (2006), and Miceli (2017).

Chapter 2

The key reference here is of course Coase (1960). A discussion of the standard economic approach to externalities (referred to as the Pigovian approach), to which Coase's paper was a response, can be found in any introductory microeconomics textbook. Demsetz (1967) examined the emergence of property rights as a means of internalizing externalities, and his related paper (Demsetz, 1972) discussed the question of when the law matters for efficiency in light of the Coase Theorem.

Chapter 3

Second only in importance to Coase (1960) in the law and economics literature is the paper by Calabresi and Melamed (1972), which introduced the distinction between property rules and liability rule as alternative ways of protecting entitlements. Kaplow and Shavell (1996) also examine the choice between these rules. Coleman (1988, Chapter 2) discusses the General

Transaction Structure as the logical culmination of the insights arising from the Coase and Calabresi and Melamed papers.

Chapter 4

The key references on the general question of whether the law evolves toward efficiency are Rubin (1977) and Priest (1977). More recent treatments are by Gennaioli and Schleifer (2007) and Miceli (2009, 2010). On selective litigation, see Priest and Klein (1984) and Shavell (1996). The mutual optimism model of litigation and settlement was first developed by Landes (1971) and Gould (1973), and is surveyed in Cooter and Rubinfeld (1989). The asymmetric information model was developed by Bebchuk (1984). Hanssen (2004) discusses the optimal degree of judicial independence.

Chapter 5

Posner (1972) first proposed an economic theory of negligence based on the Hand formula for determining due care. Brown (1973) developed the first formal economic analysis of accidents, and of the efficiency of various rules for assigning liability, in the context of non-cooperative game theory. Cooter (1985) showed the versatility of Brown's model, which he called the "model of precaution," by also applying it to problems in contract and property law. Thorough treatments of the economics of tort law based on Brown's model are Shavell (1987) and Landes and Posner (1987).

Chapter 6

The idea of sequential care accidents and the efficiency of various liability rules in that context were first formally studied by Wittman (1981) and Shavell (1983). Grady (1988) provides a non-technical discussion of how the law has dealt with the issue, with particular focus on the problem of strategic negligence.

Chapter 7

The distinction between tort and criminal law (i.e., private versus public enforcement) was first studied by Becker and Stigler (1974) and Landes and Posner (1975). See Friedman (2000, Chapter 18) for an overview. Calabresi and Melamed (1972) and Klevorick (1985) discuss the need for criminal law as a means of enforcing the General Transaction Structure. Regarding procedural rules in criminal law, see Miceli (1990) on the standard of proof for conviction; Seidmann and Stein (2000) on the rule against self-incrimination; and Posner (2003, Chapter 29) on illegal search and seizure.

Chapter 8

The modern economic theory of crime began with Becker's (1968) seminal paper. A recent survey describing the state of the art in this area is provided by Polinsky and Shavell (2007). An alternative perspective that reflects many of the points raised in this chapter is offered by Adelstein (2017). Miceli (2007) examines the interplay between the legislative and judicial roles in sentencing as enforced by the Sentencing Guidelines.

Chapter 9

Stigler (1970) suggested that first-time offenders sometimes commit crimes accidentally, and that this fact may explain escalating penalties. Agan and Starr (2017) provide recent evidence on the detrimental labor market effects of having even a minor criminal record, and Miceli and Bucci (2005) derive the link between the stigma from criminal conviction and escalating penalties. Miceli (2013) surveys the literature on escalating penalty schemes.

Chapter 10

The economic analysis of plea bargaining began with Landes (1971). Also see Grossman and Katz (1983) on the screening function of plea bargaining, and Reinganum (1988) for a formal game-theoretic treatment. Adelstein and Miceli (2001) offer a comparative perspective on the practice.

Chapter 11

Ginsburg and Shechtman (1993), Posner (1993), and Shavell (1993) analyze various aspects of blackmail from an economic point of view. Miceli (2011a) first proposed the perspective taken in this chapter.

Chapter 12

Levmore (1995a,b) and Levinson (2003) discuss group responsibility, primarily from a legal perspective, and offer numerous examples, both modern and historical. Posner (1983) discusses primitive law enforcement generally, while Parisi and Dari-Mattiacci (2004) and Miceli and Segerson (2007) examine group responsibility from an economic point of view.

Chapter 13

Posner (1977), Aivazian, Trebilcock, and Penny (1984), and Miceli (2002) analyze the enforcement of contract modifications. Kronman (1978) examines the mistake doctrine, specifically as it relates to the deliberate versus casual

Chapter 14

Shavell (1980) developed the first formal economic model of breach of contract remedies. Also see Cooter (1985), who demonstrates the applicability of the bilateral care accident model (the model of precaution) to the problem of contract breach and reliance. Bebchuk and Shavell (1991) study the economic aspects of the *Hadley v. Baxendale* rule. Polinsky (1983) examines the risk-sharing properties of breach remedies. Posner and Rosenfield (1977), Goldberg (1988), and White (1988) analyze the impossibility doctrine, and Ulen (1984) and Friedmann (1989) examine specific performance. Rogerson (1984) uses a formal model to study the efficiency of various breach remedies, including specific performance.

Chapter 15

Baird and Jackson (1984) study the general problem of protecting property rights in land under uncertainty, and Miceli and Sirmans (1995a) examine the economics of title insurance. Janczyk (1977) and Miceli, Munneke, Sirmans, and Turnbull (2002) empirically compare the registration and recording systems using their co-existence in Cook County, Illinois throughout the twentieth century as a natural experiment. Miceli and Sirmans (1995b), Ellickson (1986), Epstein (1986), and Merrill (1985) examine adverse possession from an economic perspective, and Miceli and Sirmans (1999) study the mistaken improver problem.

Chapter 16

Williamson (1975), Klein, Crawford, and Alchian (1978), Goldberg (1985), and Hart and Moore (1988) provide general discussions of the holdup problem along with possible remedies. Cohen (1991), Strange (1995), and Miceli and Segerson (2012a) likewise analyze the holdout problem. Miceli and Segerson (2012b) explicitly examine the commonalities between the two problems and their remedies.

Chapter 17

The legal and economic literature on eminent domain is extensive. See Esptein (1985), Fischel (1995), and Miceli (2012) for book-length treatments; and Michelman (1967) for a classic study with substantial economic relevance. The seminal economic analysis of takings, emphasizing its implications for land use incentives, is Blume, Rubinfeld, and Shapiro (1984). Important follow-up papers include Fischel and Shapiro (1989), Hermalin (1995), Nosal (2001), and Miceli (2008). Merrill (1986) and Miceli (2011b) specifically focus on the issue of public use.

Chapter 18

See Fischel (1995) and Miceli and Segerson (1996) for book-length treatments of the law and economics of regulatory takings. Miceli and Segerson (1994) first developed the "threshold approach" to the compensation question.

Chapter 19

For surveys of the economics of intellectual property, see Landes and Posner (2003), and Blair and Cotter (2005). Gordon (1982), Adelstein and Peretz (1985), Depoorter and Parisi (2002), and Miceli and Adelstein (2006) specifically examine the economics of the fair use doctrine. The model in the latter paper forms the basis for the approach taken in this chapter.

Chapter 20

There is a large literature on the economics of contingency fees. See, for example, Danzon (1983), Dana and Spier (1993), Gravelle and Waterson (1993), Rubinfeld and Scotchmer (1993), Miceli (1994), and Hay (1996). Stiglitz (1974) provides the classic analysis of agricultural contracts based on the trade-off between risk sharing and incentives, and Laffont and Martimort (2002) provide a survey of the principal-agent literature. Cooter (1989) first discussed the possibility of selling "unmatured" tort claims to third parties, and examined how the emergence of such a market would affect settlement and deterrence. Miller (1987) discusses agency (moral hazard) problems in the settlement of litigation. Bebchuk (1984) first examined the impact of asymmetric information in the litigation process.

References

Adelstein, Richard (1981) "Institutional Function and Evolution in the Criminal Process," *Northwestern University Law Review*, 76: 1–99.
Adelstein, Richard (1998) "Plea Bargaining: A Comparative Approach," in P. Newman, ed., *The New Palgrave Dictionary of Law and Economics*, New York: Stockton Press.
Adelstein, Richard (2017) *The Exchange Order: Property and Liability as an Exchange System*, New York: Oxford University Press.
Adelstein, Richard and Thomas J. Miceli (2001) "Toward a Comparative Economics of Plea Bargaining," *European Journal of Law and Economics*, 11: 47–67.
Adelstein, Richard and Steven Peretz (1985) "The Competition of Technologies in Markets for Ideas: Copyright and Fair Use in Evolutionary Perspective," *International Review of Law and Economics*, 5: 209–238.
Agan, Amanda and Sonia Starr (2017) "The Effect of Criminal Records on Access to Employment," *American Economic Review*, 107: 560–564.
Aivazian, Varouj, Michael Trebilcock, and Michael Penny (1984) "The Law of Contract Modifications: The Uncertain Quest for a Benchmark of Enforceability," *Osgoode Hall Law Journal*, 22: 173–212.
Akerlof, George (1970) "The Market for 'Lemons': Quality Uncertainty and the Market Mechanism," *Quarterly Journal of Economics*, 84: 488–500.
Baird, Douglas and Thomas Jackson (1984) "Information, Uncertainty, and the Transfer of Property," *Journal of Legal Studies*, 13: 299–320.
Bebchuk, Lucian (1984) "Litigation and Settlement Under Imperfect Information," *RAND Journal of Economics*, 15: 404–415.
Bebchuk, Lucian and Steven Shavell (1991) "Information and the Scope of Liability for Breach of Contract: The Rule of *Hadley v. Baxendale*," *Journal of Law, Economics, and Organization*, 7: 284–312.
Becker, Gary (1968) "Crime and Punishment: An Economic Approach," *Journal of Political Economy*, 76: 169–217.
Becker, Gary and George Stigler (1974) "Law Enforcement, Malfeasance, and Compensation of Enforcers," *Journal of Legal Studies*, 3: 1–13.
Blackstone, William (1766) *Commentaries on the Law of England*, Oxford: Clarendon Press.
Blair, Roger and Thomas Cotter (2005) *Intellectual Property*, Cambridge: Cambridge University Press.
Blume, Lawrence, Daniel Rubinfeld, and Perry Shapiro (1984) "The Taking of Land: When Should Compensation Be Paid?" *Quarterly Journal of Economics*, 99: 71–92.

References

Brown, John (1973) "Toward an Economic Theory of Liability," *Journal of Legal Studies*, 2: 323–349.

Buell, Lawrence (1986) *New England Literary Culture*, Cambridge: Cambridge University Press.

Calabresi, Guido and A. Douglas Melamed (1972) "Property Rules, Liability Rules, and Inalienability: One View of the Cathedral," *Harvard Law Review*, 85: 1089–1128.

Coase, Ronald (1960) "The Problem of Social Cost," *Journal of Law and Economics*, 3: 1–44.

Cohen, Lloyd (1991) "Holdouts and Free Riders," *Journal of Legal Studies*, 20: 351–362.

Coleman, Jules (1988) *Markets, Morals, and the Law*, Cambridge: Cambridge University Press.

Cooter, Robert (1985) "Unity in Tort, Contract, and Property: The Model of Precaution," *California Law Review*, 73: 1–51.

Cooter, Robert (1989) "Towards a Market in Unmatured Tort Claims," *Virginia Law Review*, 75: 383–411.

Cooter, Robert and Daniel Rubinfeld (1989) "An Economic Analysis of Legal Disputes and Their Resolution," *Journal of Economic Literature*, 27: 1067–1097.

Cooter, Robert and Thomas Ulen (1988) *Law and Economics*, Glenview, IL: Scott Foresman & Co.

Dana, David and Kathryn Spier (1993) "Expertise and Contingent Fees: The Role of Asymmetric Information in Attorney Compensation," *Journal of Law, Economics, and Organization*, 9: 349–367.

Danzon, Patricia (1983) "Contingent Fees for Personal Injury Litigation," *Bell Journal of Economics*, 14: 213–224.

Dawson, Robert (1969) *Sentencing: The Decision as to Type, Length, and Conditions of Sentence*, Boston: Little Brown.

Demsetz, Harold (1967) "Toward a Theory of Property Rights," *American Economic Review*, 57: 347–359.

Demsetz, Harold (1972) "When Does the Rule of Liability Matter?" *Journal of Legal Studies*, 1: 13–28.

Depoorter, Ben and Francesco Parisi (2002) "Fair Use and Copyright Protection: A Price Theory Explanation," *International Review of Law and Economics*, 21: 453–473.

De Soto, Hernando (2000) *The Mystery of Capital*, New York: Basic Books.

Doyle, Arthur Conan (1930) *The Complete Sherlock Holmes*, in 2 Volumes, New York: Doubleday.

Easterbrook, Frank (1983) "Criminal Procedure as a Market System," *Journal of Legal Studies*, 12: 289–332.

Ellickson, Robert (1986) "Adverse Possession and Perpetuities Law," *Washington University Law Quarterly*, 64: 723–737.

Epstein, Richard (1985) *Takings: Private Property and the Power of Eminent Domain*, Cambridge, MA: Harvard University Press.

Epstein, Richard (1986) "Past and Future: The Temporal Dimension in the Law of Property," *Washington University Law Quarterly*, 64: 667–722.

Feinberg, Joel (1991) "Collective Responsibility," in L. May and S. Hoffman, eds., *Collective Responsibility: Five Decades of Debate in Theoretical and Applied Ethics*, Savage, MD: Rowan and Littlefield.

Fischel, William (1995) *Regulatory Takings: Law, Economics, and Politics*, Cambridge, MA: Harvard University Press.

Fischel, William and Perry Shapiro (1989) "A Constitutional Choice Model of Compensation for Takings," *International Review of Law and Economics*, 9: 115–128.

Fitzgerald, F. Scott (1925) *The Great Gatsby*, New York: Scribner.

Friedman, David (2000) *Law's Order: What Economics Has to Do with the Law and Why It Matters*, Princeton, NJ: Princeton University Press.

Friedmann, Daniel (1989) "The Efficient Breach Fallacy," *Journal of Legal Studies*, 18: 1–24.

Gennaioli, Nicola and Andrei Shleifer (2007) "The Evolution of the Common Law," *Journal of Political Economy*, 115: 43–68.

Ginsburg, Douglas and Paul Shechtman (1993) "Blackmail: An Economic Analysis of the Law," *University of Pennsylvania Law Review*, 141: 1849–1976.

Goldberg, Victor (1985) "Relational Exchange, Contract Law, and the *Boomer* Problem," *Journal of Institutional and Theoretical Economics*, 141: 570–575.

Goldberg, Victor (1988) "Impossibility and Related Excuses," *Journal of Institutional and Theoretical Economics*, 144: 100–116.

Gordon, Wendy (1982) "Fair Use as Market Failure: A Structural and Economic Analysis of the *Betamax* Case and Its Predecessors," *Columbia Law Review*, 82: 1600–1657.

Gould, John (1973) "The Economics of Legal Conflicts," *Journal of Legal Studies*, 2: 279–300.

Grady, Mark (1984) "Proximate Cause and the Law of Negligence," *Iowa Law Review*, 69: 363–449.

Grady, Mark (1988) "Common Law Control of Strategic Behavior: Railroad Sparks and the Farmer," *Journal of Legal Studies*, 17: 15–42.

Gravelle, Hugh and Micheal Waterson (1993) "No Win, No Fee: Some Economics of Contingent Legal Fees," *Economic Journal*, 103: 1205–1220.

Grossman, Gene and Michael Katz (1983) "Plea Bargaining and Social Welfare," *American Economic Review*, 73: 749–757.

Hanssen, F. Andrew (2004) "Is There a Politically Optimal Level of Judicial Independence?" *American Economic Review*, 94: 712–729.

Hart, H. L. A. (1982) *Punishment and Responsibility: Essays in the Philosophy and Law*, Oxford: Oxford University Press.

Hart, Oliver and John Moore (1988) "Incomplete Contracts and Renegotiation," *Econometrica*, 56: 755–785.

Hay, Bruce (1996) "Contingent Fees and Agency Costs," *Journal of Legal Studies*, 25: 503–533.

Helmholz, R. H. (1983) "Adverse Possession and Subjective Intent," *Washington University Law Quarterly*, 61: 331–358.

Hemingway, Ernest (1929) *A Farewell to Arms*, New York: Scribner.

Hermalin, Benjamin (1995) "An Economic Analysis of Takings," *Journal of Law, Economics, and Organization*, 11: 64–86.

Hirshleifer, Jack (1971) "The Private and Social Value of Information and the Reward to Inventive Activity," *American Economic Review*, 61: 561–574.

Holmes, Oliver Wendell (1881 [1963]) *The Common Law*, Boston: Little Brown.

Holmes, Oliver Wendell (1897) "The Path of the Law," *Harvard Law Review*, 10: 457–478.

Janczyk, Joseph (1977) "An Economic Analysis of Land Title Systems for Transferring Real Property," *Journal of Legal Studies*, 6: 213–233.

Johnson, Dominic (2016) *God Is Watching You: How the Fear of God Makes Us Human*, New York: Oxford University Press.

Kaplow, Louis and Steven Shavell (1996) "Property Rules versus Liability Rules," *Harvard Law Review*, 109: 713–790.

Keeton, W. Page, Dan Dobbs, Robert Keeton, and David Owen (1984) *Prosser and Keeton on Torts*, 5th edn., St. Paul, MN: West Publishing Co.

Klein, Benjamin, Robert Crawford, and Armen Alchian (1978) "Vertical Integration, Appropriable Rents, and the Competitive Contracting Process," *Journal of Law and Economics*, 21: 297–326.

Klevorick, Alvin (1985) "On the Economic Theory of Crime," in J. Pennock and J. Chapman, eds., *NOMOS XXVII: Criminal Justice*, New York: New York University Press.

Kronman, Anthony (1978) "Mistake, Disclosure, Information, and the Law of Contracts," *Journal of Legal Studies*, 7: 1–34.

Laffont, Jean-Jacques and David Martimort (2002) *The Theory of Incentives: The Principal-Agent Model*, Princeton, NJ: Princeton University Press.

Landes, William (1971) "An Economic Analysis of the Courts," *Journal of Law and Economics*, 14: 61–107.

Landes, William and Richard Posner (1975) "The Private Enforcement of Law," *Journal of Legal Studies*, 4: 1–46.

Landes, William and Richard Posner (1987) *The Economic Structure of Tort Law*, Cambridge, MA: Harvard University Press.

Landes, William and Richard Posner (2003) *The Economic Structure of Intellectual Property Law*, Cambridge, MA: Belknap Press.

Levinson, Daryl (2003) "Collective Sanctions," *Stanford University Law Review*, 56: 345–428.

Levmore, Saul (1995a) "Gomorrah to *Ybarra* and More: Overextraction and the Puzzle of Immoderate Group Liability," *Virginia Law Review*, 81: 1561–1604.

Levmore, Saul (1995b) "Rethinking Group Responsibility and Strategic Threats in Biblical Texts and Modern Law," *Chicago-Kent Law Review*, 71: 85–121.

Mercuro, Nicholas and Steven Medema (2006) *Economics and the Law: From Posner to Postmodernism and Beyond*, 2nd edn., Princeton, NJ: Princeton University Press.

Merrill, Thomas (1985) "Property Rules, Liability Rules, and Adverse Possession," *Northwestern University Law Review*, 79: 1122–1154.

Merrill, Thomas (1986) "The Economics of Public Use," *Cornell Law Review*, 72: 61–116.

Miceli, Thomas (1990) "Optimal Prosecution of Defendants Whose Guilt Is Uncertain," *Journal of Law, Economics, and Organization*, 6: 189–201.

Miceli, Thomas (1994) "Do Contingent Fees Promote Excessive Litigation?" *Journal of Legal Studies*, 23: 211–224.

Miceli, Thomas (2002) "'Over a Barrel': Contract Modification, Reliance, and Bankruptcy," *International Review of Law and Economics*, 22: 41–51.

Miceli, Thomas (2007) "Criminal Sentencing Guidelines and Judicial Discretion," *Contemporary Economic Policy*, 26: 207–215.

Miceli, Thomas (2008) "Public Goods, Taxes, and Takings," *International Review of Law and Economics*, 28: 287–293.

Miceli, Thomas (2009) "Legal Change: Selective Litigation, Judicial Bias, and Precedent," *Journal of Legal Studies*, 38: 157–168.

Miceli, Thomas (2010) "Legal Change and the Social Value of Lawsuits," *International Review of Law and Economics*, 30: 203–208.

Miceli, Thomas (2011a) "The Real Puzzle of Blackmail: An Informational Approach," *Information Economics and Policy*, 23: 182–188.

Miceli, Thomas (2011b) "Holdouts, Free Riders, and Public Use: A Tale of Two Externalities," *Public Choice*, 148: 105–117.

Miceli, Thomas (2012) *The Economic Theory of Eminent Domain: Private Property, Public Use*, New York: Cambridge University Press.

Miceli, Thomas (2013) "Escalating Penalties for Repeat Offenders: Why Are They so Hard to Explain?" *Journal of Institutional and Theoretical Economics*, 169: 587–604.

Miceli, Thomas (2017) *The Economic Approach to Law*, 3rd edn., Stanford, CA: Stanford University Press.

Miceli, Thomas and Richard Adelstein (2006) "An Economic Model of Fair Use," *Information Economics and Policy*, 18: 359–373.

Miceli, Thomas and Catherine Bucci (2005) "A Simple Theory of Increasing Penalties for Repeat Offenders," *Review of Law and Economics*, 1: 71–80.

Miceli, Thomas, Henry Munneke, and C.F. Sirmans, and Geoffrey Turnbull (2002) "Title Systems and Land Values," *Journal of Law and Economics*, 45: 565–582.

Miceli, Thomas and Kathleen Segerson (1994) "Regulatory Takings: When Should Compensation Be Paid?" *Journal of Legal Studies*, 23: 749–776.

Miceli, Thomas and Kathleen Segerson (1996) *Compensation for Regulatory Takings: An Economic Analysis with Applications*, Greenwich, CT: JAI Press.

Miceli, Thomas and Kathleen Segerson (2007) "Punishing the Innocent Along with the Guilty: The Economics of Individual versus Group Punishment," *Journal of Legal Studies*, 36: 81–106.

Miceli, Thomas and Kathleen Segerson (2012a) "Land Assembly and the Holdout Problem Under Sequential Bargaining," *American Law and Economics Review*, 14: 372–390.

Miceli, Thomas and Kathleen Segerson (2012b) "Holdups and Holdouts: What Do They Have in Common?" *Economics Letters*, 117: 330–333.

Miceli, Thomas and C.F. Sirmans (1995a) "The Economics of Land Transfer and Title Insurance," *Journal of Real Estate Finance and Economics*, 10: 81–88.

Miceli, Thomas and C.F. Sirmans (1995b) "An Economic Theory of Adverse Possession," *International Review of Law and Economics*, 15: 161–173.

Miceli, Thomas and C.F. Sirmans (1999) "The Mistaken Improver Problem," *Journal of Urban Economics*, 45: 143–155.

Michelman, Frank (1967) "Property, Utility, and Fairness: Comments on the Ethical Foundations of 'Just Compensation' Law," *Harvard Law Review*, 80: 1165–1258.

Miller, Geoffrey (1987) "Some Agency Problems in Settlement," *Journal of Legal Studies*, 16: 189–215.

Nosal, Ed. (2001) "The Taking of Land: Market Value Compensation Should Be Paid," *Journal of Public Economics*, 82: 431–443.

Parisi, Francesco and Giuseppe Dari-Mattiacci (2004) "The Rise and Fall of Communal Liability in Ancient Law," *International Review of Law and Economics*, 24: 489–505.

Polinsky, A. Mitchell (1983) "Risk Sharing Through Breach of Contract Remedies," *Journal of Legal Studies*, 12: 427–444.

Polinsky, A. Mitchell and Y.K. Che (1991) "Decoupling Liability: Optimal Incentives for Care and Litigation," *RAND Journal of Economics*, 22: 562–570.

Polinsky, A. Mitchell and Steven Shavell (2007) "The Theory of Public Law Enforcement," in A.M. Polinsky and S. Shavell, eds., *Handbook of Law and Economics*, Vol. I, Amsterdam: Elsevier, North-Holland.

Posner, Richard (1972) "A Theory of Negligence," *Journal of Legal Studies*, 1: 29–96.

Posner, Richard (1977) "Gratuitous Promises in the Law," *Journal of Legal Studies*, 6: 411–426.

Posner, Richard (1983) *The Economics of Justice*, Cambridge, MA: Harvard University Press.

Posner, Richard (1993) "Blackmail, Privacy, and Freedom of Contract," *University of Pennsylvania Law Review*, 141: 1817–1847.

Posner, Richard (1995) *Overcoming Law*, Cambridge, MA: Harvard University Press.

Posner, Richard (2003) *Economic Analysis of Law*, 6th edn., New York: Aspen Law and Business.

Posner, Richard (2014) *Economic Analysis of Law*, 9th edn., New York: Wolters Kluwer Law & Business.

Posner, Richard and Andrew Rosenfield (1977) "Impossibility and Related Doctrines in Contract Law: An Economic Analysis," *Journal of Legal Studies*, 6: 83–118.

Priest, George (1977) "The Common Law Process and the Selection of Efficient Rules," *Journal of Legal Studies*, 6: 65–82.

Priest, George and Benjamin Klein (1984) "The Selection of Disputes for Litigation," *Journal of Legal Studies*, 13: 1–55.

Rawls, John (1971) *A Theory of Justice*, Cambridge, MA: Harvard University Press.

Reinganum, Jennifer (1988) "Plea Bargaining and Prosecutorial Discretion," *American Economic Review*, 78: 713–728.

Rogerson, William (1984) "Efficient Reliance and Damage Measures for Breach of Contract," *RAND Journal of Economics*, 15: 39–53.

Rubenfeld, Jed (1993) "Usings," *Yale Law Journal*, 102: 1077–1163.

Rubin, Paul (1977) "Why Is the Common Law Efficient?" *Journal of Legal Studies*, 6: 51–63.

Rubinfeld, Daniel and Suzanne Scotchmer (1993) "Contingent Fees for Attorneys: An Economic Analysis," *RAND Journal of Economics*, 24: 343–356.

Schulhofer, Stephen (1988) "Criminal Justice Discretion as a Regulatory System," *Journal of Legal Studies*, 17: 43–82.

Seidmann, Daniel and Alex Stein (2000) "The Right to Silence Helps the Innocent: A Game-Theoretic Analysis of the Fifth Amendment Privilege," *Harvard Law Review*, 114: 430–510.

Shavell, Steven (1980) "Damage Measures for Breach of Contract," *Bell Journal of Economics*, 11: 466–490.

Shavell, Steven (1983) "Torts in Which Victim and Injurer Act Sequentially," *Journal of Law and Economics*, 26: 589–612.

Shavell, Steven (1987) *Economic Analysis of Accident Law*, Cambridge, MA: Harvard University Press.

References

Shavell, Steven (1993) "An Economic Analysis of Threats and Their Illegality: Blackmail, Extortion, and Robbery," *University of Pennsylvania Law Review*, 141: 1877–1903.

Shavell, Steven (1994) "Acquisition and Disclosure of Information Prior to Contracting," *RAND Journal of Economics*, 25: 20–36.

Shavell, Steven (1996) "Any Frequency of Plaintiff Victory Is Possible," *Journal of Legal Studies*, 25: 493–501.

Shepherd, Joanna (2007) "*Blakely's* Silver Lining: Sentencing Guidelines, Judicial Discretion, and Crime," *Hastings Law Journal*, 58: 533–589.

Smith, Adam (1759 [1976]) *A Theory of Moral Sentiments*, New York: Liberty Press.

Stigler, George (1970) "The Optimum Enforcement of Laws," *Journal of Political Economy*, 78: 526–536.

Stiglitz, Joseph (1974) "Incentives and Risk Sharing in Sharecropping," *Review of Economic Studies*, 79: 578–595.

Strange, William (1995) "Information, Holdouts, and Land Assembly," *Journal of Urban Economics*, 38: 317–332.

Ulen, Thomas (1984) "The Efficiency of Specific Performance: Toward a Unified Theory of Contract Remedies," *Michigan Law Review*, 83: 341–403.

Wade, Nicholas (2009) *The Faith Instinct: How Religion Evolved and Why It Endures*, New York: Penguin Press.

White, Michelle (1988) "Contract Breach and Contract Discharge Due to Impossibility: A Unified Theory," *Journal of Legal Studies*, 17: 353–376.

Williamson, Oliver (1975) *Markets and Hierarchies*, New York: Free Press.

Wittman, Donald (1981) "Optimal Pricing of Sequential Inputs: Last Clear Chance, Mitigation of Damages, and Related Doctrines in the Law," *Journal of Legal Studies*, 10: 65–91.

Index

A Farewell to Arms 83
A & M Records, Inc. v. Napster Inc. 153
Adelstein, Richard 56, 58, 70, 74
Adverse possession 113–115, 164
Adverse selection 76–77, 80, 94, 159
Akerlof, George 76, 78, 94
Alaska Packers' Assn. v. Domenico 92–93
Anderson v. Payne 42
Anti-commons problem 120
Appropriability problem 79–80, 148, 149
Asymmetric information, and blackmail 76–80; as an explanation of trials 22, 72, 165; and the holdout problem 120; and sale of lawsuits 159; and mistake doctrine 94–100
Authors' Guild v. Google 153

Beccaria, Cesare 54
Becker, Gary 54, 55, 57, 81
Bentham, Jeremy 54, 55
Berman v. Parker 128, 133
Bilateral care situations 9, 28–35; and contract breach 104–105, 164; and lawsuits 159–160; when parties act sequentially 36–44; in regulatory takings cases 142–147
Bilateral monopoly 16
Blackmail vii, 75–80, 94, 163
Blackstone, William 82
Boomer v. Atlantic Cement Co. 15–16, 18, 120–121, 125, 134–135
Bounty system 47–48
Brady v. United States 70–71
Brandeis, Louis 139, 144
Breach of contract 34–35, 135, 164; *also see* contract law
Butterfield v. Forrester 38–40

Calabresi, Guido 4, 13, 16, 19
Call option 124, 125
Champerty 158
City of Oakland v. Oakland Raiders 136
Civil War 84
Class action 47
Coase, Ronald 4, 9–12
Coase Theorem 6–12, 14, 25, 141, 161; and contract breach 108; and land title systems 112; and mistaken improvement 116
Coercion, in contract law 75
Coleridge, Samuel Taylor 82
Coming to the nuisance 19
Common law 135, 140, 145, 146, 158; economic logic of 3, 21–27
Comparative negligence 40, 42–43
Compensating precaution 37–43, 109
Competitive market, as basis for contract law 90
Consequential damages 105
Consideration 90–93; *see also* contract law
Constitution, U.S. 16, 135
Consumer Reports 76
Contingency fees 154, 158, 160, 165
Contract law vii, 3, 34–35, 75, 89–100; and breach remedies 101–109; and doctrine of mistake 93–100, 163; and duress 91–93; and contract modification 92–93; and impossibility doctrine 106–107, 164; and specific performance 107–109, 164
Contributory negligence 38–43
Copyright Act 152
Copyrights 79; and contributory infringement 152–153; and fair use 148–153
Cooter, Robert 33, 34–35

174 Index

Criminal law vii, 35, 54–62; and boundary with tort law 20, 28, 45–53, 162; and plea bargaining 69–74

Criminal punishment 1, 3, 45–53; and the General Transaction Structure 19–20, 48–49; and group punishment 81–88; as incapacitation 67; and the proportionality norm vii, 55–61, 70, 85; and repeat offenders vii, 63–68; and sentencing discretion 60–61, 163

Darwinian evolution 27
Davies v. Mann 39–40
Declaration of Independence 16
Demoralization costs 141–142
Demsetz, Harold 7
De Soto, Hernando 113
Diminution of value test 139, 140, 144
Discovery 22
Due care, *see* reasonable care standard
Duress, *see* coercion

Easterbrook, Frank 69, 74
Efficiency norm 2, 3; as applied to the common law 21–27; as compared to other norms 17
Eminent domain 35, 120, 124, 125, 127–136, 164–165; as a liability rule 132; and regulatory takings 35, 137–147, 165
Entitlement 13
EPA 7
Epstein, Richard 140, 145–147
Exclusionary rule 52–53
Expectation damages 103–106, 109
Externalities 6–12, 13, 28, 45, 54, 103, 128, 142–143, 161

Fairness 2; and Coase Theorem 11; and criminal punishment 55–62, 68, 70, 85; and tort rules 43
Fair use 35, 148–153; as a threshold test 150, 152, 165
Federal sentencing guidelines 60–61
Fischel, William 121, 141
Fitzgerald, F. Scott 37
Free rider problem 127–136
Frivolous suits 158

Game theory 36, 41
General deterrence 55

General Transaction Structure 4, 6, 17–20, 48–49, 161–162
Goebel v. Linn 92–93, 102–105, 119
Goldberg, Victor 121
Grady, Mark 41, 42
Grand Central Terminal 139
Great Chicago Fire 113
Great Gatsby, The 37

Hadley v. Baxendale 104–106, 164
Hamer v. Sidway 90–91
Hammurabi Code 56, 82
Hand, Judge Learned 29
Hand test 29–35, 162; as applied to unreasonable searches and seizures 52; in regulatory takings cases 144
Harm–benefit rule 140, 147
Hart, H.L.A. 56, 57
Hawaii Housing Authority v. Midkiff 136
Hawthorne, Nathaniel 82, 88
Hemingway, Ernest 83
Historic landmarks 137, 139
Holdout problem 119–126, 127–136, 164
Holdup problem 119–126, 127, 164
Holmes, Oliver Wendell 1, 34, 55, 56, 112, 138–139, 144, 145
Holmes, Sherlock 75, 80

Impossibility, *see* Contract law
Inalienability rule 16–17; and criminal law 20, 49
Information, value of 79–80, 96–100, 116, 164
Injunction 13–20, 121, 134; *see also* property rule
Intellectual property 35
Invisible-Hand Theorem 23, 27, 133; and contract law 90

Joint and several liability 84
Judgment-proof problem 48
Judicial discretion in sentencing 69–70
Just compensation 127, 132
Justice 2

Kaldor–Hicks efficiency, *see* wealth maximization
Kelo v. City of New London 26, 120, 124, 127–128, 132, 133, 134
Keystone Bituminous Coal Assn. v. DeBenedictus 145

Index

Laidlaw v. Organ 99–100
Land assembly 120, 127, 129, 131; *also see* holdout problem
Land title 110–118
Last clear chance 39–43
Law of Large Numbers 46
Lease 7
Least-cost avoider 23
Legal error 50, 67, 70–74, 109, 132; and group punishment 81–88; and land title 111, 114
Legal procedure viii, 45, 49–53, 59; *see also* plea bargaining
Legal system 4
Lemons problem 76, 94; *see also* adverse selection
Leroy Fibre Co. v. Chcago, Milwaukee & St. Paul Ry. 34
Liability rule 4, 125, 131–132; as compared to property rule 13–20, 48–49, 109, 121, 125, 134, 135, 161
Loretto v. Teleprompter 138
Lucas v. South Carolina Coastal Council 140, 142, 145

Madison, James 2
Maintenance 158
Marginal analysis 4; in tort law 29–33, 34
Marginal cost liability 43
Market exchange 89–91; *see also* contract law
Market failure 6, 66, 70, 76–77, 80, 94, 130, 149; *see also* externalities
Market value 112
Mathematical models 4
Melamed, A. Douglas 4, 13, 16, 19
Mens rea (criminal intent) 45, 64
Merrill, Thomas 129, 132
Michelman, Frank 141–142, 147
Miller v. Schoene 146
Minimum wage laws 17
Mistake, *see* contract law
Mistaken improver problem 115–118, 164
Model of precaution 34, 162
Monopoly 92, 93; and holdout problem 120, 131; copyrights and patents as 148
Moral hazard 32–33, 35, 109, 143, 155, 159, 165
Mugler v. Kansas 138, 144
Mutual optimism, as an explanation for trials 22

Nash equilibrium 36, 43, 130, 143
Natural monopoly, in law enforcement 47
Negligence vii, 36, 45, 142; compared to breach of contract remedies 104–105; in sequential accidents 37–44, 142; as a threshold rule 28–34, 36, 142
New Testament 82–83, 85
New York Cent. R. Co. v. Thompson 41–42
Normal behavior standard 141
Normative analysis 3, 4, 37, 103
Noxious use doctrine 138, 139, 140, 144
Nuisance exception 140, 141, 145
Nuisance law 19, 135, 140; as basis for regulatory takings 145–146

Oedipus 82
Old Testament 56, 82–83
Open access resource 7

Paradox of compensation 33, 143, 146
Pareto optimality 2
Patents 79, 148
Peevyhouse v. Garland Coal & Mining Co. 108–109, 135
Penn Central Transportation Co. v. New York 139
Pennsylvania Coal v. Mahon 138–139, 144–145
Physical invasion test 138
Pigou, Arthur 8
Pigovian tax 8–12, 28, 30, 33, 46, 103; and General Transaction Structure 18–19
Plea bargaining 51, 69–74, 163; in comparative perspective 73–74; and deterrence 73
Poletown Neighborhood Council v. City of Detroit 128, 133
Police power 137, 138, 139
Positive analysis vii, 3, 4, 21
Posner, Richard 2, 3, 25, 26, 27, 29, 100
Precedent 25; and judicial decision making 25–27
Prediction Theory of Law 1
Pre-existing duty rule 92
Priest, George 22, 23, 24
Principal-agent contract 154–160, 165
Prisoner's dilemma 130

176 Index

Property law viii, 3, 6, 7, 35; *see also* property rights
Property rights, and choice between property rules and liability rules 13–20; copyrights as protection of 148; and Coase Theorem 6–12; and land title 110–118; and regulatory takings 137, 141, 146
Property rule 4; as compared to liability rule 13–20, 48–49, 109, 121, 125, 132, 134, 135, 161
Proportionality norm, *see* criminal punishment
Proximate cause 34; and sequential accidents 42
Public goods 127–135; information as 79, 148; *also see* free rider problem
Public use 120, 124, 127–136, 165; *also see* eminent domain
Punitive damages 46–47

Quasi-rents 122, 123, 124

Rationality 1, 4
Reasonable care standard 29–33, 45; in sequential care accidents 37–44; in takings law 141
Recording system 111–113
Registration system 111–113, 114
Regulation 12
Regulatory takings, *see* eminent domain
Rehnquist, William 139
Reliance, in contracts 34–35, 103–105, 119
Rent seeking 26
Repeat offenders, and escalating penalties vii, 63–68, 163; and three-strikes laws 3, 63; *see also* criminal punishment
Respondeat superior 84, 86
Restatement of Contracts 93
Retribution 55–56, 84
Risk-sharing 154; and conflict with incentives 109, 156, 165; in breach of contract 106–107
Roman law 56, 83, 85–86; as applied to land improvement 115
Romeo and Juliet 148
Rubin, Paul 23
Rule against self-incrimination 51–52

Santobello v. New York 71
Schulhofer, Stephen 70
Selection of cases for trial 21–22
Settlement v. trial, and the lawyer-client relationship 157–158; and legal evolution 21–27; in plea bargaining 69, 71–72
Sharecropping contract 155–157
Sherman, William T. 34
Sherwood v. Walker 95–100
Smith, Adam 23, 82, 90
Socially valuable versus purely distributive information 96–100
Sony Corp. of America v. Universal Studios 152–153
Sophocles 82
Specific deterrence 55
Specific performance, *see* contract law
Spur Industries v. Del E. Webb Development Co. 15–20, 134–135
Standard of proof 45, 49–51, 59, 85
Statistical discrimination 87
Statute of limitations 114
Stigma, from criminal conviction 49, 50, 63, 66–68, 85, 87, 163
Strict liability 23, 27, 28, 29–33; as compared to damages for breach of contract 35, 103–104
Subjective value 108–109, 112, 116, 132
Supreme Court 61, 70–71, 72, 74, 100, 120, 128, 138, 139, 140, 144, 146, 152

Takings 6; *see also* eminent domain
Three-strikes laws 55, 61, 66
Title insurance 111, 154
Torrens system 113
Tort law vii, 3, 4, 55, 145; and the Coase Theorem 8–12; and the General Transaction Structure 18, 20; and negligence rules 28–34; and sequential accidents 36–44
Tort for risk 48
Tragedy of the commons 7
Transaction costs 25, 141; and the choice between property rules and liability rules 13–20, 48; and the Coase Theorem 11–12, 108; and copyright 149; and the holdout problem 120
Trespass 19
Trojan War 84

Uniform Commercial Code 93
Unreasonable search and seizure 35, 52; *see also* exclusionary rule

U.S. v. Carroll Towing Co. 29
U.S. v. Causby 138

Veil of ignorance 2
Vertical integration 124–125
Vicarious responsibility 83, 84, 85, 86

War of 1812 99–100
Warranty 90

Wealth maximization 2
West Side Story 148
Williams & Wilkins Co. v. United States 152–153
Wittman, Donald 43
World War I 83
World War II 84, 87

Zoning 6, 137, 140, 141, 146–147